India and the Future

INDIA AND THE FUTURE

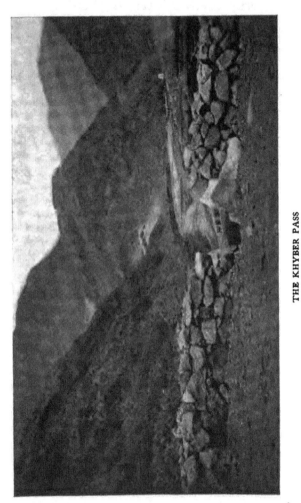

THE KHYBER PASS

INDIA
AND THE FUTURE

BY
WILLIAM ARCHER

WITH ILLUSTRATIONS

NEW YORK
ALFRED A. KNOPF
MCMXVIII

CONTENTS

	PAGE
PROLOGUE	1
CHAPTER	
I.—A BIRD's-EYE VIEW	9
II.—TWO SIDES TO THE RACIAL MEDAL	22
III.—THE UNITY OF INDIA	43
IV.—HINDU SPIRITUALITY	55
V.—CASTE AND ITS CONCOMITANTS	89
VI.—MANNERS	110
VII.—THE INDIAN OPPOSITION	127
VIII.—ART AND CULTURE	188
IX.—EDUCATION	256
EPILOGUE	295
INDEX	321

382119

ILLUSTRATIONS

The Khyber Pass   *Frontispiece*

PAGE

Tanjore: Small Temple   40

Gateway of the Temple, Trichinopoly (Trifala of Vishnu over Door)   80

Brahui, Shepherd Class   120

The Taj Mahal   160

The Palace Lake, Udaipur   200

Navigation on the Ganges (A Raft of Inflated Nilghau Skins)   240

A Ghat, Benares   280

INDIA AND THE FUTURE

PROLOGUE

THERE is a turn in the Khyber Pass, as it winds from Ali Musjid to Jamrud, where all at once you see the mountain wall drop away to its foundation, and look out over a tawny plain, stretching illimitably into a far-off purple haze.

No spot on earth is more saturated with the romance of history. For that plain is INDIA; and from here or hereabouts has it been first surveyed by the swarms of oncoming Aryans, by Alexander and his Greeks, by Scythian, Tartar and Afghan hordes, by Timur, by Babar, by Nadir Shah, and other conquerors without number. Behind that purple haze lie Kashmir, the poet's fableland; Lahore the capital, and Amritsar the holy city, of the Sikhs; the glorious mosques, palaces and mausoleums of Delhi and Agra, of Fatehpur Sikri and Bijapur; the tragic fastnesses of the Rajputs; Benares, unique in its squalid sublimity; the huge and sinister temples of the South; upstart smoke-breathing emporiums of the sea-borne invader; mighty rivers whose names are as old as history; battlefields by the score, from mythic Kurukshetra to thrice-ensanguined Panipat, from Plassey to Sobraon and Gujrat, where East came to grips with West; and, circling it all in, the white pinnacles of the most tremendous mountain barrier in the world, in whose impenetrable solitudes superstition can still place unreproved the abode of ever-living sages, holding daily commune with the gods. For the superstitions and legends of this land are as colossal as everything else within its frontiers. Hideous savageries of cult and custom prevailed in it till yesterday, and are not even now extinct. Its myths, its deities, its idols, are each more monstrous than the last; and the worship of stocks and stones is inextricably commingled with the no less superstitious worship of filmy and air-drawn metaphysical fantasies. Such is the country on the threshold whereof we stand, as Alexander stood three-and-twenty centuries ago; and working itself out in this historic and prehistoric wonderland, we can now see the most romantic adventure of modern times, a huge, precarious, blundering, heroic experiment in organization, pacification, civilization. Is there any other region in the world which makes such a multiform appeal to the vision, the imagination and the intellect?

I, at any rate, know of no other. India is the Italy of Asia; and though the past of India cannot vie with that of Italy in world-historic significance, its present is incomparably more picturesque and fraught with vaster issues.

When I landed in India, nothing was further from my thoughts than the writing of such a book as this. But the country cast an instant spell on me. Its surface aspects enthralled me, its problems became an obsession. Gradually the idea grew upon me that there was but one possible solution for these problems, but one honourable, desirable and fortunate consummation to the great adventure. It is that idea which informs the following pages.

This is not a book of travel. Of the surface aspects of India, fascinating as they are, I shall have little to say. The work of the picturesque tourist has been done to unapproachable perfection by the late G. W. Steevens, whose book, *In India*, is a masterpiece of exact observation and vivid portrayal. Excellent, too, is Mr. Sydney Low's *Vision of India;* and Mr. H. W. Nevinson's *New Spirit in India* contains many admirable pages both of description

[2]

and comment. With these writers I attempt no rivalry; and still less, of course, with the many able authorities on Indian affairs whom the civil and political services have produced.* How, then, can I justify this addition to the mountainous mass of Anglo-Indian literature? Simply by the fact that I had something to say which has not, to my knowledge, been fully, explicitly and dispassionately said before.

Not that I pretend to have made any great discovery. Many people, as I hope to show, have taken a similar view of the case. But some of them have been restrained by official traditions from speaking out very clearly. Others have spoken with a passionate partisanship, or with a querulous pessimism, which has lessened the weight of their words. I see no reason for pessimism, I see no reason for invective. What I see is an extraordinarily interesting and complicated situation, which wisdom may work out to a triumphant issue, or unwisdom may precipitate to disaster. And I feel so strong a conviction as to the course which wisdom dictates that I should regard it almost as a shirking of duty to refrain from stating my view, for what it is worth.

There is also, of course, the possibility that the situation may be inherently hopeless—one which no conceivable exercise of reason can turn to good. I do not think that this is so; but if it is—if the experiment is foredoomed to failure—at least let us fail magnanimously, and not stupidly.

I shall not here anticipate the course of my argument. But it may be well to show unmistakably from the outset that the attitude of mind which I criticize and would fain see altered is, in fact, the official attitude of mind.

* Without disparagement to others, I may mention Sir Bampfylde Fuller's *Studies in Indian Life and Sentiment* as an extremely interesting and informing work.

On August 25th, 1911, the Governor-General in Council signed a momentous despatch to the Secretary of State for India. It dealt mainly with the question of the change of capital; but the passage which was most eagerly read and welcomed in India ran as follows:

It is certain that, in the course of time, the just demands of Indians for a larger share in the government of the country will have to be satisfied, and the question will be how this devolution of power can be conceded without impairing the supreme authority of the Governor-General in Council. The only possible solution of the difficulty would appear to be gradually to give the Provinces a larger measure of self-government, until at last India would consist of a number of administrations, autonomous in all provincial affairs, with the Government of India above them all, and possessing power to interfere in cases of misgovernment, but ordinarily restricting its functions to matters of Imperial concern.

Months passed; the King-Emperor paid his memorable visit to India, a finely-inspired act of true Kingship; and it seemed as though a new era were dawning in the relations of the two peoples. Then someone in England called attention to the liberalism, cautious but explicit, of the above paragraph from Lord Hardinge's despatch; and behold! the Liberal Secretary of State had nothing more pressing to do than to disavow it. In the House of Lords, on June 24th, 1912, the Marquis of Crewe said:

There was a certain section in India which looked forward to a measure of self-government approaching to that which had been granted to the Dominions. He saw no future for India on these lines. The experiment of a measure of self-government, practically free from parliamentary control, to a race which was not our own, even though that race enjoyed the advantages of the best services of men belonging to our race, was one which could not be tried. It was his duty as Secretary of State to

[4]

repudiate the idea that the despatch implied anything of the kind, as the hope or goal of the policy of the Government.

In a later debate (July 29th) Lord Crewe was still more emphatic, laying it down in so many words that:

*The maintenance and perpetual continuance of British rule is the best way of securing the happiness of the Indian people.**

The bomb thrown at the Viceroy on December 23rd, as he entered the new capital, may probably be construed as a rejoinder to this utterance. It was an imbecile retort, condemned by all reasonable men,† in India no less than in England; yet the fact remains that, by insisting on an inconceivable perpetuity of rule, we not only inflame Indian unreason, but alienate Indian reason. Terrorism I do not regard as an important factor in the case, however unpleasant; but if the British Government thinks that even the sanest and most law-abiding citizens of India sincerely accept the principle laid down by Lord Crewe, I believe it to be labouring under a disastrous illusion.

This is, in fact, my case; and it is a case which I cannot expect to commend itself, at first blush, to British, or Anglo-Indian, opinion. Neither can I hope, unfortunately, that my argument will be read with approval in India; for I have much to say that cannot be agreeable to Indian self-complacency. Those Europeans seem to me very false friends to India who gloze over, or even treat as advantages, the historic misfortunes under which she suffers. At all events, it is an essential part of my case that India is as yet far from being prepared to take an equal place among the civilized nations of the world. A schoolboy of my acquaintance came home the other day much elated because,

* Hansard report. The *Times* report omits "perpetual."

† "Even the women deplore it," a leading Bengali journalist said to me on the morrow of the outrage.

in the singing class, he had been promoted from the best of those who sing badly to the worst of those who sing well. In the eyes of his elders the distinction did not seem very important; and, similarly, I do not think it important to decide whether India is the most forward of barbarous, or the most backward of civilized, nations. One or other, to my mind, she certainly is; and this view conflicts very definitely with the opinion of a great many Indians, who hold her to be little less than a divinity under a temporary cloud. I must face with what resolution I may the fate of the impartial commentator who exasperates both parties. But if this book should fall into the hands of any of the Indian gentlemen who treated me with ungrudging cordiality and kindness, I beg them to believe that what I learned from them was a firm faith in the ability of their race to retrieve its age-old misfortunes, and shape for itself a real future as glorious as its mythic past.

I am well aware that if any one of these gentlemen chose to apply a searching criticism to English life, he could, with no extravagance of paradox, retort at many points the reproach of "barbarism" which I am compelled to level against so many aspects of Indian life, both material and spiritual. The incompleteness of Western civilization is only too manifest, in churches redolent of myth and magic, monarchies aureoled in superstition, rank-worship only less contemptible than wealth-worship, militarism, even in times of peace, sapping the best energies of the peoples, and industrialism so iniquitously organized, or unorganized, as to engender the slum and the sweating-shop, and foster the gin-palace and the brothel. "If this be Western civilization," an Indian critic may be tempted to say, "give me Eastern barbarism!" I suggest, however, that he will do well to resist the temptation. Europe, with all its crimes and imbecilities, is many centuries further from the *Ur-*

[6]

Dummheit than un-Europeanized India. It is struggling out of the ages of faith into the age of knowledge. Some of the worst of its evils proceed from the very rapidity of its movement; whereas the evils of India are those of secular stagnation. I readily admit that the barbarism of India has picturesque and even venerable aspects to which few of the barbarisms of Europe can lay claim; but that does not make it either desirable or permanently possible in the modern world.

In the spelling of Indian names I have been guided by convenience, and have not tried to adhere consistently to any system. The accents on Sanskrit words I have entirely disregarded, as they convey no meaning except to Sanskrit scholars. By "Anglo-Indian" I mean Anglo-Indian, not Eurasian. The attempt to divert to a new and inappropriate use a word so thoroughly established in the English language can lead to nothing but confusion.

One of the following chapters—the sixth—has already appeared in the *Fortnightly Review*, and is here reprinted by permission of the Editor.

I

THE Viceroy of India rules over three hundred and fifteen million people, or in other words about one-fifth of the human race. His territory equals in extent the whole of Europe, minus Russia. It is less than half the territory of the United States; but, on the other hand, it outstrips the United States in population by more than three to one. His government, though subject to the control of the Parliament at Westminster, is absolutely autocratic in relation to the people of India. He, and the Governors subordinate to him, are bound by recent regulations to ask the advice of certain Indian gentlemen; but they are not in the least bound to follow it. The European force behind this autocracy consists of 75,000 soldiers—say, one to every 4,500 of the people. The European executive numbers some 1,500 officials, or one ruler to every 200,000 of the ruled.

Thus summarized in cold figures, the British dominion in India seems wonderful enough. But until you see it in actual working—in its habit, or habits, as it lives— the true marvel of it can be but faintly realized. The more you see of it, indeed, the more incredible it appears. Beside it the Roman Empire seems almost a commonplace affair. The organizing genius of Rome radiated from the centre outwards, and Roman civilization followed the Roman arms, either imposing itself upon barbarisms, or arriving at an amicable compromise with pre-existent civilizations. British rule in India does not radiate from a centre,

[9]

but is projected over more than 6,000 miles of sea;* and British civilization, though it is, to some extent, influencing India by sheer force of contact, remains absolutely alien to the enormous mass of the people. The Briton comes to India to govern, governs, and goes away again. His relations with a few Indians may be more or less friendly; but he no more enters into the national life of the country than the plumber who puts in your water-pipes, or the electrician who "wires" your house, becomes a member of your family. It is in this complete and deliberately-cultivated externality that the wonder of British rule consists.

The huge pear-shaped region which we call India is enveloped .from the Himalayas to Cape Comorin, from Baluchistan to Burma, in the network of the British *raj*. The meshes of the net are wide, but they are woven with great regularity and they are extremely tough. A fierce attempt to burst through them, in 1857, led only to a firmer re-weaving of the fabric. It is true that about a third part of the whole territory, with a population of 70,000,000, remains under the nominal, and in some cases the more or less real, rule of Indian princes; but to each court a British resident is attached whose word is law in all essential matters; and the proudest of the princes rules only "during good behaviour," with no power to enter into foreign relations, or to raise an efficient army of his own. In the largest of the states, Hyderabad and Mysore, the great British cantonments of Secunderabad and Bangalore are a constant reminder that the suzerain power is no effete tradition. In British territory proper, with its million square miles and its 245,000,000 people, the

* They were 13,000 miles when the British rule took its rise; and the voyage, which now occupies some three weeks, then took from six to twelve months.

[10]

meshes of the net are closer, and its foreignness, its externality, is even more apparent. Is not a net by its very nature a foreign substance, in relation to the objects which it encloses and holds together?

The great Presidency towns, Calcutta, Bombay, Madras, are European cities planted on Indian soil. All the prominent buildings are European, though in some of the more recent ones an endeavour has been made to adopt what is known as the "Indo-Saracenic" style of architecture. For the rest, the streets are called by English names, generally the names of bygone Viceroys and Governors, or of the soldiers who conquered the land and quelled the Mutiny— heroes whose effigies meet you at every turn. The shops are English shops, where English or Eurasian assistants traffic in English goods. English carriages and motors bowl along the macadamized or tarred roads of old England. On every hand there is evidence of the instinctive effort to reproduce, as nearly as the climate will permit, English conditions of life. In Bombay, indeed, the merchant princes are no longer Europeans, but Hindus and Parsis. Theirs are the most sumptuous palaces on Malabar Hill; theirs the most "swagger" motors on the Queen's Road and the Apollo Bunder. In Calcutta, though commercial competition is less keen, the great Bengali landowner is a prominent and important personage. But almost the whole life of the people of India is relegated to the back streets, not to say the slums—frankly called in Madras the Black Town. There are a few points—clubs and gymkhanas specially established to that end—where English men, and even women, meet Indian men, and even women, of the wealthier classes, on a basis of social equality. But few indeed are the points of contact between the Asian town and the European city which has been superimposed upon it. The missionary, the Salvation Army outpost, perhaps the

[11]

curiosity-hunting tourist, may go forth into the bazaars; but the European community as a whole cares no more for the swarming brown multitudes around it than the dwellers on an island care for the fishes in the circumambient sea.

Leave the Presidency towns and go to the provincial capitals or to the smaller stations, and what do you find? Go to Allahabad, to Lucknow, to Lahore, to Poona, to Agra, even to Delhi itself—everywhere you are in a British town, with British street names, British shops, British churches, British statues, British red-pillar-letter-boxes, British "Standings for Hackney Carriages," British "No Thoroughfare" and "Trespassers will be prosecuted" notice-boards, British customs, conventions and traditions rampant on every hand. Everywhere, no doubt, there is a "native" town, more or less adjoining the British civil station and military cantonment. Sometimes, as at Delhi and Benares, this town is a show place which everyone visits; but in other cases neither travellers nor the ordinary run of residents give it so much as a passing thought. Externally the British station is extremely unlike a town in the old country. Land was apparently of no value when these settlements were laid out; so that each bungalow stands in a spacious "compound," often acres in extent, and the dwellings of a hundred Europeans, with their servants, will often occupy an area that would accommodate many thousands in the adjacent bazaar, or in a city of Europe or America. It must be owned that the Anglo-Indian leads a spacious life. His settlements realized the ideal of the "garden city" before that term was invented. Miles of roadway, from 70 to 130 feet wide, are densely overarched by those wonderful trees which are the incomparable glory of India. In many places there are three rows of trees, and a tan-covered ride skirts the macadamized

[12]

driving-way. Every house has its own embowering trees; and there are often—as, for instance, at Lahore and Amritsar—spacious public gardens as well. The result is, of course, that distances are enormous, and walking, even when the temperature admits of it, is impossible. Everybody rides or drives, and of late years the motor-cycle is much in evidence. Even the shops stand in their own compounds, and you approach your tailor's by a carriage drive that would do credit to a duke's town-house.

The life of these stations, though comfortable and pleasant, is by no means extravagantly luxurious. But whatever else it may be, it is utterly, aggressively British. The sahib generally rises early, has his "chota hazri," or morning cup of tea, and goes off for his still more indispensable morning "exercise." If the hounds do not meet, he and his "memsahib" are probably content with a canter along the tan-track of the Mall, round the race-course, and back by Dalhousie Road, Lytton Avenue and Lansdowne Park —some six or eight miles in all. Then he has his bath, and runs through a few official files before breakfast. After breakfast he sets to work in earnest to govern the country, as magistrate, as revenue assessor and collector, as conscience-keeper to an Indian prince, as head of some huge district, or, it may be, as governor of a province more populous than Great Britain. He leaves off governing for tiffin at two, and then governs again till tea-time. Between tea and dinner he goes to the Club, meets the other sahibs of the station, male and female, civil, political and military, plays tennis, and (after dusk) Badminton by lamplight, listens to the regimental band discoursing melodies from "The Up-to-Date Girl," and looks at the English illustrated and sporting papers. At eight he goes home to dress for dinner at eight-thirty. For a domestic meal he puts on a "short coat" and a black tie, and the same if

[13]

he is dining out "quite quietly." If that deprecatory formula does not occur in the invitation, he arrays himself in swallow-tail and white choker, and expects to drink champagne. Often, before he goes to bed, he will again plunge into the "files" which are always awaiting him, and burn the midnight oil over reams of conflicting perjuries in some case that has come before him on appeal. For it is no easy job this governing of India, nor does the British official take it easily. His innocent recreations are not more than enough to keep him "fit." The routine above sketched is, in many cases, varied by periodical excursions "into districts," when the official lives for weeks in tents, moving from village to village, and investigating on the spot questions of revenue, police, irrigation, public works and what not. This, however, must be regarded, not as a hardship, but as a pleasant variety in his duties; for the Indian servant has mastered the art of tent life, and can generally make his sahib extremely comfortable, even under unpromising circumstances.

I am not, for the moment, either praising or dispraising the government thus conducted. For the moment the point to be noted is its undisguised and systematic foreignness. India is administered from a network of foreign townships, planted in her midst, in close association with another network of cantonments, or foreign military camps. Of the heads of the Government not one is an Indian. A very few Indians hold moderately high appointments, especially judicial; but they are, to the mass of the civil and political services, at the outside, as one in twenty. In subordinate civil functions—in the secretariats, in the police, the post-office, the telegraphs, the railways, and so forth—millions of Indians are employed, but always under the eye of European superiors. A considerable number of British

[14]

officials do their work not only conscientiously but enthusiastically. They study the people they are set to rule over, encourage and develop the better sides of their character, master their languages, even their dialects, and govern, in a word, not only capably but sympathetically. These, however, are necessarily exceptions. The average British official, though honest, hard-working and efficient according to his lights, does little to mitigate the crude fact of racial domination. He seldom dreams of wearing a velvet glove on the iron hand. He sincerely believes that the Oriental character understands and appreciates nothing but despotism; and he consistently acts up to that belief—for which, indeed, there is a great deal to be said. I am not, I repeat, either praising or condemning him. I am simply trying to throw into relief the astounding fact that we have in India three hundred million people whose political life consists in "obeying orders given in a foreign accent."

And who are these people? A brutish, savage race, born to tutelage as the sparks fly upwards? Let us hear Edmund Burke on the point:

This multitude of men does not consist of an abject and barbarous population. . . . [They are] a people for ages civilised and cultivated; cultivated by all the arts of polished life while we were yet in the woods.

I shall have to argue later that this is a violent and mischievous overstatement; but the fact that it could be made with any sort of plausibility by such a man as Burke is sufficient for my present purpose. And one thing is certain: namely, that every educated Hindu knows this passage by heart, and has rubbed its flattering unction into the very pores of his nature. Nothing is more frequent in intercourse with Indians than to have them courteously

[15]

checking themselves on the brink of a reminder that their
ancestors were monarchs and sages while ours were woad-
stained cave-men or lake-dwellers.* Whether the statement be true, and what, if true, should be deduced from
it, need not here be considered. The point is that this
race, or rather these races, are far from having no pride
of ancestry, far from being congenitally predisposed to
admit the superiority of a Western people.† It is true
that not even in their wildest moments of arrogance can
they claim to have enjoyed, at any period of their past,
what we of the West call political freedom. But this does
not render them less accessible to democratic ideals and
dreams, less sensitive to the *diminutio capitis* involved in
obeying a caste of foreign rulers. History, in short, ex-
plains the origin, and accounts for the possibility, of the
British dominion in India, but offers no adequate basis for

* The late Mr. G. K. Gokhale, speaking at the National Liberal Club,
London, on November 15, 1905, said: "The people of India are an ancient race who had attained a high degree of civilization long before the
ancestors of European nations understood what civilization was. India
has been the birthplace of great religions. She was also the cradle and
long the home of literature and philosophy, of science and arts."

† As a small illustration of this fact take the following passage from
The Heart of Hinduism by Sir Narayan Chandavarkar, a Judge of the
Bombay High Court: "From Hindus Englishmen have borrowed the
habit of daily bathing. Other nations in Europe are still backward;
but they, too, are slowly learning." At no period of history have Indians
been inclined to admit or to realise that they had anything to learn from
the outside world. It is surprising to observe how little they profited
by the Greek influences which came home to them pretty closely in the
centuries after Alexander's invasion. They learned something in sculpture, but that was all. The theory that their drama shows Greek influences I believe to be mistaken. "Asoka," says Mr. Vincent Smith,
"was much more anxious to communicate the blessings of Buddhist teaching to Antiochos and Ptolemy than to borrow Greek notions from them."
And again: "The Indians were impressed by both Alexander and
Menander as mighty captains, not as missionaries of culture, and no
doubt regarded both these sovereigns as impure barbarians, to be feared
but not imitated." *Early History of India*, p. 235.

[16]

the theory that it is providentially adapted to the unalterable psychology of the Indian people. To any Indian with a gleam of intelligence, it can only appear the final outcome and symbol of a series of historic disasters, stretching back into the very dawn of recorded time.

To such an Indian, and indeed to any moderately unbiased and thinking person, the British rule may seem tolerable, and even indispensable, as a means to an end. But it is hard to understand how any thinking person, English or Indian, can regard it as an end in itself, a thing desirable for its own sake. If England recognizes in time this plain and simple distinction, many of her hardest problems in India will gradually solve themselves, and the history of her Indian Empire will always be to her a legitimate source of pride. But if she declines to recognize it, and obstinately stakes her national prestige upon the endurance for ever and ever of her autocratic rule in India, she is heading towards certain disaster for herself and for all the millions whom Fate has entrusted to her care.

It is not in human nature that such peoples as those of India should rest permanently content to lead their lives under the domination of an alien, unsympathetic, uncomprehending and uncomprehended race. Actual political disaffection may be as yet confined to a small minority; but there are and will always be plenty of definite and material subjects of discontent, coming home to vast numbers of people; and, rightly or wrongly, the *Sirkar*, the Government, will always be held to blame for whatever is amiss. Thus "unrest," though it may simmer down for a time, will always be latent and easily revived; and if England should ever, for a single month, lose the command of the sea, and find her communications cut off by a hostile Power, there can be little doubt that India, if still in her present temper, would burst into a blaze of rebellion.

[17]

This prophecy may seem surprising in view of
displayed during the European War by the Ind
and the Indian army; but though that loyalty
able it does not alter the fundamental facts. 1
are naturally a conservative aristocracy, who
are bound up in the existing state of things,
position in a revolutionary, democratic India wo
difficult, not to say impossible; but they could
stem a revolutionary movement if once it got
The army is loyal to the hand that feeds it, s
It is loyal so long as it feels itself a part of
smoothly-working machine, deriving its pow
distant, vaguely-realized source. But once let
be cut off, once let the machine cease to functio
and the army would be at the mercy of th
and the demagogue. The very participation of l
German War has placed a weapon in the ha
revolutionist, who can represent as black ingr
England's part any tardiness in fulfilling the e
of Indian nationalism, however premature or
If rebellion should break out, all sanely pa
dians would be plunged in grief, realizing th
successful or not, it could have none but disastr
But sane patriotism would have no chance a
headed enthusiasm, asking "Are we to submit for
autocratic domination and exploitation of a
arrogant foreigners?" There would be suff
ciousness in this view of the case to render it
to over-wrought brains. But if, on the other han
ernment had, for a series of years, in word and in
that it sincerely realized its true mission, not
on its present routine to all eternity, but of mak
nation and gradually preparing it for self-g
there would be a reasonable probability that, e
[18]

land's direst straits, sane counsels would prevail, and India
would be in no undue haste to cut the leading-strings and
prematurely declare herself an adult and self-sufficient political entity. This she is far enough from being, all reasonable
people admit; but, thanks to British rule, she is much
nearer to political cohesion and competence than she ever
was before in the whole course of her history. It lies with us
to decide whether we shall recognize and consciously forward this process of evolution, or stupidly attempt to
check it, in the interests of an unimaginable permanence
of things as they are. We have before us a great opportunity and a great danger; if we neglect the one, we shall
infallibly rush headlong into the other.

There is nothing paradoxical, nothing even novel, in this
view of England's opportunity in India. It has been held
and uttered, more or less explicitly, by many English
and Anglo-Indian statesmen. It may even be said that
the sempiternity of British domination is a recent pseudo-
ideal, begotten of that thoughtless Imperialism which regards not only the Indian Empire, but the whole Empire of
Great Britain, as an end in itself, and not as a means to a
higher end. I am no Little Englander; on the contrary,
I regard the British Empire as one of the greatest, and
possibly one of the most beneficent, facts of history. Even
in India, I have not the slightest sympathy with those
who indiscriminately applaud everything Indian, and have
nothing but carping disparagement for the great work
England has done. I admire it whole-heartedly; but that
does not prevent me from recognizing that it must ultimately go to ruin if it is inspired by a false and imprac-
ticable ideal.

The time is ripe for the open recognition and promul-
gation of a juster view of England's duty and opportunity.
Without making too much of the well-meant but rather

[19]

ineffectual efforts at social approximation between the East
and the West, one may safely say that the brutally contemptuous attitude of the West to the East—never the
attitude of good or intelligent men—has had its day and
survives only among the dregs of the European population.
Bad manners are no longer good form, and it is being
generally realized that racial superiority, if it exists at
all, is not to be demonstrated by bluster and swagger.
And as outward manifestations cannot change without a
corresponding change in inward feeling, it is certain that
the decline of swagger in manner is not unaccompanied
by a decline of swagger in thought. Respect for the human
rights of the Indian cannot be quite divorced from respect
for his political aspirations; and even in the most unlikely
official quarters one does already find the germs of such
respect. Oddly enough, the outward, if not the inward,
change is probably to be traced back to the execrated
viceroyalty of Lord Curzon; but it has been greatly promoted under that statesman's successors. What is needed
now is an explicit recognition in the highest quarters of a
change of attitude which, though hitherto unrecognized,
is already in great measure accomplished. There is no
need for definite pledges, or rash speculations as to the
probable rapidity of progress. The essential point is that
British rule should be openly confessed and authoritatively
proclaimed to be *a means, not an end*. As soon as this idea or
ideal had percolated, as it rapidly would, from the centre to
the extremities of the governing body, a happy change in the
relations of the two races would, naturally and without
effort, manifest itself. I do not mean a social approximation, which seems to me difficult and unimportant. What
I mean is that the Indian in official life would feel a new self-
respect, and that this feeling would react upon the
European attitude towards him. Indian patriotism, in a

[20]

word, would no longer have to choose between querulous opposition to the Government at every possible point, and pessimistic acquiescence in foreign rule, simply "lest worse befall." There would still be plenty of friction, plenty of difference of opinion as to the best means of attaining the common end; but they would be the differences of normal political life, not of irreconcilably conflicting purposes and ideals.

This is, in outline, the view of England's opportunity which I propose to develop in the following pages. I need not, at this point, further anticipate the course of my argument. But one question which will certainly be asked I can answer quite briefly and without delay. "British rule," it may be said, "is, according to you, a means to an end, that end being a united and self-governing India. Do you propose that this self-governing state should be part of the British Empire, or independent of it?" My answer is: "Sufficient for the day are the problems thereof." Many a long year will have to pass before India is ripe for self-government; and who can tell what may be the state and constitution of the British Empire when that date is reached? It may have broken up into its component parts; it may be merged into a larger synthesis; all we know is that it will be a very different thing from the Empire of to-day. It is sheer waste of time to wrangle over the formula "within or without the Empire." So much alone is certain: we are far more likely to keep India within the Empire by fostering than by obstinately thwarting her natural aspirations. A nation of 300,000,000 cannot be held in permanent subjection, against its will, by a nation of 40,000,000; and India, thanks to our rule, is rapidly becoming a nation and developing a will of her own.

II

THE first thing to be done if we would understand the Indian problem aright is to determine the true status of the Indian peoples among the races of the world. The instinct of the European is to assume without further inquiry the inferiority of everyone who wears, like Othello, "the shadowed livery of the burnished sun." Even the olive complexion of an Italian or Spaniard is a little suspicious to the peoples of the North. In America to-day, Dante and Cervantes would be contemptuously bracketed as "dagos." But when the olive tint deepens into chocolate, there is no longer any question, in some minds, as to the racial inferiority it implies. When Mr. Dadabhai Naoroji, a Bombay Parsi, stood for the borough of Central Finsbury, Lord Salisbury sneered at the notion that a British constituency should ever return "a black man;" and it is likely enough that Mr. Naoroji would not have been elected had his complexion in any way justified Lord Salisbury's epithet. The time is not so long gone by when Englishmen used to lump together the peoples of India as "niggers;" and though that stupidity has been stamped out,* the inveterate habit of associating a dark skin with congenital inferiority still lies at the root of a great deal of our thinking and feeling with regard to India.

* Mrs. Besant says that it still survives; and, as she would not speak without warrant, I presume there must be isolated Rip Van Winkles who have not yet awakened to its enormity. They have not even read their Kipling.

[22]

On the other hand, as I have already said, many Indians return the compliment by looking down on Europeans as an inferior and upstart brood, mere parvenus in the domain of civilization. Hindustan—"Aryavarta"—is the nursery and home of all true religion, philosophy and culture; and, when her present period of eclipse is past, India is to arise in her glory for the salvation of the world. Such is the sentiment expressed by that very cultivated woman and true poetess, Sarojini Naidu, of Hyderabad, in her ode:

TO INDIA

Oh, young through all thy immemorial years,
  Rise, Mother, rise regenerate from thy gloom,
And, like a bride high-mated with the spheres,
  Beget new glories from thy ageless womb.

The nations that in fettered darkness weep
  Crave thee to lead them where great mornings break. . . .
Mother, oh Mother, wherefore dost thou sleep?
  Arise and answer, for thy children's sake.

The Future calls thee with a manifold sound
  To crescent honors, splendors, victories vast;
Waken, oh slumbering Mother, and be crowned,
  Who once wert empress of the sovereign Past.

It is only fair to assume that "the nations" who are represented as waiting to be liberated by India are nations within her bounds, she being conceived for the nonce as an ideal entity, distinct from the geographical or racial divisions of which she is composed. But even if we thus limit the meaning of the second stanza, we can scarcely interpret in so limited a sense the line "Who once wert empress of the sovereign Past." The poetess does not mean that India was empress of her own past, but of the past of the world; and, as it is manifest that this was never true in a political sense, we must interpret it spiritually, as an assertion of bygone but recoverable supremacy in the realm of intellect and soul. And to thousands of Indians this is an article of faith. Far from being conscious of any drawback of race, they hold themselves a chosen people, the depositories from of old of all the highest wisdom of the world. In this belief, moreover, they are encouraged and established by plenty of Western testimony. For instance, the Central Hindu College at Benares, founded by an Englishwoman and (until recently) controlled by an Englishman, publishes *An Elementary Text-Book of Hindu Religion and Ethics,* on the second page of which the novice is assured that

No other Religion has produced so many great men—great teachers, great writers, great sages, great saints, great kings, great warriors, great statesmen, great benefactors, great patriots.

It would be easy to quote scores of testimonials to a like effect, from Western as well as Eastern sources, often combined with vague allusions to a political Golden Age, at some undetermined point in the misty regions of Indian antiquity. One need scarcely add that these crude stimulants to national self-esteem are greedily swallowed, with such effects as crude stimulants are usually apt to produce.

If we clear our minds of unreasoning prejudice on the one hand and visionary sentimentality on the other, we shall arrive without too much difficulty at the plain truth of the matter. The Indian races, take them all round, are not low, but very high races. They are not "black men" as the negro is black, but sunburnt white men.* Colour is an

* Recent research is said to discountenance the idea that the heat of the sun has anything to do with dark pigmentation. Nature, in that case, seems to have taken some trouble to put us on a wrong scent.

accident in India; in Africa, and Afro-America, it marks a radical difference. In some districts of India there is, no doubt, a slight negroid infusion, but it is scarcely more influential than the negroid infusion in Europe. A large part of the Indian people is admittedly of the same stock as ourselves; but I am not claiming any necessary superiority for the "Aryan brother." It is pretty clear that many of the races whom the Aryans found in possession of India, and with whom they intermingled, must have been nearly, if not quite, their equals in racial development. At any rate, it does not seem possible, at the present day, to declare the presumable Aryan a better man than the presumable Dravidian. There is no part of India which does not produce a considerable percentage of notably fine men—fine in stature, in features, in facial angle, in physical development—and is there any country in Europe for which a larger claim can be advanced? The military pageants of recent years have made Londoners familiar with the magnificent specimens of humanity who abound in our Sikh, Punjabi, Rajput, Maratha, Pathan regiments; but these might be assumed to be picked men. They were, no doubt, exceptional in the sense that they were well fed and athletically trained; but the raw material of such men abounds in every Indian village. As for the women of India, is not their grace proverbial? In the North (under Muhammadan influence, I presume) they often contrive to conceal it by wearing hideous trousers; but in the South every girl who drapes herself in her *sari*, and goes forth to the well with her shining brass pitcher on her head, is a model for either sculptor or painter—perfect in contour, brilliant and yet harmonious in colouring. It is true that their grace is short-lived, and that they age before their time; but it is also true that the children whom they carry astride on their hips are often divinely beautiful. Physically, then—whenever their circumstances are such as to give them a fair chance of development—the peoples of India stand high among the races of the world. They stand high in stature, proportion, power, dignity, delicacy; and—judged by the highest standards known to us—they often excel in beauty. Some of the noblest types of manhood I have ever seen were—or rather are—Indians.

"Even if all you say be true," the reader may object, "you refer only to physique; and the place of a people in the racial scale cannot be determined by physique alone." Certainly not; and we shall come presently to other considerations. But when we talk of "a fine race," we mean, in the first instance, physically "fine;" and it seems important to make it clear that in this respect the Indian is at no disadvantage as compared with the ruling races of the world. His physique denotes (shall we say?) the highest potentialities of development. One is forced, however reluctantly, to recur to a comparison with the African races. In moving among negroes, one has constantly to avow— perhaps to struggle against—a sense of their fundamental, inherent, ineradicable inferiority. Whatever may be their amiable and even admirable qualities, one cannot resist the conviction that they are some degrees nearer the brute; nor can one wonder at their proved incapacity to evolve for themselves any approach to civilization. In moving among Indians, on the other hand, what is constantly borne in upon one is a sense of their fundamental equality, and a vague wonder as to how they happen to have sunk to a position of apparent, and to some extent real, inferiority. The difference between the negro and the Indian is so enormous that the comparison seems cruel to the one and insulting to the other; but I know not how else to make clear the absurdity, as well as the brutality, of in any way associating the dark races of Asia with those of Africa.

[26]

Even in point of complexion, many of the Indian stocks are much nearer to ourselves than to the negro.

But now we come to a distinction which it is easier to feel than to explain. The sense of high potentiality is constantly overborne in India by a sense of actual, practical, palpable low development—more painful than that of the negro, inasmuch as it is the low development, not of one who has failed to rise, but of one who has fallen. I am not speaking, of course, of selected individuals—of a few thousands or hundreds of thousands at the top of the social, educational, economic tree. I am speaking of the hundreds of millions who are the real people of India—who must form the Indian nation, if such a nation is ever to exist in any true sense of the word. Look at the life of the villages, the fields, the bazaars; study the crowds at railway-stations, at bathing-ghats, at places of pilgrimage; and you cannot but feel nearer to barbarism than in any other country that makes the slightest pretence to civilization. It is not wholly or mainly a question of caste. The "depressed castes," indeed, are very depressed; but the stranger does not with any certainty recognize caste distinctions. Many of the personages who strike one as most barbarous are, in fact, Brahmins; and from some of the scenes in which barbarism is rampant, pariahs and "untouchables" are fiercely excluded. It may be an open question whether this sense of melancholy backwardness is justified, and whether it is, as some maintain, in great part an illusion due to Western prejudice. But even those who take up this position must surely have moments of oppression and dismay in viewing the sheer multitudinousness of the Indian populace. These swarming myriads, vegetating, and content to vegetate, under the dominion of noxious traditions and grotesque superstitions—by what magical influence are they or their children's children to be rendered capable

[27]

of self-conscious, self-respecting national life? By education? Yes, that is the sole resource. But in how many years or centuries can education undo the work of enervating, soul-sapping millenniums?

This, then, is my reading of the racial status of the Indian people. Fundamentally they are inferior to none; but a long chain of prehistoric and historic circumstances, ultimately traceable to geographical conditions, has reduced the masses to a condition of stagnant barbarism, and "the classes" to an even less desirable state of inveterately self-satisfied pseudo-civilization, which must be radically amended before India can reasonably aspire to take her place on a footing of equality among the nations of the world. Far from being the most favoured region of the earth, as sentimental patriotism is fond of asserting, India has been, from the very dawn of history, among the most unfortunate. That is the key to her past and her present: it is by realizing that, and striving to repair her misfortunes, not by talk about reviving a mythical Golden Age,* that her sons and her sympathizers can hasten the coming of a united and (so to speak) an adult India. If it be asked whether the British rule is to be placed to the account of

* There have been two periods, of a little over a century each, when the greater part of India was at any rate nominally united under Indian rulers, and when some approach to good government seems to have been attained. The Maurya Empire covered the third century B.C. and the Gupta Empire, roughly speaking, the fourth century A.D. The earlier period, described by Megasthenes, produced a really great monarch in the person of Asoka, and is certainly the nearest approach to an Indian Golden Age of which we have any record. Much less is known of the later period. Indeed, its greatest figure, Samudragupta, has left no trace in written records, his history having to be pieced together from inscriptions and coins. But even if we take the most romantic view of the civilization of these misty "empires," it is obvious that they lacked one important element of political well-being—namely, stability. They were transitory gleams in a dark and stormy internal history, constantly diversified by foreign invasion.

[28]

good or of evil fortune, the answer must be paradoxical and yet (I think) obvious. It is—or at any rate we trust it will prove to be—an extraordinary piece of good fortune; but at the same time it is the outcome and final evidence of no less extraordinary ill-fortune. That country must be hapless indeed of which it can be said that the best thing that could possibly befall it was a protracted period of foreign domination; yet all reasonable Indians admit that, whatever may be the shortcomings of the British rule, this is the truth of the matter. If India will but realize the immense leeway she has to make up, and take patient, strenuous advantage of the opportunity for doing so afforded her by the British rule, she may one day come to date the dawn of her regeneration from the Battle of Plassey.

But I have strayed away from my immediate theme: the high racial potentialities of India, contrasted with its actual state of degradation. By way of bringing the contrast home to the reader, let me jot down two impressions that came to me immediately before and immediately after I first set foot on Indian soil.

Ceylon is not India, but may be called its vestibule or outer court; and Colombo swarms with Indians of many tribes and castes, from Pathans of the north to Tamil-speaking people of the south. Coming from Japan and China, I spent a few days in Colombo, and noted on the one hand the white people around me at my hotel, on the other hand the brown types I encountered in the streets. And quite sincerely—without the slightest tinge of preconceived theory or paradox—I found myself almost blushing for my race. These Orientals, with their noble carriage, their dignity and distinction, seemed incomparably the finer breed of men. I do not mean the Sinhalese, but more par-

[29]

ticularly the Indian immigrants. One saw sinister faces, one saw fanatical faces, one saw heavy and rather stupid faces, but not one of the unfinished, shapeless potato faces so common in a European crowd—so common in the crowd at my hotel. I must confess that, for some reason or other, that crowd was an exceptionally insignificant set of people. As I looked round the dining-room of an evening, and saw the dapper little men in their dinner-jacket uniform, and the overdressed or underdressed women, chattering about the day's racing or the morrow's hockey, and complacently listening to the imbecile jingles ground out by the band—I could not but ask myself by what possible right we posed as a superior race. Outside, in the streets, I had seen Shylock, I had seen Othello, I had seen Sohrab and Rustum, I had seen a hundred stately and impressive figures. I had even seen two or three men who might have sat to a realistic painter as models for Christ—not, of course, the bland and lymphatic Saviour of pictorial convention, but the olive-browed, coal-eyed Enthusiast of historic probability. Surely it was a strange topsy-turvydom that reckoned the races which had produced these figures essentially inferior to the trivial mob around me—devoid of dignity, devoid of originality, devoid of earnestness, all cut to one dull pattern, all living up to the ideals of the vulgarest sporting papers, the only literature to which they appeared addicted.

I do not attribute any evidential value to this somewhat splenetic mood. I own that it never recurred with equal strength in India itself, where, take them all round, the sahibs look like sahibs in whatever environment they may be placed. They are often by no means such "fine men" as the Indians around them; but they and their forefathers for many generations have lived an intenser, a larger, a saner life, and it has left its imprint on their features. I

[30]

speak particularly of the men in the upper grades of the
services, who are, in a very real sense, picked men; while
my fellow-sojourners at the Colombo hotel were (I know
not why) distinctly below the fair British average. Per-.
haps, too, my keen admiration for the Indian types to be
seen in Ceylon was partly to be traced to my recent
recollections of the Japanese and Chinese, whose warmest
admirers will scarcely claim for them great dignity of carriage or nobility of feature. I admit, in short, that this
early impression of positive physical superiority in the
races of India is subject to a good deal of discount; but I
note it for what it is worth. Oddly enough, the one place
where it definitely recurred to me was Calcutta. The
physical type of the average Bengali as you meet him in
the streets—tall, bare-headed, with his toga-like garment
lightly draped around him—seemed to me remarkably
distinguished.

Now take another impression of only two days later.
From Colombo to Tuticorin you cross in a night; and the
early afternoon finds you in the city of Madura, famous for
its giant temple. The railway platform and all the purlieus
of the station are densely thronged with pilgrims, a motley,
scantily-attired, clamorous throng. Each family group
has its rope-tied bundle, its brass water-jar and simple
cooking utensils. Some are rushing aimlessly about;
others squatting patiently to await a train which may not
be due, perhaps, till next day; others, and these are many,
have stretched themselves on the ground, here, there and
everywhere, and are blissfully asleep, without even a pillow
for their heads. The first thing you learn in India, especially
in Southern India, is that you must walk warily for fear of
treading upon a slumbering fellow-citizen. But what is
it that gives the crowd such a strange and savage aspect?
Unless you are prepared for it (as I was not) you almost

[31]

gasp as you realize that everyone has his or her forehead daubed with some garish device, for all the world like the war-paint of the Indians of the West. But this is not war-paint, it is religion-paint. One commonly sees these devices alluded to as "caste-marks," but that they are not, at least as a general rule. They are sect-marks—marks of devotion to one or other deity of the swarming Hindu pantheon. Many men—perhaps most—have a huge trident plastered on their foreheads: one red prong between two white. This is the *trifala*, the mark of a Vaishnavite—a devotee of Vishnu. The devotees of Siva, at Madura at any rate, wear a comparatively chaste and unobtrusive device—a large round spot of bright carmine. But the daubs and blotches are endless in their variety—I never mastered the significance of more than two or three of them. Some people go about with three horizontal stripes of red or yellow across the whole breadth of their foreheads. Others wear two narrow vertical lines of vermilion with a white spot between them. Some wear a lozenge, others a triangle, others a circle with a spot in its centre. The sect-marks of the women are generally less obtrusive than those of the men, and the wearing of sect-marks at all seems to be on the decline in Northern India. But in the South it is practically universal, and it gives to the people a strange air of savagery combined with fanaticism. No doubt this does them some injustice; for, fanatics though they be, they are not usually savage fanatics. Nevertheless, explain and explain-away the custom as much as we please, it marks a low stage of spiritual development. True, it has its analogies in civilized life. There are people in Europe, not even of religious profession, who obtrude their "views" by wearing some sort of ecclesiastical ornament or badge. I have in my mind's eye at this moment a large cross aggressively pendent from the watch-chain of a prominent and rising

[32]

British politician. But to show that isolated survivals of savagery lurk here and there in civilized countries is not to prove that a whole population which plasters itself with religious war-paint* can be placed in the forefront of human development—or anywhere but sadly in the rear.

So, too, the fact that many European women wear earrings does not render the jewellery of their Southern Indian sisters any the less hideous. I say nothing of the anklets and bangles, finger-rings and toe-rings, worn in extravagant profusion. It is unreasonable, no doubt, to carry these pounds and pounds of metal on the person; but one cannot call the effect positively ugly; it has even a certain barbaric charm. But what of the ear-decorations and nose-jewels? Outside of Darkest Africa, there is probably only one more repellent manifestation of a perverted sense of beauty, and that is the tortured feet of the women of China. The women of Southern India carry in their ears not only enormous hoops and clusters of hoops—that would be a trifle—but often great carven bars of gold, three or four inches long and an inch thick, for the insertion of which not only the lobe of the ear but the upper cartilage is pierced and horribly distorted. There is a fantastic variety in these ornaments. You often see an ear in which half a jeweller's stock seems to be ingeniously inserted and suspended, the other half being in the other ear. And sometimes the same woman will wear in her nose either a gold ring three or four inches in diameter or a sort of aigrette of pearls and rubies drooping over the left side of her upper lip and coming well over the mouth. Not all women, of course, wear so much gold as this; not all bedeck both nose

* These marks, I believe, are not really of paint, but of sandal-wood paste dusted over with the required colours. In some cases they are drawn on the devotee's forehead (no doubt for a consideration) by the Brahmin who is his spiritual guide.

and ears; but it seemed to me in Madura that all women, down to the very humblest, had either silver or gold pendants or attachments, either in nose or ears, and generally of monstrous size. I have seen little girls of ten or twelve with clusters of silver hoops in their ears that must have weighed nearly as much as their heads.

But stay! not all women are so decorated. You see in Southern India not a few whose ear-lobes are monstrously expanded, so as to consist of a mere strip of cartilage round a hole three or four inches long, but who have nothing at all to fill the holes, their hoops and bars and ingots having all vanished away. I presume they are for the most part widows, whose finery has been confiscated by their deceased husband's relatives; but they may also be married women who have gone bankrupt and been forced to part with their treasures—to "live upon their capital." In any case, they are pathetic spectacles.

The south of India is more extravagant than the north in the variety and weight of its adornments; but huge ear-hoops and more or less elaborate nose-jewels are common everywhere. Now I do not forget the parable of the mote and the beam, and I grant that a traveller from India might find many relics of barbarism in European fashions of feminine adornment, for some of which I have not a word to say. But I submit that it is no mere local prejudice which holds a nose-jewel fit only for savages, and which sees all the difference in the world between a featherweight pendant at the ear and a golden dumb-bell which drags the lobe almost down to the shoulder. Even the pendant seems to me an undesirable survival, and I imagine that the civilized woman of the future will reject all such ornament. But no array of arguments of the "tu quoque" type can alter the fact that the boasted "civilization" of India has left its women, in their use of jewellery, at a very primitive

[34]

stage of development. Their innate grace and nobility of carriage bear testimony to splendid racial potentialities; but in this matter of personal adornment they have stood still for a thousand years. And the nose-ring, it need scarcely be added, is not only an obtrusive fact, but a symbol of profound significance.

Discussing caste-marks and nose-rings, we have not yet got beyond the platform of the Madura station. If we follow the stream of pilgrims, five minutes' walk will bring us to a street at the further end of which towers one of the huge *gopuras* of the temple. The *gopura* is a gateway surmounted by a wedge-shaped tower, 150 feet high; and, as you approach it, you see that the whole surface of the tower is one mass of human or quasi-human figures, ranged in horizontal rows. They are mitred, hawk-faced figures, wasp-waisted, and posed in a sort of affected prancing attitude, so that they are not only grotesque, but vaguely suggest some sort of sophistication or corruption. The main figures are, I fancy, something over life-size; and there are numberless subsidiary figures around them. Whether they are in high relief or absolutely in the round, I cannot say; but the relief, if relief there be, is certainly very high. The material, I take it, is some sort of terra-cotta; the general colouring a reddish yellow. I tried to count the figures on a small section of the tower, but found it quite impossible; at a rough guess, I should say that on one *gopura* alone there must be well over a thousand. In the distance, its mere mass is impressive; close at hand it is no longer impressive, but oppressive in the highest degree. This senseless reduplication to infinity of one mincing, prancing figure produces an indescribably nightmare-like effect; and what can be said for it, from the point of view either of art or of religion, I, for my part, cannot conceive. Who the figures represent I am not sure; they may be guardians of the

temple, they may be *Gandharvas*, they may be Siva himself.
I forgot to mention that, to the best of my belief, they have
either four or six arms apiece; at least, if these particular
figures have not, they strangely depart from the usual type.
It may seem odd that my memory should be uncertain on
such a point; but where all is monstrous, a few extra arms
or heads are mere details that easily escape attention. And
here, assuredly, all was monstrous, from the general conception of the gateway to the smallest subsidiary figure.
I had seen fragments of such monstrosity before, in museums
such as that of Mexico City, where are preserved the relics
of extinct barbarisms. But to come face to face with it
on so enormous a scale—not fragmentary, not under a
glass case, but towering under the open sky, an adjunct to
a living cult, a "going concern"—this was an experience
which positively took my breath away.* Does it show gross
ignorance on my part that I should have come upon it
unprepared? Was the reader, by chance, better informed?
There are thousands of Europeans in India itself who know
nothing of the wonder and the horror of these great temples
of the South.

Yes, the horror—that is the only word for it. I do not
mean that nowadays any particular horrors are perpetrated
in the grim recesses of these giant fanes. I do not know
that at any time they were the scenes of great cruelty or
other abominations, though certainly they present the com-
pletest *mise-en-scène* for such excesses.† What I do know

* Pierre Loti calls these *gopuras* "pyramids of gods," and says: "The
inconceivable abuse of detail is as disquieting as the excessive mass.
All that one imagined one knew, all that fairy-plays and spectacles
had tried to reproduce, is amazingly surpassed."

† Sir Alfred Lyall writes in his *Asiatic Studies*, Vol. I. (1882): "The
more cruel and indecent rites of Brahmanism have hitherto owed their
reformation principally to ordinances of the English police, who have
suppressed suicide, self-mutilation, and other unsightly or immodest

is that, from the corner-stone to the coping of the highest *gopura*, they are the product of gloomy, perverted, morbidly overwrought imaginations, revelling in the most extravagant features of the most monstrous of all mythologies. This temple of Madura is by no means the oldest of its kind: it dates, for the most part, from the sixteenth and seventeenth centuries. It is not the largest, though to make its circuit you have to walk a good mile. But it easily surpasses the others I have seen—Trichinopoly and Tanjore—in its labyrinthine gloom. As you pass along its lofty corridors, between monolith granite pillars carved into all sorts of fantastic shapes, you can readily imagine yourself in Nineveh or Babylon three thousand years ago. And on every hand, in its swarming courts and alcoves, you see the lowest fetichism intent on its grovelling rites. Here is a huge elephant-headed idol—Ganesh, the God of Luck—shining as though freshly black-leaded, because his devotees keep him constantly anointed with *ghee* (clarified butter) and other unguents. Yonder is a band of women decking with flowers the *lingam*, an emblem of procreation, known, indeed, to most primitive cults, but surviving unabashed (so far as I am aware) in India alone. In the sacred water of a great green tank, surrounded with colonnades (the one feature of the temple which can by any stretch of language be called beautiful) men and women

spectacles. . . . Our police drag people from under Jagannath's car, and fine the whole township if a man kills or mutilates himself. Human sacrifices are still perpetrated under the cloaks of mysterious, unaccountable murders." Here the writer is probably thinking of sacrifices to obscure deities of the village or the jungle. I have heard nothing to connect the great temples of Southern India with any such practices. But one cannot but wonder how much the police knows of what goes on in the dark penetralia of these labyrinths of stone, jealously guarded against intrusion on the part of low-caste or casteless persons, whether Indian or European.

are washing away their sins: but where is the fire-hose that
ought to be turned on them to wash away the filth of the
sacred tank? In the neighbourhood of the Holy of Holies,
a half-naked group of shaven-headed Brahmins are squatting on the ground, twining the thread that marks their
"twice-born" caste, and discussing (let us hope) some of
those metaphysical mysteries that are believed to underlie
the "allegories" of Hinduism. Not far off, a long wall is
covered with miniature frescoes, old and new, childish in
drawing, crude in colour, illustrating various grotesque and
horrible, but doubtless edifying, legends. The only one I
remember depicted the impaling of certain Jain heretics.
I did not know before what "impaling" meant, and the
reader will do wisely not to inquire. That there were any
actual obscenities in the frescoes I cannot aver; but the
carving of several of the pillars represented unspeakable
aberrations of sensual imagery, which the guide pointed out
with modest satisfaction.* The atmosphere of the whole
vast building was heavy with the emanations of cows, the
scent of camphor, and the sickly smell of decaying marigolds
and other flowers. For it is the dominant characteristic of
Hinduism, not in the South alone, that whatever it touches
it soils. Flowers enter largely into its ritual, but I have
never seen them used with the smallest sense of beauty.
Generally, as here at Madura, they are left rotting around,
bedraggled and faded, like torn bouquets on an ash-heap.†

* These carvings were, no doubt, some three centuries old; but in
another temple of the South I saw a quite new Jagannath Car, still under
the hands of the artist, one panel at least of which represented a revolting obscenity.

† Lest it be thought that I have achieved the impossible and exaggerated the hugeness and the squalor of the temple at Madura, I
append a page from Pierre Loti's masterly description of it: "I have
to give up all attempt to keep track of the ways by which the priests
guide me through the labyrinth of vaults. The further we advance, the
more does everything seem to me overwhelming and superhuman. Every-

[38]

As I walked along one of the outer corridors, I heard a curious rapid shuffling behind me. Thinking that a beggar with loose sandals was following at my heels, I turned round to send him away, when, behold! I stood face to face with a giant elephant, swaying his gorgeously painted trunk almost over my head. I looked with respect upon the mighty brute. He seemed to me the most dignified, the most sane, the most wholesome among all the denizens of the temple—and certainly not the worst theologian.

Then I took a gharry and drove, past a wonderful banyan-tree that might have sheltered an army, to a really beautiful square tank with an island fane in its middle. Under some trees on the farther shore, stood a little yellow temple. It consisted of a shadowy cella, wherein a figure of the goddess Kali was dimly visible, and a long narrow portico, the roof of which was crowded with rude plaster figures—votive offerings, I conceive. But these are not the offerings in which Kali or Durga chiefly delights. In front of the portico stood an altar, and the earth around it was sodden with blood. Four newly severed heads of kids lay at the altar foot; and as I stood there a burly Brahmin caught one of several live kids that were skipping around,

thing is constructed of more and more enormous blocks. The gods with a score of arms, the gods of colossal and manifold gestures, swarm in the gloom. . . . I move, as if in a dream, through the realm of giants and hobgoblins. . . . The sculptures grow ever more prodigious, the magnificence ever greater, and at the same time there is more of barbarous slovenliness, more of filth. . . . Here is a gallery consecrated to Ganesh, the elephant-headed god, whose monstrous person is lighted from below by some smoky rushlights burning at his feet, underneath his trunk. Here, again, in a sinister recess, as dark as night, is a lazy family of sebu-cows. . . . One slips about in their dung with which the pavement is littered; but no one would dare to throw it out as an unclean thing, for whatever proceeds from their entrails is as sacred as they are themselves. And every moment great broad-winged bats flap about in alarm above our heads."

douched it with water from a brass pot, threw it down, placed his foot on its head, and gashed its throat with a knife. Then he turned back the head so as to make the muscles of the throat tense and, with another slash, completed the decapitation. It was quickly and skilfully done. Far worse cruelties are perpetrated, I daresay, in slaughter-houses; infinitely worse on battlefields. But it was the first time I had seen innocent blood shed in the name of religion; and I drove back to Madura radically revising the illusion, to which I had well-nigh yielded in Colombo, only forty-eight hours before, of the racial superiority of the Oriental. My present feeling was very like that of the hero of *Locksley Hall:*

"For I hold the grey barbarian lower than the Christian child."

Barbarian, barbarism, barbarous—I am sorry to harp so much on these words. But they express the essence of the situation. The potentially noble peoples of India have, by an age-old concatenation of inauspicious circumstances, been baulked of adequate opportunity of development, and arrested in a condition of barbarism. There are, of course, many thousands of individuals who have risen and are rising above it; but the plain truth concerning the mass of the population—and not the poorer classes alone—is that they are *not civilised people.* The tokens of barbarism in manners and religion on which I have been dwelling are, indeed, superficial. They might conceivably cover, if not a highly developed, at least a healthy and progressive social state. But it need scarcely be said that this is not the case: even the strange Europeans who are attracted by Hinduism as a religion are but half-hearted in their defence of the social institutions associated with it. The more we look into it, the more clearly do we realize that these institutions have spelt disaster for the peoples of India.

TANJORE: SMALL TEMPLE

No intelligent Hindu would contest this statement, though many, if not all, would contend for a soul of goodness in Hinduism. Perhaps they are right. At all events they are probably wise in attempting to base their efforts at reform on the conservation of whatever elements of good they can find in the national traditions. These reforming movements are in many ways admirable and deserving of all sympathy; but the task before them is dishearteningly huge. It seems to me manifest beyond all argument that India must at least be well advanced towards social salvation before she can dream of attaining a stable political organization, unbuttressed from without. If circumstances enabled her to throw off British rule before the leaven of social reform had thoroughly permeated her system, she would simply add a crowning calamity to the long series of which her history consists. Another recent observer, not to be suspected of British bias,* has noted in the following terms the contrast between racial potentialities and actual development, which I have been trying to illustrate in the present chapter:

"Some of these dark people," he writes, "have the faces and the port and carriage of power; but it is hollow, the shadow of an inheritance, not the real substance. It is as though the masks of warriors and sages were walking about untenanted. The character and power have become exhausted, leaving the husk of a great civilization gone to seed."

This is a picturesque image, but, in my view, scarcely a just one. There never was a "great civilization" in India; but there must have been, in the epic ages, a splendid barbarism. In the course of hapless centuries, it sank into the Hinduism we see to-day; but the survival in so large a

* Price Collier: *The West in the East, from an American point of view,* p. 332.

measure of the noble physical characteristics of the race warrants the hope that the development, arrested so many ages ago, may be successfully resumed, and, once fairly under way, may proceed with great rapidity. That is an optimistic view; but there are moments when one can hold to it without too much effort.

III

IT is the fashion to preface all accounts of India with the statement that it is not one country but a "sub-continent," and to enlarge upon the diversities of race and language contained within its boundaries. We are told, for instance, that the people of India speak one hundred and forty-seven idioms, reducible to fifty clearly different languages, which, again, belong to twelve families or types. The Abbé Dubois, though his travels did not extend beyond the southern third of the country, tells us that "A careful observer would see less resemblance between a Tamil and a Canarese, between a Telugu and a Maratha, than between a Frenchman and an Englishman, an Italian and a German." It would indeed be a very careless observer who should fail to note the difference between the Bengali and the Baluch of Sind, the Madrasi and the Rajput.

The implied and often explicit deduction from these facts is that India is incapable of unity unless it be imposed on her from without. But this is a dogma which demands careful scrutiny.

To the naked eye, so to speak, examining the map of the world, India seems rather conspicuously a geographical unit. She holds in Asia a position curiously analogous to that of Italy in Europe: she is the midmost of three south-ward-stretching peninsulas; she has a great island attached to her toe; and her northern river-plains are bastioned by a gigantic mountain range, the highest in the continent. We now hold Italy beyond all question a natural unit; but

[43]

little more than half a century ago, theorists were declaring that she could never be one; that her people were a hotch-potch of invading races; that the Neapolitan could not understand the Venetian, the Calabrian the Piedmontese; and that local jealousies would always frustrate the purely factitious aspiration towards unity. Events have shown that the centripetal forces were immensely stronger than the centrifugal, and that geographical unity meant much more than the theorists were willing to allow. May it not prove so in India as well?

"Encircled as she is by seas and mountains," writes Mr. Vincent A. Smith, "India is indisputably a geographical unit, and, as such, is rightly designated by one name. Her type of civilization, too, has many features which differentiate it from that of all other regions of the world, while they are common to the whole country, or rather continent, in a degree sufficient to justify its treatment as a unit in the history of the social, religious and intellectual development of mankind."

Sir Alfred Lyall writes to the same effect: "Although the Indians are broken up into diversities of race and language, they are as a whole not less distinctly marked off from the rest of Asia by certain material and moral characteristics, than their country is by the mountains and the sea. The component parts of that great country hang together, physically and politically; there is no more room for two irreconcilable systems of government than in Persia, China or Asiatic Turkey." Sir Alfred is here accounting for the failure of England's perfectly sincere and repeated efforts to check the spread of her dominion over the whole geographical area—to lay down for her proconsuls a "thus far and no further." But from the fact that India could never be at peace save under one rule, it does not necessarily follow that that rule must forever be a foreign one.

[44]

I am disposed to think—though on this point the historians give us no very clear guidance—that India's chief misfortune may be found to have lain in the very fact of her indisputable unity, coupled with her huge and unwieldy size. Every potentate, native or foreign, who achieved a certain measure of strength within her borders, was irresistibly tempted to extend his sway over the whole area. Owing to the lack of strong natural frontiers, he might find no great difficulty in nominally subduing a vast extent of country; but "effective occupation" was a different matter; and still more impossible was permanent organization under one central control. Thus empires rose and fell to pieces again like waves in a tumbling sea. There was no political rest or stability; and men, unable to attain any national cohesion or organization, fell back upon that caste cohesion which has proved so disastrous to healthy development.

It might have been a great deal better for India if her geographical unity had not been so incontestable—if she had been broken up into clearly-marked states of manageable size, within whose natural frontiers nations might gradually have differentiated, while they defended with patriotic spirit their own territory and institutions. As it is, this region, as large as all Europe minus Russia, has no predestinate and easily defensible internal partitions. Rivers are nowhere a good frontier, and least of all in India, where so many of them dwindle in the dry season into a mere trickle from pool to pool. The Vindhya mountains, though they clearly mark off the Indo-Gangetic plain from the southern table-land, are not comparable, as a strategic frontier, to the Alps or the Pyrenees; and the hills of Rajputana, the fantastic outcrops of the Deccan, rarely encompass what may be called definite and convenient kingdoms. They make fine fortresses, but poor barriers. The

[45]

strips of coast country east and west of the Ghats are too narrow to form strong political units. We see, as a matter of fact, that the districts into which India was divided before the British rule, were always vague and fluctuating. Many of the names were purely regional, with no distinct political significance—such as the Malabar coast, the Coromandel coast, the Deccan, even the Punjab. Rajputana was parcelled out among clans whose frontiers were, for the most part, arbitrary and unsettled. Many of the existing provinces and native states were administrative divisions of the Moghul Empire, with about as much geographical individuality as may be claimed for Norfolk, Suffolk and Essex. It is true that when Lord Curzon, presuming upon the fluctuating quality of India's internal frontiers, decreed the partition of Bengal, he raised a hornets' nest about his ears; but that was the outcome of a new spirit with which he declined to reckon, begotten of British rule. As Sir Thomas Holderness observes: "An Indian province is not what we mean by a nation, though it tends to create a provincial spirit which is not far removed from national life."

It is a little difficult to see why, with this absence of natural frontiers and feeble development of national life, there should be such great diversity of language in India. That the Aryan languages should fail to oust the Dravidian and other aboriginal tongues is comprehensible enough; but why. did the Aryan speech itself break up into so many widely different idioms? Why is there one language in Russia, one language (even though its dialects differ widely) in China, and more than two score distinct languages in India? I do not know that this striking difference has ever been explained.

But the tragic paradox of India's fate is this: she is unified by that which at the same time divides and enfeebles her. Over all her kindreds, peoples, tribes and tongues, except a few lingering savages in her mountains and a few emancipated folk in her modern cities, the great institution of Caste holds sway, and has done so from time almost (though not quite) immemorial. Even the Muhammadans, whose religion is theoretically equalitarian, have caught from Hinduism the contagion of caste; as the Hindus, whose religion does not require the seclusion of women, have been confirmed by Islam in the purdah habit. Hapless, indeed, is the country which instinctively fastens upon whatever is worst in its contending religions, and makes it a rule of life.

This is not the place to discuss the merits and demerits of caste. I merely point out that an institution which nowhere else in the world exists in anything like the same form, has ruled for something like three thousand years throughout the length and breadth of India. It sprang, perhaps, as above suggested, from the absence of national life; and, once established, it effectually barred the development of national life. Not country, but caste, was, and in great measure still is, the object of loyalty. Under the dominance of caste, every community is divided against itself. The very idea of a common-weal is excluded where one social stratum would disdain to have anything, whether weal or woe, in common with another. Therefore, as a patriotic Indian writer * points out, the vernaculars of India possess "no single simple word" to express the idea of patriotism. "One result of contact with the Occident has been the development of this feeling," so that "the dialects now possess specially coined terms for it." Caste, then, goes far to explain India's lack of political cohesion and power of resistance to foreign conquest. Nevertheless, even a common vice forms, in its way, a bond of union. Caste is a

* Saint Nihal Singh in the *Hindustan Review*. December, 1912.

vice which affects India, all India and—in its extreme development—nothing but India. Its tyranny will have to be broken before India can become a nation among other modern nations; but the very struggle against it, affecting as it does all regions and all classes, is the mark of a real, indefeasible unity. When caste is nothing but a memory, it will be a memory common to all India, in which the rest of the world will have no share.

So, too, with religion, of which, indeed, caste is little more than an offshoot. It is true that there are two religions in India, and that their antagonism is supposed to have promoted in the past, and to facilitate in the present, the rule of a foreign race. Some people will even tell you that relations between the two bodies are becoming more and more embittered, and that any real community of thought or action between them is out of the question. "An individual cat may get on with an individual dog," a high official said to me, "but the race of cats and the race of dogs will never get on together." I do not pretend to decide whether this gentleman saw deeper into the essence of the existing situation than the numerous Hindus and Muhammadans who are labouring to improve the relations between their communities; but I believe that when the time is ripe for Indian self-government, Hindus and Muhammadans will find some means of adjusting their differences more dignified than querulous appeals to the British *sirkar*. Is it not partly because both are, so to speak, suitors before an external judgment-seat that each is so determined not to let the other over-reach him?

In any case, the presence of Islam in India scarcely lightens the enormous unifying pressure of Hinduism. An emanation from the sacred soil of Aryavarta, it has absorbed all previous cults, and has constituted, from the beginning of recorded time, the whole mental atmosphere of

[48]

an overwhelming majority of the population. If we include
some 3,000,000 Sikhs, 1,250,000 Jains, and about 250,000
members of the Arya and Brahmo reforming sects, the
Hindus of to-day number nearly 222,000,000, as against
something less than 67,000,000 Mussulmans. And the pre-
dominance of Hinduism is by no means expressed in these
numbers. Millions of the Mussulmans are extremely ignorant of their own religion and enormously influenced by sur-
rounding Hinduism. To many adherents of each creed, in
fact, the only salient and tangible difference between them
lies in the circumstance that the one holds cows sacred and
the other does not. Again, the educated Mussulman does
not withhold his admiration from the religious, philosophic
and epic literature of the Hindus. He takes pride in it as
the literature of India: just as the educated Hindu reckons
the Taj and Fatehpur Sikri among the glories, not of Muslim, but of Indian architecture. In short, the fact that
India has in Hinduism an indigenous and extremely ancient
religion, absolutely peculiar to herself, is in no way cancelled
by the fact that about a quarter of the population have, in
comparatively recent centuries, become dissenters from it.
Hinduism is, and will remain, a mighty bond of union. There
is nothing local or parochial in its spirit. "To the Hindu of
all provinces, his Motherland is the seat of holiness, the
chosen home of righteousness, the land of the seven sacred
rivers, 'the place to which, sooner or later, must come all
souls in quest of God.' "

After my account of the temple at Madura and of the
sacrifice to Kali, I shall scarcely be suspected of an exaggerated esteem for Hindu ritual. In another chapter, I
shall have to go further and confess to the gravest doubts
as to the supreme value of Hindu philosophy, and, in
general, as to the spiritual genius which Hindus are fond
of claiming for themselves, and which we Westerners, I

[49]

cannot help thinking, too lightly admit. Still more heretically, perhaps, I shall have to inquire whether the great epics, the Mahabharata and the Ramayana, are, in fact, wholesome mental sustenance for a people which aspires to play an independent part in the drama of the future, upon the stage of the real world. But whatever may be our private doubts as to the value of Indian literature, especially in relation to the problems of the coming age, there is not the least question that India does possess a literature of immense historic interest, to which many great scholars, and some great critics, have assigned a very high rank among the literatures of the world. We are assured, too, that the influence of this literature has filtered down through the whole mass of the people—that the most illiterate, fetish-worshipping peasant is conversant with lofty spiritual ideas, and (more credibly) that he is familiar with the doughty deeds of the Pandus, and with the romantic fortunes of Rama and Sita. As to the depth of his metaphysics I remain unconvinced; but there is no doubt that all Indians are conscious of having behind them a great religious and legendary—or, as they think, historic—literature. To the Brahmins has been confided the care of the spiritual treasures left behind by their forefathers, while the loves and exploits of the national heroes have, in one form or another, become common property. The unifying influence of this living literary tradition must be apparent; and it cannot be supposed that even low-class Muhammadans remain quite outside it. Many of those who, in the Mohurrum, rend the air with their frenzied shouts of "Ya Hasan! Ya Hosein!" are perhaps, in reality, more intimate with Arjuna and Krishna than with the saints of their own religion.

We see, as a matter of historic fact, that no outside influence is needed to make the two religions pull fairly well together. The horrors of Muslim conquest and the

[50]

persecutions of Aurungzebe are things of the remote past. Before we established ourselves in India, Muhammadan princes ruled over Hindu subjects, and Hindu princes over Muhammadan subjects, with very tolerable impartiality of rule or misrule. And the same is true in the native states of to-day, not merely as a result of British overlordship. At no time since the days of Aurungzeb has either religion seriously tried to overpower and cast out the other. The attempt, supposing it possible, would have been too manifestly ruinous and suicidal. That there should be friction and occasional rioting between Hindu and Muhammadan is only natural. We have seen ignorant fanaticism lead to religious faction-fights nearer home. Nor is there anything surprising in the bitter squabbles of the two creeds over the loaves and fishes of government employ. The greater suppleness and (as a rule) the better education of the Hindu, to say nothing of his numerical superiority, give him an advantage which is naturally galling to the Muhammadan; while in every preference shown to the Muhammadan, the Hindu is apt to find confirmation of his belief that the great maxim of British statecraft is "divide and rule." That this maxim has any conscious weight in our councils I do not believe. The difficulty of holding the balance between the two persuasions is no fault of ours, and I believe we try to hold it true without any ulterior motive. But when British officials, undreaming of any other ideal than the perpetuity of the *raj*, assure us that "cat and dog will never get on together," I would not swear but that the wish may be father to the thought.

Cat and dog got on well enough together in 1857. It was not any religious dissension that saved the sahibs from being driven into the sea.

In one regard, however, it must be admitted that England has in effect, though not in outward form, adopted the principle of "divide and rule." In her policy of maintaining nearly four score native states * under her suzerainty, she has, not exactly divided, but deliberately abstained from unifying. The rulers of these principalities, large and small, are, as a whole, genuinely loyal to the Empire, and sincerely opposed to any idea of self-government. They see in British rule (quite justly) a conservative force, and they dread and shrink from the New India, unknown, untried, and to them unimaginable, which is germinating in the brains of political agitators. In a double sense, then, the native states are bulwarks of the Empire. They not only strengthen it in the present, but they make it difficult to conceive the place they are to occupy in any non-autocratic organization of the future. Nor do they render it possible to dream of a national autocracy, an Indian Empire under an Indian Emperor. Not one of them is, either in historic prestige or in actual wealth and power, sufficiently predominant to afford a rallying-point for any aspirations of this order; and, in fact, no such aspirations exist. There are no Indian Jacobites or Carlists. It is conceivable, no doubt, that a United India might choose to call itself an Empire, and might enthrone as Emperor one of its princes. But if so, it would be by reason of some personal merit or preponderance, not of any revival of historic loyalty.

If England had incorporated all the native states with her own immediate dominions, she would have enormously facilitated the movement towards national unity. The mingling of moderation and astuteness which prevented her from doing so will probably prolong her rule in India, and that, very likely, to the great ultimate benefit of the country. The chief danger which India has to fear is the premature dissolution of her dependence on Britain. But

* Their area is over 700,000 square miles, their population over 70,000,-000.

the obstacle of the native states cannot for ever bar the way to unity. Times change and even maharajas change with them. It was a maharaja, who, speaking to Mr. Price Collier, "hinted at a federation of states under a central government."

To sum up the argument of the present chapter: India is one of the most clearly-marked geographical units in the world. Nature could scarcely have individualized her better if, instead of a half-island, she had made her a whole-island. There is, indeed, much diversity of race and language within her bounds, but that has not hindered a very marked unity of cult and custom. All Indians have been Indians, and as such, definitely related to each other and distinguished from the rest of the world, for a much longer time than Englishmen have been English, Frenchmen French, or Germans German. The numerous attempts to translate into terms of political organization the geographical unity of the country have hitherto failed disastrously, for the simple reason that the country was too huge. In the days when there were few roads and no railways, it was impossible for a central power to hold its lieutenants in control, and an empire was no sooner formed than it began to disintegrate. But roads, railroads and telegraphs have changed all that. The British rule, bringing these things with it,* reduced India to a manageable size. It has made unity a

---

* Indian malcontents are apt to resent such statements as this, on the ground that India would no doubt have had railroads and telegraphs even if British rule had never existed. That is true: European capital would no doubt have rushed in to some extent, whatever had been the political conditions of the country. But the spread of these material adjuncts and forerunners of civilisation has been enormously facilitated by the unity and peace of the country; and unity and peace it would certainly not have had except under British, or some other external, rule. And undoubtedly the necessary capital has been obtained at a far cheaper rate than would have been possible under other political conditions.

political as well as a geographical and spiritual fact, and it has thereby begotten a sentiment of unity which it is folly to ridicule as factitious or denounce as seditious. Why should we dream that three hundred millions of people who are, in the main, able-bodied, and whom we are honestly, if not too efficiently, striving to render able-minded, should go on to the end of time "obeying orders given in a foreign accent?" Why stake our national prestige on achieving so undesirable a miracle? Especially when our national glory so obviously lies in the opposite direction—in the building up of a united, self-controlled, virile and responsible India.

IV

THE common task which English and Indians have before them—that of bringing India into line in the march of civilization—will not be facilitated by false ideals on either side. And the Indian is at least as liable to them as the Englishman.

The Abbé Dubois, a Catholic missionary who spent the best part of his life in the most intimate contact with the peoples of Southern India—who adopted their dress, spoke their languages, and came to be accepted by them almost as one of themselves—wrote of them nearly a century ago as "a vain and self-sufficient people, filled with the idea of their own moral ascendancy." This is plain speaking, but there is a great deal of justice in it even to-day. Indeed, if the worthy Abbé had said "moral and intellectual ascendancy," he would not have been far wrong. Until Hindu patriotism is dissociated from irrational arrogance, and associated with rational humility, the advance of the mass of the people towards self-respecting intelligence must inevitably be slow.

I do not say that the same remark is not justly applicable to many other people nearer home. That is not the question: two blacks do not make one white. Nor do I say that the reproach applies to all Indians. On the contrary, the leading intelligences of the country prove their claim to that position by seeing things in juster proportions. But the general tendency is to regard India as a sort of divinity

[55]

under a cloud: a heaven-born paragon of genius, valour, piety and learning, who has only to cast off an evil spell in order to shine forth in the eyes of all the world, resplendent, incomparable, the saviour of the human species. Now the evil spell is real enough: another name for it is the history of India. The illusion lies in supposing that the races which have undergone that spell were in any way specially favoured at the outset, and that the ban can be lifted in any other way than by a patient and resolute struggle gradually to undo its effects.

It cannot be said that India is self-hypnotized into this illusion. I have already given one or two specimens of the flatteries—or if that word begs the question, let us say eulogies—which have been heaped upon her by Western writers. These eulogies may be roughly divided into two classes: those of scholars whose painfully-acquired knowledge of Sanskrit literature naturally inclines them to make the most of a treasure which has cost them so much; and those of a recent school of enthusiasts who find in the arcana of Hinduism the basis of certain esoteric doctrines which they believe to be the ultimate truths of religion. Of neither group of eulogists would I be understood to speak with disrespect. Certainly not of the latter group: I believe that its leader, Mrs. Annie Besant, has done much good in India, and I know that she has uttered a great deal of sound sense on education and other topics. But when it comes to making India the birthplace and home, not only of all spirituality, but of all science, I can no longer follow either the learned or the illuminated.

Listen to the late Colonel H. S. Olcott, lecturing at Amritsar in 1880 on *India, Past, Present and Future*. After claiming for the Aryans "a system of telegraphy without either poles, wires or pots of chemicals"—in other words, a probable enough knowledge of telepathy—he proceeded:

[56]

"And then the Aryans—if we may believe that good man the late Bramachari Bawa—knew a branch of science (*Viman Vidya*) about which the West is now speculating much, but has learnt next to nothing. They could navigate the air, and not only navigate but fight battles in it, like so many war eagles combating for the dominion of the clouds. To be perfect in aeronautics, as he justly says, they must have known all the arts and sciences related to that science, including the strata and currents of the atmosphere, their relative temperature, humidity and density, and the specific gravity of the various gases. At the Mayasabha, described in the Bharata, he tells us, were microscopes, telescopes, clocks, watches, mechanical singing birds, and articulating and speaking animals. The *Ashta Vidya*—a science of which our modern professors have not even an inkling—enabled its proficients completely to destroy an invading army by enveloping it in an atmosphere of poisonous gases, filled with awe-striking shadowy shapes, and with awful sounds."

The late Bramachari Bawa, one imagines, must have been a spiritual kinsman—possibly a former incarnation—of Mr. H. G. Wells. If the proficients of the *Ashta Vidya* had indeed at their command this short and easy method of dealing with invading armies, it seems a pity that they were so chary of exercising it—there was ample opportunity in Indian history.

Colonel Olcott, it may be said, was a well-known visionary, credulous of all marvels. But similar credulity is by no means uncommon in India. "I have known an educated Indian," says Professor Oman, "to maintain with much warmth that in the Golden Age the *rishis* and others were well acquainted with the art of aerial navigation, and probably with other rapid modes of locomotion unknown to us moderns. I have heard him assert boldly that even the telephone, microphone and phonograph were known to the Hindu sages, up to the time when the sciences and arts of

[57]

the ancient world perished . . . on the fatal field of Kuruk-shetra." Some maintain that the art of constructing aeroplanes, and other marvels of applied science, was deliberately withdrawn from human ken by the *rishis*—a mysterious race of semi-divine sages—because they held them inappropriate to a dark age (*Kali Yuga*) which they saw to be impending over the world. Why did they not apply their stupendous powers to averting the dark age, instead of giving us the trouble of conquering Nature all over again?

On such insanities, however, it is profitless to dwell. The glory which is claimed for India by serious Western thinkers —in words re-echoed a thousandfold by Indians themselves —is that of high spirituality, a unique genius for grasping and expounding the realities behind the phenomenal world, and the innermost meanings of life.

One finds traces of this idea in the most unexpected quarters. I have heard a British civilian, high in place and rich in experience, say that in the daily work of administration and legislation he often had to deal with Indians of greater intellectual capacity than his own; and on inquiring into his reasons for so esteeming them, I have found it to lie mainly in the fact that they were familiar with regions of thought which were to him untrodden ground, and ground, moreover, on which his robust practical intellect could find no foothold. Now it is probable enough that he did, as a matter of fact, have to meet, in discussion, "foemen worthy of his steel"— perhaps quicker and suppler-minded than he. But I contested, and still contest, his assumption that familiarity with metaphysical conceptions—perhaps even the power of arguing with some subtlety on metaphysical points—is necessarily a proof of great mental capacity. I am sceptical of the value of thought in a region where there is no possible test of values.

Another proof of the widespread acceptance of India's

claim to supreme religio-philosophic genius may be found in a very judicious book by a highly qualified student and observer of Indian affairs—*The Economic Transition in India*, by Sir Theodore Morison. The very last words of that book are these: "We can only hope that India may be warned in time by the example of Europe, and that her industrial revolution may not be disfigured by the reckless waste of human life and human happiness which has stained the annals of European industry. Most of all must we wish that, in the fierce struggle for material wealth, she may not lose the lofty idealism by which she has hitherto been so nobly distinguished."

What is this "idealism?" What is its meaning? What does it amount to? These are questions to which I have been unable to find a very satisfactory answer.

The extraordinary interest of the early religio-philosophic literature of India is beyond all doubt. Beginning with the four Vedas (hymns, invocations and magical formulas) it proceeds through the Brahmanas (ritual prescriptions) and the Aranyakas (literally "jungle books," for the use of anchorites) to the Upanishads or philosophical treatises, explaining, allegorizing or supplementing the primitive nature-worship of the Vedic hymns. The meaning of the word "Upanishad" is much disputed, but Deussen interprets it as "secret word" or "secret text." The Upanishads, or their doctrines, are sometimes termed the Vedanta—the end or consummation of the Vedas.*

Everyone admits that as documents in the history of the human spirit the Vedas are invaluable. They can be dated only within very wide limits; their text is thought to have been much "worked over," and is so obscure as to lend itself to ludicrous divergences of interpretation; but, after all

* I trust there is no gross error in this paragraph; but very confusing explanations are given of even the nomenclature of this literature.

deductions, they remain, I take it, the earliest religious out-
pourings that have assumed anything like literary form.
Some of the hymns are said to be beautiful; a few certainly
show a gift of philosophic penetration, rare among primitive
peoples. I shall quote in a later chapter an utterance of a
sort of agnosticism, very striking in a work of such early
date. But to place the Vedas as a whole on the summits
of literature is to confuse historic with æsthetic and spiritual
values. It has been well said that "two classes of persons
entertain the most exalted notions of the Vedas: those who
know nothing of them, and those who know nothing else."
Let us hear Max Müller on this point—an authority certainly not apt to depreciate the wisdom of the Orient. He
says:

> There have been silly persons who have represented the devel-
> opment of the Indian mind as superior to any other, nay, who
> would make us go back to the Veda, or to the sacred writings of
> the Buddhists, in order to find there a truer religion, a purer
> morality and a more sublime philosophy than our own. . . . That
> the Veda is full of childish, silly, even to our mind monstrous
> conceptions, who would deny?

And again, in another place:

> The historical importance of the Veda can hardly be exagger-
> ated, but its intrinsic merit, and particularly the beauty or ele-
> vation of its sentiments, have by many been rated far too high.
> Large numbers of the Vedic hymns are childish in the extreme:
> tedious, low, commonplace. . . . The Veda contains a great deal
> of what is childish and foolish, though very little of what is bad
> and objectionable. * Some of its poets ascribe to the gods sen-

* Here Max Müller is, of course, thinking of the Rig-Veda, and the
same remark may probably apply to the Sama and Yajur Vedas, which
closely follow the Rig-Veda. But of the later Atharva Veda we are told
that it is "full of magical verses, some to remove disease, cause hair to

timents and passions unworthy of deity, such as anger, revenge, delight in material sacrifices; they likewise represent human nature on a low level of selfishness and worldliness. Many hymns are utterly unmeaning and insipid, and we must search patiently before we meet, here and there, with sentiments that come from the depth of the soul, and with prayers in which we could join ourselves.

No one, assuredly, who looks into the translations of the Rig-Veda can fail to admire the indomitable industry which has sustained scholars in their struggle not only with the obscurities but with the extreme tediousness of the greater part of the hymns. The Rev. K. S. Macdonald, a missionary, no doubt, but a very liberal-minded one, writes:

The same prayers for the gratification of sensual, carnal and worldly desires occur so continuously that it is a positive pain to read any large number of hymns at a sitting. One becomes sick of such praises and prayers, and longs to see men and women go about their ordinary occupations. . . . The horizon of the *Rishi* is confined almost invariably to himself. He prays for the happiness of neither wife nor child, not for the good of his village or his clan, nor yet for his nation, or people. He manifests no common joys, any more than common sorrows.

The evidence of high idealism in such literature as this is certainly scant. Of the "monstrous conceptions" occurring in the Vedas the following specimen may suffice. In one hymn, says Max Müller:

Indra is praised for having made Heaven and Earth; and then, when the poet remembers that Heaven and Earth had been praised elsewhere as the parents of the gods, and more especially

grow on bald heads, and to abate the nuisance caused by vermin. . . . The incredible filthiness of some of these symbolical and magical rites is almost beyond belief, and the first part of the Aitareya-Aranyaka rivals the most obscene Tantras of the worshippers of *Shakti.*" Burnell, p. xxiii.

as the parents of Indra, he does not hesitate a moment, but says: "What poets living before us have reached the end of all thy greatness? for thou hast indeed begotten thy father and thy mother together from thy own body."

"That is a strong measure," Max Müller continues, "and a god who could once do that was no doubt capable of anything afterwards." Already we see at work the tendency to monstrous generation- and incarnation-stories that runs through all Indian mythology. Yet of the documents wherein such mere ravings occur, otherwise sane people are actually found to declare that they are "faultless from all eternity, evident by themselves, and, as they were revealed, unaffected by the shortcomings of human authorship."

Something will have to be said in a later chapter of the "Back to the Vedas" movement, which finds its chief expression in the Arya Samaj. But though, in the orthodox conception, the seeds of India's spirituality are thought to be sown in the Vedas, it is only in the Upanishads that they reach their full flower. Now the interest of the Upanishads is incontestable. They are, perhaps, the earliest philosophical writings in the world; and even if this be not so, they are unquestionably original, evolved entirely in the Indian mind, not sprung from wandering foreign thought-germs. They reveal an extraordinary intensity and ingenuity of speculation, a wonderful power of applying to appearances the solvent of thought. No one can read Deussen's great book on the Upanishads without marvelling at the luxuriance of sheer cerebration displayed in the literature he summarizes. That it proceeded from subtle brains there is no doubt whatever. On the other hand, I do not see how any one can fail to observe that, on its constructive side, Indian thought merely built up a new, and fantastic, and often self-contradictory, mythology, in which speculative concepts took

[62]

the place of anthropomorphic deities. This was, indeed, inevitable; it is the process of all metaphysical thought that
is not merely destructive; but India then fell into the error
of thinking that it had fathomed the unfathomable, and presenting speculation in the guise of dogma. Wherever its
teachings can be tested—as in its cosmology, physiology,
psychology—they are found to consist of just what one
would naturally expect, namely, baseless classifications and
ingenious guesses. Its wildest fancies are often interesting
and suggestive; for the power to think erroneously is better
than mere brutish incapacity for thought. It is better to
let the mind grope in the darkness than to keep it torpid and
incurious. But to mistake groping for seeing, guessing for
knowing—that is the very unspiritual habit into which India
has fallen.

Whatever may have been the genius of the individual
thinkers to whom we owe the Upanishads, their dogmatism
must have had a cramping rather than a stimulating effect
upon the minds of their disciples. The relation of *guru*
and *chela*, still admired by many as the basis of India's intellectual greatness, is in fact destructive to all criticism and
therefore to all healthy life. "Since the knowledge of the
atman," says Deussen, summarizing one of his documents,
"is contrasted with the reality of experience as the realm
of ignorance, it cannot be gained by mere speculation
(*tarka*) concerning it, but only by a revelation communi-
cated through the teacher." * This is surely the very reverse
of a sound doctrine. Teaching may, indeed, put the mind
on the track of philosophical realization, may even bring
it up to the threshold; but the threshold can be crossed
only by an unteachable act of apprehension, taking place
in the individual mind. Nevertheless this conception of

* Deussen, *The Philosophy of the Upanishads,* p. 78. "Atman" may
be roughly rendered as "world-soul."

truth as something that can be poured mechanically from one mind into another lies at the base of Indian philosophic teaching. Here is another (later) utterance: "As the Purana says, 'Do not apply reason to what is unthinkable! The mark of the unthinkable is that it is above all material causes.' Therefore the cognition of what is supersensuous is based on the holy texts only." "The holy texts!"—here we touch the heart of the matter. If to look to the past for all wisdom, whether divine or human, be a spiritual tendency, then the spirituality of India cannot be contested. But neither is it doubtful that her spirituality, in this sense, has been one of her greatest misfortunes. She has also displayed an unequalled diligence in thinking about the unthinkable, that being an exercise agreeably compatible with physical immobility and living upon the alms of the faithful. But of what possible value even to the individual himself (to say nothing of his fellow-men or his country) is this mechanical and morbid rumination of "the holy texts," or of the mystic syllable "OM," * confessed by Deussen to be "entirely meaningless," but "precisely on that account especially fitted to be the symbol of Brahman"? May it not fairly be suspected that this much-vaunted habit of meditation is often a cloak for sheer blankness of mind?

The absolute value of India's contribution to metaphysical thought is of course a matter on which specialists only can give a competent opinion. Several Western philosophers, and particularly Schopenhauer and Cousin, have spoken with warm admiration of the Upanishads; and the influence of these and later speculations is traceable in a good many quarters—notably among the New England transcendental-

> *As when we dwell upon a word we know,
> Repeating, till the word we know so well
> Becomes a wonder, and we know not why.
> *Tennyson.*

ists. In fine, there is no difficulty in admitting that individual Indians, some nameless, some known by name, one—
Gautama Buddha—world-renowned, have played a more or
less distinguished part in the history of philosophy. But
between this admission, and the pretension that India as a
whole—the Indian people—has manifested a unique religio-
philosophic genius, there yawns an immeasurable gulf. The
genius which the Indian people, from the Brahmin caste
downwards, has displayed to great perfection, is a genius
for obfuscating reason and formalizing, materializing, degrading religion.

This may seem a hazardous assertion in the face of a cloud
of witnesses. But the witnesses themselves may be cited on
both sides; and where they advance anything like proof, as
distinct from the mere repetition of stereotyped formulas,
it is all on the negative side of the case. Take Mr. Romesh
Chunder Dutt, for example. He assures us, on an early
page of his *History of Civilization in Ancient India*, that
"The history of the intellectual and religious life of the
ancient Hindus is matchless in its continuity, its fullness and
its philosophical truth." But a little further on he tells
us that immediately upon the Vedas followed the Brahmanas,
"inane and verbose compositions" which "reflect the enervation of the people and the dogmatic pretensions of the
priests;" and that later, in what he calls the Epic Period
(B.C. 1400 to 1000?) "the gradual enervation of the Hindus
was the cause of the most important results in religious
and social rules. Religion changed its spirit. The manly
but simple hymns with which the sturdy conquerors of the
Punjab had invoked nature-gods scarcely commended themselves to the more effete and more ceremonious Hindus of the
Gangetic valley." Later, again, in the Pauranik Period
which followed the expulsion of Buddhism:

[65]

An unhealthy superstition and social system warped the national mind and paralysed the national vigour. Worshippers were divorced from religious learning, warriors were divided from the people, professions and sects were disunited for ever and enfeebled. Men were subjected to unmeaning restrictions and hurtful rules. Women were encouraged to perish on the pyre. A monopoly of knowledge was established, social and religious freedom was extinguished, and the lamp of national life was quenched with the light of freedom and of knowledge. The Hindu who can deservedly boast of the religion of the Upanishads and the ethics of Gautama Buddha, owes it to Truth and to History to confess to the degeneracy of later times.

On this candid passage one comment seems called for, namely, that the ethics of Gautama Buddha were themselves a protest against the "degeneracy" of earlier times, and that the revival they effected was partial and transitory. In talking of the "extinction" of social and religious "freedom" and so forth, Mr. Dutt falls into the inveterate Hindu habit of assuming a past Golden Age, for which the evidence is of the scantiest. Otherwise the passage is sound enough; but what becomes of the "matchless continuity and fullness" of the "intellectual and religious life" of the Hindus? *

When we look into it closely, we can trace the general estimate of Hindu spirituality to two very different sources: to what may be called the lower and the higher Hinduism. We have on the one hand the spectacle of a people intensely devoted to an infinitude of cults and observances which may be classed as religious inasmuch as they show a constant preoccupation with the supernatural, and belief in its ac-

* It may be said that Mr. Dutt's assertion refers only to the *ancient* Hindus, an expression which might conceivably denote only the Aryans of the Vedas. But the context puts this interpretation out of court: "ancient" must be understood in its widest sense as simply meaning "not modern,"

tivity in ordinary life. On the other hand, we know that
the thinkers of this same race have evolved certain religio-
philosophical ideas, of great interest and importance. Putting these two facts together, people vaguely conclude that
the religious life of India is at once intimate and exalted—
that the average Hindu carries into his daily life religious
conceptions of the highest order, even if they be, perhaps,
expressed in outward forms that, to an unsympathetic eye,
may savour of idolatry.

The fact is, unfortunately, that the lower Hinduism knows
and cares very little about the higher, while the higher is
so contaminated by the lower that, except in small reforming sects, it can scarcely be said to exist. The "spirituality" manifested in the lower Hinduism is that to which
anthropologists have given the name of animism. It is
the spirituality of the savage who fears and seeks to propitiate, not only ghosts and demons, but every natural
object or phenomenon that can possibly influence his life.
New gods and new worships grow like weeds from the teem-
ing soil. They are growing to-day, if not quite with the
old luxuriance; and the higher Hinduism makes no attempt
to keep them down. Listen to what "The Saint Ramdas,"
as quoted by Mr. Justice Chandavarkar, of Bombay, has to
say on the subject: "Many gods have risen and run riot;
it is a medley of ghosts and deities; the One Supreme God
has been forgotten; so all has become a hotch-potch of
worship. Hence the thinking power has been destroyed.
Who knows the difference between the true and the false
in this market cry of the *Shastras* and the noises of the
gods?" The Saint, as is natural, assumes that this chaos
results from the corruption and degradation of a once pure
faith; but, historically, this is not the case. The lower
Hinduism is simply an unweeded jungle of indigenous cults
and cult-making tendencies which the higher Hinduism has

[67]

adopted, and to which it has largely assimilated itself. If it be spirituality to think of the whole world as being at the mercy of myriads of capricious powers which may be placated by sacrifices and sometimes dominated by spells, then all one can say is that savagery and spirituality are closely akin.

The higher Hinduism, or Brahminism in the stricter sense of the term, is descended from the religion brought into India by the Aryan invaders, but has, in the course of ages, changed beyond recognition. It has thrown off, so to speak, philosophies the appraisement of which we have agreed to leave to experts. But the philosophy which inheres in it as a workaday religion, which underlies such definite doctrines as it can be said to possess, is neither technical nor recondite, and may be discussed without presumption. A little scrutiny will show us, I think, that on this side, too, India has achieved a reputation for spirituality which the facts are far from justifying. Great thinkers she may have possessed, but she has not extracted from their thoughts a rational, an ennobling, or even a morally helpful religion.*
Hinduism is defined in the Census of India (1901) as "Animism more or less transformed by philosophy," or, more briefly, as "Magic tempered by metaphysics." To my thinking the animism and the magic are much more palpable than the transformation and tempering.

From the holy texts, then, what has actually been extracted? Three fundamental doctrines, which may be described as the essence of the higher Hinduism. They are:

---

* Deussen, indeed, says: "The Vedanta, in its unfalsified form, is the strongest support of pure morality, is the greatest consolation in the sufferings of life and death—Indians, keep to it!" Even if we could accept this opinion as authoritative, we should have to inquire how many Indians now, or at any time, have made the Vedanta "in its unfalsified form" their guide in life and death.

(1) The doctrine of *Karma* in association with the transmigration of souls.

(2) The doctrine that life is an incurable ill, from which we can be relieved only by attaining re-absorption into the All, or the Self, or That, as the inexpressible is sometimes expressed.*

(3) The doctrine of the supreme and all-conquering efficacy of asceticism.

Can we, then, recognize in these doctrines symptoms of high spirituality or idealism in the people which has evolved and lived upon them?

TRANSMIGRATION AND KÀRMA.

The first is not a metaphysical doctrine at all, but an assertion of what may be called ethico-physical fact, which might conceivably be proved by such evidence as would satisfy a court of law. For my part, I know of only one objection to it, namely, that satisfactory evidence, or any evidence beyond the assertions of the holy texts, is entirely lacking. No one seems to know precisely how or when the doctrine of transmigration implanted itself in the Indian mind—it is not to be found in the Veda, nor did it come from Greece. It was in all probability borrowed from the aboriginal tribes; for it is a concept that has occurred to the untutored savage fancy in almost every region of the world. It is, of course, impossible of disproof. No one can say that his vital principle, whatever it may be, has not at some time inhabited other bodies, animal or human, and may not pass through a further series of incarnations. But as it is

---

* There appears, indeed, to be some distinction between "the Self" and "That." Brahma as "That" would seem to include Brahma as "the Self." The one is unmanifested, the other is manifested. The reader will, perhaps, pardon me for not going more at large into the matter.

scarcely asserted, and certainly not proved,* that memory ever links-up these existences, so as to establish their identity with one another, it is hard to see what is the value, or indeed the meaning, of an identity which never represents itself in consciousness. My memory is me: what is outside my memory is not me, in any sense that matters to me; and if an angel from heaven assured me that once upon a time I was Julius Cæsar or Judas Iscariot, I should be politely interested—no more. It would be otherwise if we were promised, and believed, that, at the end of our series of avatars, we should suddenly recall them all, and see and realize the thread of personality running through them. That would be a consummation of unique interest: a cinematograph-show of the ages, which we could turn on at will in the theatre of our sublimated brain. But what we are actually promised when we have "dreed our weird" to the end, is, not memory, but forgetfulness, or something practically indistinguishable from it: so that we should toil up a Himalaya of experiences only to close our eyes to the view. Lafcadio Hearn somewhere relates a Buddhist legend of a disciple and Master— a *chela* and *guru*—painfully ascending a mountain which seems to crumble away under their feet, until at last the disciple realizes that it is not on loose stones he is treading, but on skulls—the mountain is entirely composed of them. "Whose skulls are these?" he asks; and the Master replies: "They have all been your own." One could not desire a better parable of the transmigration theory: each of us is to climb up a mountain of his own skulls in order to merit the privilege of nirvana at the top.

As for *karma*, it is simply the transmigrationist form of the old moral: as a man sows, so shall he reap. It is cer-

* Theosophists, I understand, sometimes profess to recall, or otherwise identify, their previous incarnations; but I am not aware that they adduce anything that can be called evidence.

[70]

tainly more consonant with abstract justice than the theory
which allots us only one brief seed-time on earth, to be followed by a singularly disproportionate harvest of eternal
bliss or pain. Assuming that our actions are not the mathe-
matical result of their antecedents, but are in some measure,
at any rate, originated by a free moral agent within us, there
is doubtless a sort of fair-play in giving us an indefinite
series of lives in which to struggle upwards, through temporary error and defeat, to some ultimate goal of spiritual
perfection. If there were the smallest evidence that such
was the lot imposed upon us, we could accept it, if not with
rapture, at any rate with tolerable fortitude—on condition
that in undergoing this series of adventures, the soul should
be conscious of its identity. The admitted non-fulfilment of
this condition robs the scheme of all its virtues. Why should
I care what I sow when it is (to all intents and purposes) a
stranger who will reap, I myself, as a conscious individual,
having ceased to exist? No doubt, as the world goes on, the
idea of the welfare of coming generations takes more and
more hold of us, and we are more and more willing to
make strenuous exertions, and even to sacrifice what may
seem our immediate personal good, for the sake of that idea.
But who is so fantastically self-centred as to feel his benevolence towards posterity reinforced by the notion that one
of the partakers in the good time coming will, in some inconceivable and wholly unrealized fashion, be he himself?
Such identity is surely immaterial in every sense of the word.
A man who has children, may, indeed, tell himself that the
"posterity" he works for will probably be, in some measure,
his very own; but does that idea perceptibly stimulate his
endeavours? To think so would be to take an extravagantly
cynical view of human nature. Egoists we may be, but not
such morbid egoists as to think more of our own great great
great great grandsons than of the descendants of other peo-

ple. Do we find, as a matter of fact, that the man who has children is apt to be more concerned about the future of humanity than the childless man? No, we do not: it might rather be argued that, from Jesus Christ onwards, the most passionate workers for the kingdom of heaven on earth have been celibate or childless. And if the real, though attenuated, continuance of our personality in our distant offspring be not a sensible spur to benevolence, why should an unrealizable, unthinkable identity between me and some man, woman, or animal a thousand years hence—an identity for which there is no evidence save "the holy texts"—furnish me with an ethical motive of any measurable efficiency? * I suggest, then, that the theory is not deep, but shallow—that it founds an illusory spiritual law upon an imaginary natural law, conceived at a venture by some primitive people.

It is said by some who know the Indian character well that the foregoing argument is rebutted by the facts—that, whether it ought to or ought not, the theory of *karma* does in practice supply "an ethical motive of measurable efficiency." For instance, Mr. Burn, of the United Provinces, one of the workers in the Census of 1901, writes as follows:

"It has been stated that the ordinary Hindu peasant has practically no belief in the doctrine of transmigration; but this is contradicted by my own experience and by all the reports that have been supplied to me. I believe that the doctrine of *karma* is one of the firmest beliefs of all classes of Hindus, and that the fear that a man shall reap as he has sown is an appreciable element in the average morality." This may very well be true: though, like the

---

* Professor Hyslop, late of Columbia University, puts the matter briefly and forcibly: "An identity of subject or substance without a retention of our memories would have neither interest nor moral importance for us." *The Borderland of Psychical Research*, p. 368.

fear of hell, the doctrine of *karma* (which, by the way, does not exclude the fear of hell) has probably much more effect on the naturally good than on the naturally evil. At all events, I am not concerned to deny the efficiency of *karma* as a factor in Hindu morality, such as it is. My point is that the doctrine is not one which testifies to any spiritual genius on the part of those who conceived and elaborated it; and that point is rather strengthened than otherwise if all their brooding on "the holy texts" has not shown the Hindu people its insubstantiality. If the theory is an empty one, there is little proof of spiritual genius in having evolved it, and still less in having clung to it for three thousand years.

PESSIMISM.

We come now to the second characteristic of Hindu thought—its deep-seated pessimism. Here, again, the credit of mere priority cannot be denied to the thinkers of Aryavarta. As they were the first to seek the reality behind the appearances of things, so, too, were they the first to frame a systematic indictment of life, and to aver, like Leopardi, that "men are miserable by necessity, though resolute in declaring themselves miserable by accident." The mere formulation of this theory shows considerable acuteness of thought—a substantial advance upon the primitive attitude of mind which accepts life, as a dog accepts it, with unreflecting acquiescence. Until man has acquired the faculty of conscious discontent, he is a mere thrall to his destiny. And, discontent once born, it was inevitable that it should be carried to its logical issue in systematic pessimism; even though, for the mass of mankind, psychology gives logic the lie, and re-asserts the value of life, spite of "age, ache, penury and imprisonment."

But it is not in the mere formulation of a pessimistic

philosophy that Indian spiritual genius is supposed to have manifested itself; it is rather in the discovery of a method of releasing the soul from the treadmill of innumerable reincarnations. Wherein lies the evil of life? What is it that binds us to the wheel? Why, desire, the thirst for this, that or the other gratification, which, being attained, cloys; not being attained, tortures. "There are only two tragedies in life; not getting what you want—and getting it": that is the kernel of Indian wisdom. Consequently, as the soul is indestructible and cannot be simply extinguished, the evil of life must be circumvented by the extinction of desire, the cultivation of detachment, indifference, until nirvana, or re-absorption into Brahma, the Self, from which all being emanates, be ultimately achieved. The exact conditions of nirvana, and whether the soul, after re-absorption, retains any sort of individuality, I have never been able to make out. The oracles are either dumb or contradictory. But if individuality be not retained, nirvana would seem to be little more than a euphemism for death.

Many people imagine that this pessimistic philosophy, culminating in the dogma of nirvana, is peculiar to Buddhism; but that is not so.* It was characteristic of Hinduism long before Gautama was born; and it remains an integral part of Hinduism, though Buddhism is practically extinct in the land of its birth. The Bhagavad-Gita, though of comparatively late origin, and outside the pale of the so-called "inspired" books, is nevertheless recognized by the modern Hindu as a work of the highest authority: so that the following quotations from it may be accepted as presenting an orthodox view of the theory of detachment. The speaker is the god Krishna, an incarnation of Vishnu; and he is supposed to be addressing Arjuna, the leading hero of

* Buddhism, rejecting the doctrine of the Self, and denying the individual soul, has to adopt a still more elusive conception of nirvana.

[74]

the Mahabharata, on the eve of the battle of Kurukshetra. Thus, then, saith Krishna:

"Humility, unpretentiousness, harmlessness, rectitude, service of the teacher, purity and steadfastness, self-control,

"Indifference to the objects of the senses, and also absence of egoism, insight into the pain and evil of birth, death, old-age and sickness,

"Unattachment, absence of self-identification with son, wife or home, and constant balance of mind in wished-for and unwished-for events,

"Unflinching devotion to Me by *yoga*,* without other object, resort to sequestered places, absence of enjoyment in the company of men,

"Constancy in the Wisdom of the Self, understanding of the object of essential wisdom: that is declared to be the Wisdom; all against it is ignorance."

"One should neither rejoice in obtaining what is pleasant nor sorrow in obtaining what is unpleasant; with Reason firm, unperplext, the Brahma-knower is established in Brahma.

"He whose self is unattached to external contacts, and findeth joy in the Self, having the self harmonised with Brahma by *yoga*, enjoyeth happiness exempt from decay."

"He who is happy within, who rejoices within, and who is illuminated within, that *yogi*, becoming Brahma, goeth to the Nirvana of Brahma. . . ."

It may be noticed that in these passages there is no reference to transmigration. The theory, indeed, is so hard to work out in detail, that Indian sages often forget to use the language appropriate to it. But none of them, so far as I am aware, explicitly renounces it; and the most modern

* *Yoga*, in this aspect, is defined as "ecstatic union of soul with the supreme spirit."

exponents of Hinduism cling to it with desperate tenacity. Witness this passage from *Sanatana Dharma*, a work from which I have already quoted, under its sub-title of *An Elementary Text Book of Hindu Religion and Ethics*:

A Jiva [that is, practically, a soul] may slip backwards for a time, and stay awhile in a stage that he has long left behind him. There is something he has not quite learned, some power he has not quite evolved, and he falls by this into a lower stage again, as a boy at school, if he were idle, might be put back into a lower class. A Jiva which has reached the human stage may be attached to an animal or to a plant, or . . . even to a stone, till he has learnt to use the human form better. . . . But the Jiva is not to be tied for ever to the wheel of births and deaths. The ropes that tie him to this wheel are his desires. So long as he desires objects that belong to this earth, he must come back to this earth in order to possess and enjoy these objects. But when he ceases to desire these objects, then the ropes are broken and he is free. He need not be born any more: he has reached liberation.

This is the stage of development indicated by the Buddha himself, in the following passage: "The man who is free from anger, endowed with holy works, virtuous, without desires, subdued and *wearing his last body*, him I call a Brahmin."

Can we, then, accept as a great discovery, a lofty ideal, a proof of rare spiritual genius, this concept of salvation through the annihilation of desire? Is it not, on the contrary, the glorification of a simple device for "hedging" against destiny, which most of us discover for ourselves, and the strong man discovers only to abandon as being cowardly and ineffective? There is something, no doubt, in the rule of practical philosophy which bids us not to found the livability of life upon external satisfactions, subject to the caprice of fortune, but rather on internal resources of which nothing can deprive us. Up to a certain point, this is true wisdom; carried beyond that point, it lands us in sheer insanities of egoism which strike at the very root of all human association. This is so evident that Indian thinkers have expended a great deal of ingenuity on the attempt to reconcile a philosophy which denies all value to life with an ethical system based, as all ethical systems must be, on the assumption that life is supremely valuable, and the test of all other values. A good act is, ultimately, one which tends to make life livable; a bad act, on the contrary, one which tends to make life unlivable. That is so in Indian as in all other ethics: but if life be inherently evil, why should that which makes for life be good? To this question there is no rational answer. A consistently pessimistic ethical system is a contradiction in terms.

If we wish to see how Indian thought escaped, or tried to escape, from this dilemma, we may turn again to the Bhagavad-Gita. The argument, so far as I can follow it, amounts to this: since nothing matters to the wise man, and since he must do something (for even he who passes his life in contemplating the end of his own nose, is performing action of some sort), he may just as well act virtuously as the other way:

"The man who rejoiceth in the SELF, with the SELF is satisfied, and is content in the SELF, for him verily there is nothing to do.

"For him there is no interest in things done in this world, nor any in things not done, nor doth any object of his depend on any being.

"Therefore, without attachment, constantly perform action which is duty, for by performing action without attachment man verily reacheth the Supreme."

It does not, at this point, occur to Arjuna to inquire

what duty is, or why it is duty. If he did, he would probably be referred to the holy texts, or to the will of Brahma. A few lines further back, Krishna has told him that "all things which have life are generated from the bread they eat: bread is generated from rain, rain from divine worship and divine worship from good works"—so that the sanction of good works lies ultimately, even for Krishna, in their making for life. It is only fair to add that the particular good work which Krishna is enjoining upon Arjuna is that of slaughtering as many as possible of his kinsmen and former friends in a gigantic battle, arising out of a family feud: a work which certainly cannot be said to make for life. But this does not appreciably help us to find any stable foothold in a region of logical quicksands and whirlpools.*

The upshot, as it seems to me, is something like this: The doctrine of detachment, passionlessness, indifference, as a cure for the inherent evil of existence, is not a profound one at all, but is merely the exaggeration of a common and somewhat pusillanimous rule of prudence. In its exaggerated form, it is violently anti-social, and consequently incompatible with any rational system of ethics. If, nevertheless, we find in the Hindu writings many admirable ethical doctrines, it is only because Hindu philosophy is, after all, too human to be logical. This is not the place to discuss that problem so strangely overlooked by the theologians— the Origin of Good. Suffice it to say that good is a plant which springs from every soil, along with the beginnings of social cohesion and co-operation; and according as it flourishes or sickens we say that a people rises or falls in the

---

* It might, perhaps, be possible to construct a scheme of moral values in which actions should rank as more or less laudable according as they did or did not tend to promote in others that subjugation of will and detachment from desire in which the highest good is assumed to consist. But I am not aware that this has been seriously attempted.

scale of humanity. That it has at times flourished greatly
on the soil of India is beyond question. One day, perhaps,
when a world-standard of "good" has been evolved, it may be
possible to measure with some accuracy the comparative
values of the ethical achievements of India, Judea, Greece,
Rome and the modern world. In the meantime all we can say
with confidence is that India has lived an interesting and
chequered moral life, with a fair share of victories and perhaps more than a fair share of disasters. But to base any
claim to special genius upon her attempt to reconcile a high
conception of moral activity with a flat negation of the value
of life is surely an extravagant paradox.

ASCETICISM.

The third fundamental doctrine of Hinduism is the supreme and all-conquering virtue of asceticism. Can this be
accepted as a token of spiritual genius?

Asceticism has entered more or less largely into the practices of every religion, and in some cases, no doubt, we must
recognize it as a measure of spiritual hygiene. "Plain living," carried even to the point of abstinence, may conduce
to "high thinking"; and in times of rampant luxury and
sensuality, the ascetic's protest is at any rate well meant.
Of more questionable value, but still respectable, is the asceticism which finds in physical privation a means of spiritual
illumination, insight, intuition. This is sometimes, no doubt,
the motive of the *yogi;* but Indian asceticism was, in its
origin, neither a protest against luxury, nor an aid to clair-
voyance, but very patently a branch of magic. Not that it
was peculiar in this respect; a magical element is everywhere
traceable in ascetic practices; but in India that element is
particularly prominent and persistent. The *rishis* whom
modern Hinduizers would have us mention with bated breath,

figure in popular legend, not as beneficent sages, but as peculiarly irritable ascetics who, by dint of hideous "austerities," have acquired a power of cursing which they use with the utmost freedom, often on very slight provocation. Nor can it be said of their comminations that "nobody seems a penny the worse." On the contrary, the gods themselves cannot stand up against "the potent curse of a holy ascetic." Here is a characteristic story—one of hundreds—from the Mahabharata. An ascetic, under a vow of silence, was accused of receiving the stolen goods of a gang of robbers. Debarred by his vow from pleading not guilty, he was impaled along with the bandits. With the stake in his body, he "serenely devoted himself to contemplation," and lived on as though nothing had happened. This miracle being brought to the notice of the king, he humbly apologized to the skewered sage, and ordered his immediate release. It was found impossible to extract the stake from his body, so it was sawn off, "and the ascetic, apparently none the worse for this addition to his internal economy, went about as usual." He was not grateful, however, for so notable an addition to his stock of "merit," and called the God of Justice to account for his misadventure. That deity explained that the ascetic had once, in his childhood, impaled an insect on a blade of grass, so that the punishment exactly fitted the crime. The holy man was not of that opinion, "particularly as the *Shastras* exempted children from responsibility for their actions." Feeling that such maladministration of an important department must not be overlooked, he uttered the following curse, "Thou shalt, oh God of Justice, be born among men, and in the Sudra (or servant) caste." Hence followed an incarnation of the erring deity, through the human agency of another renowned ascetic, whose amour with a maid-servant need not be here related. It is not the

[80]

GATEWAY OF THE TEMPLE, TRICHINOPOLY.   (Trisûla of Vishnu over Door.)

least repulsive of the nauseous birth-stories in which Hindu mythology abounds.

These, it may be said, are late and debased legends, and the irascible and malignant *rishis* of the epics are not to be confounded with the *rishis* of the Vedic hymns. Perhaps not; but the mass of the Indian people has for ages drawn its spiritual nourishment, not from the Vedas, but precisely from these monstrous epics which attribute to sages and holy anchorites unlimited powers of maleficent magic.* "Devotion and asceticism impress," says Sir Alfred Lyall, "because they are found to connote influence with heaven, rather than as ethical examples." And assuredly it is from the worser, not the better, side of asceticism that the ascetics of to-day draw their inspiration. They are of two classes: the comparatively clean sturdy-beggars, with shaven heads and saffron robes, who perambulate the country; and the filthy and disgusting creatures, daubed with ashes, and wearing their uncut hair in matted chignons, who haunt sacred places and are, I imagine, more or less stationary. Some of them, no doubt, are sincere fanatics; but many, by the admission of everyone, are simply noxious ruffians. Mrs. Annie Besant's enthusiasm for Hinduism makes her tolerant of many strange things; but even she cannot away with the common fakir. Addressing the Hindu people, she says: "You are not too poor to build colleges and schools for your children while you are able to maintain, as you are doing, large crowds of men as mendicants, in the full strength of vigorous life, who are innocent of all sacred learning, innocent of the light, who have nothing of the sannyasi but the cloth that covers them, and who are yet fed and sheltered by the crore."

* The plot of the celebrated *Sakuntala* of Kalidasa turns upon a curse uttered by a holy ascetic, merely because Sakuntala was a little tardy in opening the door of her cottage to him.

[81]

The Census of 1901 showed that 5,200,000 *sadhus* and persons of like character lived by begging. "Taking the cost of their upkeep at the low average of R.3 a month [a little more than three-halfpence a day], this means an annual tax of £12,500,000 which the workers of India pay to the drones." The alleged "drain" upon India, due to her association with Britain, amounts, at any reasonable reckoning, to little more than half this sum. Whether it is really a "drain" at all is a question to be afterwards considered. In any case, the politicians who are so loud in their complaints that India pays too dear for the services rendered her by Britain, would do well to inquire what services are rendered by the *sadhus* and *sannyasis* for whom she pays nearly twice as much. The answer that the upkeep of the mendicants does not go out of the country is nothing to the point. Unless they render some equivalent service, it is just as though rats every year devoured grain to the value of twelve and a half millions.

On examination, then, it would seem that India's claim to spiritual genius rests, not on any exceptional value in her contributions to the intellectual heritage of the world, but simply on priority of date in some of her philosophical speculations. There seems to have been a considerable body of religio-philosophical thought in India some centuries before any similar body of doctrine can be shown to have existed in other parts of the world. But the question of priority is more curious than important. We do not call a man a good worker merely because he rises at six. If the man who rises at eight does a better day's work, it is he who merits the palm.

India's real distinction lies, not in evolving, but in killing, the germs of sane and virile spirituality. The fact that she, so to speak, got up at six, is not her glory but her reproach.

[82]

What has she made of her long working-day? Has she evolved a noble, pure, progressive religion, in intimate relation with high social and individual morality? There are a few fanatics who would answer this question in the affirmative, but I can imagine no wilder perversion of staring, glaring, incontrovertible fact. The popular Hindu religion of to-day is the lowest professed and practised by any people that purports to have risen above savagery. Beside it the devotion of the Russian or Spanish peasant is rational and enlightened. As for Muhammadanism, one leaves India with (comparatively speaking) an enormous respect for it. Even its fanaticisms are reasonable compared with those of the Hindu; and in its everyday aspect, it is a clean, a dignified, a manly cult.

It is sometimes said that Hinduism has at least the merit of being marvellously suited to the character of the people. As well might we marvel at the nicety with which a man's skin fits his flesh. Hinduism *is* the character of the people, and it indicates a melancholy proclivity towards whatever is monstrous and unwholesome. This may seem an absurdly sweeping "indictment of a nation;" and so it would be if it were not for the well-known fact that people are always, in many respects, better than their religion. That there are fine and admirable qualities in the Hindu character I do not for a moment deny: else were the future of India hopeless indeed. It is precisely on the religious side that the character of the Indian people, as I read it, is conspicuously defective. They have always gravitated towards the lower rather than the higher element in religion, towards the form rather than the substance, towards the letter rather than the spirit. That is why I hold it the very acme of paradox to claim for them an exalted spirituality.

Does not the matter lie in a nutshell, when we find the most enlightened religious thought of to-day concentrated on a movement "back to the Vedas"? What a confession of the only too patent fact that the religious history of the people has been one long downward drift, scarcely interrupted by heroic but futile attempts to stem the tide! It is hardly fair, however, to speak as though the Hinduism of to-day were a lineal, though degenerate, descendant of the Vedic religion. It is much rather to be regarded as a product of the welter of fetishism and witchcraft into which the Aryan settlers plunged on their arrival in India. In phrases, names and forms, a good deal of degenerate Aryanism no doubt survives; but the substance of Indian popular religion is little more than the rank crop of superstitions which have always grown, and which continue to grow, out of the sun-baked soil. These superstitions, says Sir Alfred Lyall, "are not so much the offspring of Brahminism as its children by adoption;" * but assuredly they have overrun and taken possession of the house.

In the Vedas we have a wholesome, primitive, nature-religion, free from sacerdotalism, free from asceticism, knowing nothing of metempsychosis, and based on a simple, natural form of social organization. A few centuries elapse, and we find religion the property of a hereditary priest-

---

* See Sir Alfred Lyall's "classification of beliefs" in his *Asiatic Studies*, Vol. I., p. 7. The same highly qualified authority says in another essay: "The masses have preserved their immemorial polytheism; they worship innumerable gods directly by prayer and sacrifice; the middle class adores the great gods of the Hindu pantheon as the signs and figures of ubiquitous divinity." And again, "In India you may behold at this moment an immense and intelligent society much given to dreamy meditation over insoluble problems, and practically unanimous in rejecting any solution that stops short of Pantheism." He is here writing in the assumed character of a Brahmin; but though the whole essay (*Asiatic Studies*, Vol. II., Chap. i.) is ironical, these passages are doubtless intended as sober statements of fact. Presumptuous as it may appear, I cannot but wonder whether, if he could be cross-questioned, Sir Alfred might not be moved to qualify one or other of the two epithets "immense" and "intelligent."

[84]

hood; ceremonial so tinctured with magic that the misplacing of a syllable or an emphasis in a sacred *mantra* is supposed to annul its efficacy; asceticism rampant and arrogant; the theory of metempsychosis morbidly overstraining the imagination, and leading men to look upon life as an illimitable, fantastic, more or less cruel fairy-tale; and, to crown all, a social organization the most elaborately anti-social that the mind of man ever conceived. Caste and its concomitant abuses we must consider in another chapter; for the present it is sufficient to note that they are of the very essence of Hinduism, growing with its growth and strengthening with its strength. A few more centuries pass, and great efforts are made to remedy the worst of these abuses. Two almost contemporary movements, Buddhism and Jainism, have a certain measure of success. But Brahminism, tenaciously invincible, soon rears its undiminished head. Buddhism is cast out,* and the Jains survive as a comparatively small sect, worshipping a different set of idols, and more fanatical on the point of not taking animal life, but otherwise much on a level with orthodox Hindus. And so it goes with a hundred attempts at reform, the Sikh propaganda in the seventeenth century being perhaps the most notable. They find many adherents at first, generally among the castes whom Brahminism treads under foot; but they soon sink back almost indistinguishably into crass superstition and inveterate social prejudice. The result is that the spiritual genius of the Indian people is to-day found expressing itself, not here and there, but everywhere, in forms which not only the Western world but China and Japan have for ages outgrown. The whole country is populated with myriads of monster-gods, many-headed, many-armed, often colossal,

* Not without persecution it would appear, though as a rule Brahminism is too vague, too unformulated and unorganized, to be a persecuting religion.

always hideous; to say nothing of the animal gods, Ganesh and Hanuman, the elephant and the monkey, who are even more popular than their quasi-human rivals. If a census of idols—even confined to objects of public, as distinct from domestic, worship—could be taken in India, the result would be amazing, certainly running into millions. Nor do the rites whereby these idols are worshipped bear testimony to any superabundant spirituality. Of obscene and licentious practices I say nothing. I did not witness any; and though they certainly prevail to some extent, it is hard to say how far they leaven the mass of Hinduism. Even if they did not exist at all, the ordinary daily practices of the cult are sufficient to place it beyond the pale of civilization. Not in out-of-the-way barbarous corners, but wherever you turn, you meet with repulsive performances of piety. A twopenny tram will take you from the centre of Calcutta to the "Kalighat," from which some suppose that the city takes its name, where you may see, in the slimy, swarming precincts of the temple, the ground crimson with the blood of sacrifices, while in a filthy but very sacred backwater of the Hooghly men, women and children not only bathe in their hundreds, but drink the yellow ooze in which their bodies and their garments have been steeped.* Hinduism has, indeed, a marvellous gift for extracting bad effects from good intentions, actual ugliness from potential beauty. It is always washing and never clean; some of its practices have probably been hygienic in their origin, yet it is innocent, and often bitterly resentful, of sanitation; it professes a superstitious respect for animal life,† but it raises no finger to

---

* This is not, however, the most disgusting beverage prescribed by Hindu piety. The urine of cows, with other scarcely less nauseous ingredients, enters largely into their "purificatory" doses.

† The Jains cover their mouths with a respirator lest they should inadvertently inhale, and so kill, an insect. "Pinjrapole" hospitals for

check the most callous cruelty to animals.* It is, in short, the great anachronism of the modern world. There is a synagogue in Prague which claims special sanctity on the ground that it has never been cleaned for seven centuries. For "seven" read "thirty" and you have the history of Hinduism.

What is the distinguishing characteristic of all the great religions of the world—at any rate of the three now prevalent over three-fourths of the globe? Is it not that each has been filtered, at a definite historic period, through one or more great minds? The historic individuality of the Buddha and the Christ may be doubtful: perhaps they are legendary personifications of the purifying forces, rather than real personages. But even if we take this view (and it seems to me by no means established) we cannot deny the reality of the movements associated with their names. At all events, St. Paul and Muhammad are incontestably historic personages, and in them we see the process of filtration very clearly at work. It is true that, in all these cases, corruptions have subsequently crept in, and that attempts at refiltration have been only partially successful. Here and there, indeed, all three religions have relapsed into something very like primitive fetishism. Still, the character of the (real or ideal) founder of the cult has always set a standard to which reformers might appeal, and placed a certain check

animals are, it is said, "so administered as to cause more suffering than they prevent." They have been known to contain wards for bugs, lice and scorpions.

* See an article by the Hon. Mrs. Charlton in the *Nineteenth Century* for September, 1912. Sir Bampfylde Fuller says, "No one teases animals in India;" but this is certainly far too sweeping. On the very first day I spent in India, I saw some boys tormenting a poor sick squirrel, mangy, ragged and evidently dying. I reproached myself for not putting it out of its misery; but perhaps, if I had done so, there would have been a riot.

[87]

upon the worst degenerations. Hinduism, on the other hand, is a wholly unfiltered religion—a paganism which has resolutely declined filtration. If it includes in its pantheon any personage holding a position in the least analogous to that of Gautama or Jesus, it can only be Krishna—and what a difference is there! It is this tendency towards pollution rather than purification that assigns it its place—incomparably the lowest—in the scale of world-religions. Until Hinduism has somehow got itself filtered, India cannot reasonably claim fellowship on terms of equality with the civilized nations of the earth.

V

In the foregoing chapter, Hinduism has been regarded in its religious, as distinct from its social, aspect. Our object was to ascertain how far it bore out the widespread belief in the innate spirituality, the "lofty idealism," of the Indian character. But Hinduism is much more than a religion. It has begotten, and it continues to enforce with all the power of sacerdotal sanctions, an extremely elaborate social system. Of this social system what are we to say? Is it one which justifies the people who adhere to it in claiming an independent and equal place among the nations of the world? And, if not, what chances are there of any effectual amendment within reasonable time?

It is beating at an open door to demonstrate the evils of ' caste. If Hinduism had been in other respects the loftiest and purest religion imaginable, its intimate association with caste would have rendered it a calamity to the Indian people. I have earnestly endeavoured, by reading and personal inquiry, to discover the good side of caste—I will not say any general justification of the system, but even any appreciable set-off against its manifest evils. The endeavour has been almost fruitless. Is a caste a benefit society? Scarcely, if at all: caste comradeship manifests itself much more in ostentatious "treating" than in systematic helpful charity.* Is a caste a trade-guild? Occasionally, in a very

* Sir Bampfylde Fuller (*Studies of Indian Life and Sentiment*, p. 202), speaking of the extraordinary power of resistance to famine if it be not

limited degree. The purposes of trade-protection are much better fulfilled by organizations specially directed to that end. It is said that caste secured a high level of hereditary skill in arts and handicrafts. I am not a sufficiently convinced adherent of Weissmann to deny the possibility of inherited aptitude; but the probability is that the alleged effect was due simply to the influence of caste in promoting early and assiduous apprenticeship. So much merit may be allowed it; but a good apprenticeship-system has been evolved elsewhere, without enforced heredity of function. Even if, in these or other respects, some odds and ends of benefit may be shown to have resulted from caste, they are as nothing compared to the mountainous evils it has entailed upon unhappy India. It has enfeebled her politically by substituting class-exclusiveness for solidarity, class-vanity for patriotism. It has impoverished her physically by fostering a marriage system which is thoroughly unhealthy both in its obligations and in its restrictions. It has corrupted her morally by making insensate arrogance a religious and social duty. It has paralysed her intellectually by forcing her to occupy her mind with infantile rules and distinctions, and to regard them as the most serious interests in life.

Nor is there any defence for caste in the "tu quoque" argument. It is true that class-distinctions, class-vanity and class-arrogance obtain to a certain extent throughout the world, and that in many countries—in England among

too long continued, says, "It is due in the main to the efficacy of the family and the caste as institutions for mutual relief. There is no man but has some one to turn to in misfortune. . . . Indeed it might perhaps be argued that caste owes its extraordinary development to apprehension of famine. Caste certainly establishes some such responsibility for relief as was thrown upon English villages by the Poor Law settlement." This is the most plausible plea for caste that I have come across; but most authorities declare it to be a very inefficient Poor Law. Mutual helpfulness within the limits of the family is, of course, a different matter.

the rest—they manifest themselves in noxious and ridiculous forms. Certainly there is too much of caste in Europe and America, where, moreover, it is accompanied by a paltry wealth-worship which is at any rate less conspicuous in India. But apart from the fact that caste is infinitely more complex, more rigid and more inhuman in India than anywhere else in the world, there is a fundamental difference which deprives the comparison of all validity. It is simply that in Christian and Muhammadan countries religion fights against caste, or, failing to do so, neglects its manifest duty; whereas in India religion is so inextricably identified with caste that one may almost reverse the order of the concepts and say that caste is religion. In the West, people are of many minds as to the permanent value and necessity of class distinctions. Some hold social equality to be an idle dream; a few even believe that hereditary aristocracy is an institution of high social value. But scarcely anyone would openly deny that

> The rank is but the guinea stamp,
> The man's the gowd for a' that.

Scarcely anyone would openly deny that homage ought to be paid rather to worth than to birth, and all the more to worth if it has not enjoyed, from the outset, the advantages of birth and station. Religion and social theory, in a word, both profess to be equalitarian, whatever defects of practice we may have to admit and deplore. But in India the most inhuman snobbery is a religious duty. In India alone, of all countries in the world, are millions of human beings placed outside the pale, not only of society, but of religion, by the mere fact of their being born to useful and necessary but conventionally degrading functions. Other countries share the benefits or evils (as the case may be) of a hereditary

[91]

aristocracy; in India alone there is a hereditary and exclusive priesthood, a hereditary and hopeless sediment of
"untouchables." * India has the monopoly of the Brahmin
and the Pariah.

"During times of conquest and migration," says Max
Müller, "such as are represented to us in the hymns of the
Rig-Veda, the system of castes, as it is described, for instance, in the Laws of Manu, would have been a simple impossibility. . . . On the other hand we do find in the gramas
of the Five Nations, *warriors*, sometimes called nobles, leaders, kings; *counsellors*, sometimes called priests, prophets,
judges; and *working-men*, whether ploughers, or builders, or
road-makers. These three divisions we can clearly perceive,
even in the early hymns of the Rig-Veda." These divisions
manifestly correspond to the Kshattryas, Brahmins and
Vaisyas of later times; and when we add the Sudras, or servile caste, originally consisting, no doubt, of the conquered
aborigines, we have the four castes of classic tradition. So
far, the origin of caste is clear enough and normal enough:
the problem which no one has satisfactorily solved is to
account for the innumerable ramifications of later days, and
the absolute tyranny which caste prejudice and exclusiveness came to exercise over the mind of the whole Indian
people. It is not difficult to trace several of the influences
which have gone to the building up of the system. Totem-
ism, for instance, played its part; and clan-practices of endogamy and exogamy are familiar to anthropologists all
over the world. But the fact that many of the elements
of caste are to be found elsewhere and everywhere, only
renders it harder to understand why in India alone the
system should have run into such monstrous developments.

* "The term untouchable, as applied to over 50,000,000 Indians, is in
no sense merely metaphoric." Saint Nihal Singh in *Contemporary Review*, March, 1913.

To say that, in India, everything runs into exaggeration and monstrosity is only to re-state the problem, not to solve it. "The system arose out of weakness and lifelessness among the people," says Mr. R. C. Dutt, "and to a certain extent it has perpetuated that weakness." One can understand that enervation begotten of climate might render the mass of the people easy victims to the exorbitant pretensions of the priestly caste; but why should "weakness and lifelessness" generate the fantastic multiplication of mutually exclusive groups throughout the whole social system? There is surely a good deal yet to be done in tracing out, not only the historic, but the psychological origins of caste.

In its practical effect, it may be likened to a virulent epidemic. It seems as though the Indian peoples were peculiarly susceptible to the bacillus of arrogance. Generated among the Brahmins, the microbe spread, by way of servile imitation, through all classes, until a passion for having someone to despise and look down upon became universal and ineradicable. Snobbery has been defined as a mean admiration for mean things; but here we have an inverted and much more inhuman snobbery, which consists in aggressive contempt, without any semblance of a rational basis. "The Brahmin won't take water from me; therefore it is necessary to my self-respect that I should find someone from whom I may decline to take water"—this, or something like it, appears to have been the instinctive feeling which lay at the root of caste. The desire to hand on a humiliation is one of the common foibles of human nature; but in India alone has it become a ruling principle of life. The infection has penetrated to the very depths of the social scale, so that one of the difficulties in the way of raising the "depressed" castes, is that no one is so "depressed" but that he will object to having his children educated along

[93]

with the children of someone whom he imagines to be a hair's-breadth lower than himself.*

The Census of 1901 recognizes 2,378 "main castes" as distinct from minor and fluctuating sub-divisions. As to precedence:

"It is impossible," says Sir Herbert Risley, "to draw up any scheme for the whole of India. One might as well try to construct a table of social precedence for Europe, which would bring together on the same list Spanish grandees, Swiss hotel-keepers, Turkish Pashas, and Stock-Exchange millionaires, and should indicate the precise degree of relative distinction attaching to each."

Yet some sort of classification may be attempted in accordance with the following criteria:

"That particular castes are supposed to be modern representatives of one or other of the castes of the theoretical Hindu system (Brahmins, Kshattryas, Vaisyas); that Brahmins will take water from certain castes; that Brahmins of high standing will serve particular castes; that certain castes, though not served by the best Brahmins, have nevertheless got Brahmins of their own . . . ; that certain castes are not served by Brahmins at all, but have priests of their own; that the status of certain castes has been raised by their taking to infant marriage, or abandoning the remarriage of widows; that the status of some castes has been lowered by their living in a particular locality; that the status of others has been modified by their pursuing some occupation in a special or peculiar way; that some can claim the services of the village barber, the village palanquin-bearer, the village midwife, etc., while others cannot; that some castes may not enter the courtyard of certain temples; that some castes are subject to special taboos, such as that they must not use the village well, that

* Dubois speaks of a case in which a serious riot had nearly arisen because a shoemaker at a public festival had stuck red flowers in his turban, which the Pariahs—mark that!—insisted that none of his caste had a right to wear.

[94]

they must live outside the village, or in a separate quarter, that they must leave the road on the approach of a high-caste man, or must call out to give warning of their approach. . . . In Western and Southern India Brahmins will as a rule take water only from Brahmins. In Northern India they will take water and certain sweetmeats from some of the better class of Sudra castes. In Madras the idea of ceremonial pollution by the proximity of a member of an unclean caste has been developed with much elaboration. In Cochin a Yayar can pollute a man of a higher caste only by touching him, the Kammalan group (masons, blacksmiths, carpenters and leather-workers) pollute at twenty-four feet, toddy-drawers at thirty-six feet, Pulayan or Cheruman cultivators at forty-eight feet, Paraiyan (Pariahs) who eat beef, at sixty-four feet."

There is a caste of Brahmins in Bengal who are permanently degraded by the fact that four centuries ago their forefathers were compelled to eat, or as some say only to smell, the beef-steaks that had been cooked for a renegade Brahmin, the *dewan* of a Muhammadan prince.

Nothing would be easier than to fill pages with instances of the absurdity and cruelty of caste.* It would be difficult,

---

* Men will die in famine-time rather than accept food from a low-caste or casteless person. At Lahore, only a year or two ago, a *chuprassi* was mortally injured by a bomb explosion. As he lay on the ground in agony, someone brought him a glass of water; but "a man in the crowd said that he was a brother of the dying man, and that, as he was a Brahmin they ought not to give him anything to drink." At Kohat, not long ago a group of women were drawing water at a well, when a child fell in. The only man at hand was a "sweeper" who wanted to go down to its rescue; but the women would not suffer him to pollute the well, and the child was drowned. It has been remarked that Nana Sahib, at Cawnpore, did not lose caste by engaging butchers to slaughter some hundred and fifty women and children in the Bibi Garh; but if he had let one little girl live, and taken a glass of water from her hands, he could scarcely have expiated the pollution. In Southern India it used to be a law that no man of the degraded castes might enter a village before 9 a.m. or after 4 p.m., less the slanting rays of the sun should cast his shadow across the path of a Brahmin.

however, to find a clearer example of what it really means than the following account, given by a Hindu reformer, Pundit Rambhaj Dutt, of his efforts to raise the depressed classes in the Punjab, whom the barbers refused to shave and who were forbidden to draw water from the wells which the higher castes regarded as their exclusive property:

"The Pundit's first difficulties were with the people whom he was striving to help. They suspected him of mercenary motives, and declined to have anything to do with his propaganda. At the principal meeting at which he was to have opened his campaign not a single Dhoomna attended. But the Pundit was equal to the occasion. Instead of delivering his address, he at once betook himself to the quarters of the town in which the untouchables dwelt, and was able to induce many of them to follow him to the place of meeting. He assured them that he had no intention of demanding money from them or of taking away their women, but that his sole object was to have their rights accepted by the higher castes. The Pundit went from shop to shop and from house to house appealing to the Hindus to admit the low castes to the privileges mentioned above, and his words seem to have carried conviction. In the presence of thousands of Hindu men and women the great work of *shuddi* or purification was performed on hundreds of the untouchables. 'For two days,' writes the Pundit, 'we went on shaving and purifying crowds of men, women and children. More than 1,400 were admitted into the Arya or Hindu community. We had distributed the twenty-seven razors which I had purchased for the purpose, while several barbers were working with their own razors.' But the most touching part of his account relates to the inception of the reform permitting the low castes to draw water from the wells of the village community. The Pundit called a meeting of the several *biradaries* or caste groups, and, in moving language, prayed them to admit their low caste brethren to this privilege so vital in a tropical country. His prayer was granted. In a body the whole assembly arose and proceeded to the heart of the Hindu quarter of

[96]

Sujampur where the incidents related here took place. Thousands of Hindus stood round the well when the Pundit called upon one of the Dhoomna leaders to draw water from it. What followed is best told in the Pundit's own words. 'It was too much for him. He took off his shoes, and with folded hands trembling with emotion he asked the *biradari* if he could really go up to the well. They cheerfully assented. I helped him up the stairs, and told him to ask their permission three times. He did so thrice, each time the permission was granted, the brotherhood becoming more and more enthusiastic and full of feeling in their sympathetic reply to his petition. On this I asked the man to fall at the feet of the brotherhood who had raised him. He obeyed and drew water from the well amidst cheers.' " *

This, be it noted, is not an event of fifty, twenty-five, or even ten years ago, but of the year of grace 1912; and there are in India from fifty to sixty millions as abject as these Dhoomnas.

In this case we see reform at work, as, indeed, it is in many quarters; but it moves very slowly and with many relapses. Time out of mind, attempts have been made to expel the virus of caste from the Indian body politic;† but often the sects which thought to abolish it have ended in themselves becoming castes, as exclusive as all the rest. The founders of the Sikh religion declared against caste, with very little effect. Of the three sections of the Brahmo Samaj, a reforming body founded by Rammohun Roy about 1830, only one does not recognize caste. The Arya Samaj, a younger and much more vigorous sect of re-

---

* *Times of India*, September 11, 1912.

† Dr. Hoernle, however, points out that "Neither Buddhism nor Jainism represents a revolt against the tyranny of caste, but only against the caste exclusiveness of Brahmin ascetics; caste, as such, was fully acknowledged by them. The Buddhist or Jain priest only acted as the spiritual guide of his followers; for their religious and ceremonial observances, Brahmin priests had always to be called in."

formers, professes to reject caste altogether; but, says Sir
Herbert Risley, "the preaching of members of the Samaj is
in advance of their practice." I myself heard of a case in
which the members of a local branch of the Samaj were
violently excited by the discovery that a *chamar*, or leather-
worker, had intruded among them under false pretences. In
another place, a leading member of the community declined
to sit at table with me, not, it was explained, because he
himself had any objection, but because it might have scan-
dalized the weaker brethren. The idea that the spread of
railways, and the popular taste for railway travelling, tends
to break down the barriers of caste, is, as we shall presently
see, only partially true.

As regards eating and drinking, it is said that in Bengal
the restrictions have almost disappeared; but this is far
from being the case elsewhere.* The Aryan Brotherhood
in Bombay recently gave a dinner to which invitations
were issued in deliberate disregard of caste distinctions,
Sir Narayan Chandavarkar occupying the chair. The
occasion was most harmonious, but many of the guests got
into sad trouble with the *panchayats*, or committees, of
their castes. Apparently it was the presence of one man,
known or suspected to be an "untouchable," that caused
the scandal. Some of the offenders were "out-casted,"
others made their peace by doing penance, or in other
words going through a particularly nasty process of purification.† It is characteristic that in discussing this dinner
one of the "Anglo-Vernacular" papers of Bombay approved
it in an English article, but condemned it in its vernacular

---

* It seems to be pretty commonly recognised that neither ice nor
soda-water counts as water for the purpose of conveying pollution; while
biscuits and patent medicines are also exempted from the strict operation
of caste rules.

† It includes swallowing a bolus composed of the *panchagavya*, the
five products of the cow—milk, curds, ghee, urine and dung.

columns. One of the evils of the present condition of
affairs is that it engenders hypocrisy: lip-service to enlightenment while the heart is still in the bondage of prejudice, or (more commonly perhaps) conformity to social
prejudice without any conviction behind it.

But even in Bengal, though restrictions on the *jus
convivii* may be almost extinct, the *jus conubii* is extending
much more slowly—and this, of course, is a far more serious
matter. For it is one of the gravest of India's many misfortunes that, while social custom makes marriage an imperative obligation and celibacy a disgrace, caste sets narrow bounds to the field of choice, and so leads to infant
marriage, and the prohibition of widow re-marriage, not to
mention darker, though less wide-spread, evils. In assuming
these things to be evils, do I imply that Western ideas as to
marriage and the relations of the sexes are the last word
of social wisdom? Certainly not; no one doubts that in
these matters our practices, and even our principles, stand
in glaring need of amendment. But again, the "tu quoque"
plea is of no avail. Our habits are not, like those of India,
mere crystallizations of barbarism; and, even if they were,
would that make the Indian habits any better? In the
Vedas there is no trace of infant marriage; free courtship
of the modern type is recognized: and widow re-marriage
is so far from being prohibited that there are special words
for "a man who has married a widow," "a woman who
has taken a second husband," "a son of a woman by her
second husband." As for suttee—the burning of widows
—there is some trace of its having existed in pre-Vedic
times, and having been replaced by a symbolic and innocent
ceremony. One passage in the Rig-Veda was made by the
Brahmins to justify the practice: literally "made" by the
deliberate alteration of the word *Agre* into *Agne*—"perhaps
the most flagrant instance," says Mr. R. C. Dutt, "of what

can be done by an unscrupulous priesthood." But the Vedic period had not long passed before all three practices were firmly established. The Laws of Manu prescribe that a man of thirty shall marry a girl of twelve, a man of twenty-four a girl of eight. The custom of ancestor-worship, the necessity of having an heir to do *sraddha* to your ghost, rendered marriage imperative; while endogamy forced you to marry within your clan; exogamy (in many cases) forbade you to marry within your group; and hypergamy frequently (though not universally) forbade a girl to marry a man of a group lower than her own in social standing. It is not quite clear how the idea arose that to have a marriageable daughter unmarried was the direst of social reproaches; but it can readily be understood that when once it was firmly rooted in the popular mind, a father would take no risks of finding a daughter left on his hands, and would be especially anxious to get her disposed of before she could possibly develop a will of her own. Where hypergamy was added to the other difficulties of the marriage market, the birth of a daughter came to be regarded as a calamity; whence the prevalence of female infanticide* in many parts of India, but particularly among the Rajputs. Nor is this an ancient horror, dragged from the archives of anthropology. Mr. E. A. Gait, the director of the Census of 1911, tells us that a friend of his was discussing with the Durbar of a native state the amount which ought to be expended on the marriage of the Chief's sister, and, as there was some difference of opinion, he asked how much had been spent on similar occasions in the past. "He was told in reply *that there was no precedent.* The girl was the first in the family that had been allowed to live!" The

---

* The practice, however, is not entirely due to the artificial restrictions on marriage begotten of the caste system. There are clear traces of it in the Vedas.

same authority goes on to say: "A middle-aged Punjabi gentleman recently told me that he had been compelled, as a boy, to assist at the murder of an infant sister, and that an aunt had had seven daughters and had killed them all." Even now infanticide is kept in check in Rajputana only by making things unpleasant for a village which cannot show a fair proportion of girls. I asked one of the officers who had taken the 1911 census in this district whether the practice was really a thing of the past. "They vow and swear that it is," was his reply, "but the statistics are against them." That female children are much neglected there is no doubt. "Girls," says Mr. Gait, "are neither so well-fed nor so well-clothed as boys, nor, if they are ill, are they carefully looked after. In Gujarat there is a proverb, 'The parents look after the boys and God looks after the girls.' "*

The ban upon widow re-marriage is clearly due to the same cause as female infanticide: where it is so difficult, and at the same time so necessary, to get a girl married at once, it is naturally regarded as unfair that any woman should add to the glut in the wife-market by getting married twice. Suttee was, of course, a conclusive safeguard against widow re-marriage; but it was more than that. It was a sacrificial rite, comparable with the burying of his horse and arms along with a dead chieftain; it obviated all difficulties as to property and dower; and it was a useful deterrent for any lady who might be tempted to compass the death of her lord and master by witchcraft or poison. I do not know that the latter motive was ever avowed in India, as it is in some parts of West Africa; but it is not in human nature that so obvious an advantage should

* The exposure of female infants used to be very common in Bengal, where, too, the caste of Kulin Brahmins used to make a profession of "marrying" girls by the score, and so relieving the parents of the reproach attaching to their celibacy.

not have contributed to render the institution popular— with husbands.

An unsympathetic Government made suttee illegal in 1829; but it is said that cases of it still occur. In the matter of child-marriage, the Government is practically powerless, though in British territory the consummation of such a marriage before the wife has reached the age of twelve is now a penal offence. Enlightened Indian opinion is alive to the physical and moral evils arising from the practice, as well as to the cruelty of forbidding the re-marriage of widows, thousands of whom have never been wives. But enlightened opinion, in India, is pathetically powerless against the sheer inertia of immemorial habit. Moreover, qualified observers hold that the influence of railways and the printing-press is helping the ingrained snobbery of caste to introduce these abuses into social strata which were formerly innocent of them.

"The strength of the Hinduizing movement," says Sir Herbert Risley, "has been greatly augmented by the improvement of communications. People travel more, pilgrimages can be more easily made, and the influence of the orthodox section of society is thus much more widely diffused." And again: "The extension of railways which indirectly diffuses Brahmanical influence; the tendency to revive the authority of the Hindu scriptures, and to find in them the solution of modern problems; and the advance of vernacular education which increases the demand for popular versions of and extracts from these writings—these are among the causes which, in my opinion, are tending on the one hand to bring about the more rigid observance of the essential incidents of caste, especially of those connected with marriage, and on the other to introduce greater laxity in respect of the minor injunctions which are concerned with food and drink."

Imitation of the higher by the lower castes being "the ultimate law of the caste system," and child marriage and

[102]

widow non-marriage being tokens, from of old, of social distinction, they are thought to be spreading in India, very much as the habit of dining in evening dress is spreading in England. Can enlightened opinion make head against such a tendency?

One would answer in the affirmative with greater confidence if enlightened opinion were not so afraid of its own enlightenment, and so determined to make out that—a few trifling defects apart—Hindu civilization is on the whole the most exalted and enviable the world has ever seen. One cannot but be a little sceptical of the regeneration that is to be founded on such very imperfect conviction of sin.

I take up a book entitled *Hindu Progress* (1904), consisting of "Papers collected and edited by N. Subbarau Pantulu Garu, B.A., B.L., Fellow of the Madras University, and formerly Member of the Legislative Council, Madras." The fourth of the twenty essays included in this work is entitled "The Aims of Hindu Social Life," by Mr. N. Ramanujachariar, M.A. In it I read:

"Every one who has in any way studied ancient India with profit knows how well and harmoniously this mighty and complex social organization of the Hindus has worked for thousands of years, and how it has always tended to help on peace, order and progress. Can the history of the world point out one other instance of a social organization which has worked so successfully for so long a time? Even to-day it is as full of strength and vitality as it was in ancient times. But owing to various causes, internal and external, it is not now in perfect working order."

Before such an utterance of inveterate and insensate racial vanity, one is almost tempted to despair. The social organization of India "tended to help on peace;" yet the country was, from the beginning of history, and almost without respite, torn by cruel wars. The social organiza-

[103]

tion promoted "order:" yet, from sheer lack of any approach to order, India fell into the hands of a European trading company, who had to crush whole armies* of marauders, and to put down, with great difficulty, organized dacoity and the amiable religion of the Thugs. The social organization made for "progress:" yet, in another mood, the panegyrists of Hinduism will mourn the decay and disappearance of the splendid civilizations of the past; while the evidences, if not of decline, at least of age-old stagnation, are written broad over the face of the land. The social organization has worked with unexampled "success:" yes, if it be a sign of success to render the country incapable of self-defence or self-direction, and to subject her for a thousand years to the domination of one foreign conqueror after another. If Mr. Ramanujachariar represents the frame of mind of the friends of "Hindu progress"—and he not unfairly represents a considerable section of them—one can only wonder what may be the mental attitude of those who are not friends of progress, but conservatives. Truly there seems to be some ground for the opinion of many who know the Indian character well, that if British rule were withdrawn to-day, suttee† would be revived to-morrow.

* Literally armies—sometimes as many as 30,000 men, horse, foot and artillery, attached to no state or government, and openly living on rapine.

† Many educated Indians look back to suttee with pride and a sort of sentimental regret. Note the spirit in which it is treated in *The Prince of Destiny, a Drama of India*, by Sarath Kumar Ghosh. I was at first inclined to regard the opinion that suttee would revive on the withdrawal of the British, as an irresponsible suggestion to which little weight was to be attached; but further inquiry has led me to modify this view. Sir Bampfylde Fuller, a close and competent observer, who always weighs his words, says that "beyond all doubt" suttee is "popular," and would be revived at the first opportunity. (*Studies in Indian Life and Sentiment*, p. 161.) The recent suicide by burning of several Bengali girls points in the same direction.

[104]

A similar, though less extravagant, strain of ultra-conservative liberalism runs through a recent speech of the Honourable the Maharajadhiraja Bahadur of Burdwan, at the opening of the ninth All-India Kshattrya (Warrior-Caste) Conference at Agra. The Maharaja, I should state, is not a ruling prince, but a great land-owning potentate. He speaks severely of several members of the Kshattrya community who, in marrying their children, "ignored the resolutions that we have been carrying year after year about the curtailment of expenditure, the restriction of 'nautches,' and the avoidance of fireworks at marriage festivities." He deplores with evident sincerity "the ignorance of the uneducated among us, and of the poor unfortunate women of our community from whom enlightenment has been withheld." He urges the removal of barriers to intermarriage between sub-sections of the caste.

"In all this," he says, "I am with you. But for God's sake don't go further. What I advocate is not mixed marriages. I only mean taking into our fold Kshattryas of every grade and subcaste, whilst the other means a deluge. It means sowing the seeds of confusion and chaos. . . . If you lean too much on the delicate reed of social emancipation of the West, you will go under, you will eventually be committing a racial suicide, so great, so stupendous, that I tremble even to think of it. I therefore say, brethren, advance, but advance cautiously: but, on the other hand, revive the glories of the past."

Alas for those "glories of the past"! They are like to prove a terrible hindrance to the greatness of the future.* The Hindu who could persuade his countrymen to listen

* The Rev. C. F. Andrews, a writer animated by the most ardent sympathy with India's national aspirations, says that some years ago "a paralysing recollection of India's greatness in the past took the place of hopeful optimism in the present." I hope he is right in thinking that the paralysis is passing away.

to the plain truth about the past would do more for *swaraj* than any number of political declaimers.

Not, of course, that one would ignore the inherent difficulties of the case, or look for a sudden and general abandonment of secular tradition. It is neither surprising nor discouraging that the mass of the people should move very slowly, if at all, towards a saner social system; the discouraging part of the matter is that the enlightened classes should be so half-hearted in their enlightenment. With conservatism in religion one can feel a good deal of sympathy. It is even possible that many people do, as a matter of fact, penetrate the rather revolting husk of Hinduism, interpret allegorically its multitudinous idolatry, and cling to the lofty spiritual creed which is understood to lurk behind it. But where is the spiritual substratum of caste? What sympathy can we feel with conservatism in infant marriage*—that practice whereby "a child awakens to conscious life—married"? What respect for the habit of mind, which, admitting that there are a few little adjustments to be made, yet defends and even boasts of the Indian social system as a whole? There was, indeed, something to be said for caste so long as it was not caste: before it took on the characteristics which now give the word its meaning. But these character-

---

* Though the modern tendency is, no doubt, to make boy and girl marriage equivalent to our betrothal, and postpone cohabitation until the parties are at any rate well in their teens, the fact remains that, in many parts of the country, "girls become mothers at the very earliest age that is physically possible." Deussen, an observer more than willing to make the best of everything Indian, writes, "The actual married life begins too early for the girls, before the bodies have attained a sufficient power of resistance. The consequence is that, not only do the women fade very quickly, pine and die, but they bring very delicate children into the world; and this, with the absence of animal food, is probably the chief reason why the Indian, though not less intelligent, is both physically and mentally unable to compete with the European." *My Indian Reminiscences*, p. 89.

[106]

istics, and the social habits ensuing from them, are nothing more nor less than a disease of the body politic; and the frank recognition of this fact is the beginning of wisdom for every Indian who wishes his country to take rank among the great nations of the future.

I once asked one of the leading European Hinduizers, why it was that the writings of that school contained, so far as I could see, no outspoken condemnation of caste. The reply ran thus:

"I do not think the four great castes stand in the way of national growth. Caste has become inflexible, and *there* lies its evil: if it regained the flexibility of its earlier days, so that men might change their caste, it would be very useful. Class is rigid in Germany: the nobles do not inter-marry with the bourgeoisie or the peasantry, yet Germany has very strong national feeling. As to Hinduism at large, I laid much stress, in past years, upon its greatness, because it was vitally necessary to implant self-respect in the people; without this no building of a nation was possible."

To this interesting utterance, there are three pretty obvious rejoinders: (1) Flexible caste, with penetrable partitions, would no longer be caste, but simply class in the European sense of the word. (2) Not in Germany alone, but throughout Europe, inter-*class* marriages are of doubtful advantage, because marked differences of education and social tradition are not conducive to married happiness. But it is no such consideration which forbids inter-*caste* marriages in India. It is simply an inveterate clinging to rules, for the germs of which the anthropologist may discover some justification in the dim dawn of society, but which have long hardened into a rigid system of prejudice, quite out of touch with reason. (3) As for the implanting of self-respect in the people, that, if we take "self-respect" in its higher sense, is eminently

[107]

desirable. But I very much fear that the efforts of European sympathizers have tended rather to the fostering of self-esteem and self-glorification, which need no outside encouragement.

At a congress of pundits, held a few months ago at Conjeevaram, in Southern India, the following views were elicited:

"On the question of sea voyage, eighteen pundits held that sea voyage is sinful in itself, twenty-seven were of opinion that it becomes sinful only under special circumstances, and *one pundit only decreed that it is not sinful at all.* On the question of post-puberty marriage for Brahmin girls, eight pundits declared that the Shastras prescribe such marriages; twenty-one pundits were of opinion that they are permitted by the Shastras under certain circumstances for a period of three or four years after puberty; while *seven held that the Shastras prohibit post-puberty marriages.*"

It is said that the comparatively limited support (in money at any rate) given in India to the movement on behalf of the Indians in South Africa is due to the fact that so many Hindus have no sympathy with the man who sacrifices his caste by crossing the *kala pani* (black water) and settling in the land of the *Mlechchas.*

So long as the thoughts of a people are seriously pre-occupied with such considerations as these: so long as they make a religion of snobbery, and a moral obligation of practices from which science and common sense alike revolt: so long as even their educated and thinking classes are more or less prone to regard with complacency all that is most barbarous and disastrous in their historic record: can it be said that that people is ready to take rank on equal terms with the intelligent and civilized nations of the world? I do not see how any unprejudiced person can answer this

[108]

question in the affirmative. It is true that there are vices and stupidities among the nations of the West from which the Hindu is comparatively free; but that is rather because they do not come in his way than because he rises superior to them. It might be argued that a people may as well be pre-occupied with caste as with "sport"; but such a sophism will scarcely bear examination. Sport is, after all, a distraction of a minority, though a large one; it is not the essence of the national religion. It may be, in many cases, a more or less deleterious distraction;* it may be a by-product and symptom of undesirable social conditions; but it has also its good and healthful aspects, and, at worst, it is not incompatible with very high intelligence in the serious business of life. Caste is, to many millions of Indians, the most serious thing in life, and pre-occupation with its incidents and accessories is the very negation of intelligence. What people can hold its own in the struggle for existence which has not the mental energy to shake off such an ancestral obsession?

I should be disposed to accept the success of the social reform movement as a very fair test of India's moral and intellectual regeneration. In freeing herself from caste and its subsidiary evils, she will give the best possible proof of her fitness for political enfranchisement. But she will never work out her salvation while she continues to think and talk in this strain: "Ours is the eternal ideal of spiritual perfection for the individual and for humanity; and there is not the least fear that the nation which has been working for the last six thousand years and more towards the achievement of such an aim . . . will ever die so long as it clings firmly to its great social ideal."

* If the Hindu is not a "sportsman" it is not because he lacks the gambling instinct. Even the *rishis* of the Vedas acknowledged the irresistible fascination of the dice-box.

VI

OF the Europeans who visit India, probably three-fourths
land at the Apollo Bunder, Bombay. As they stand on that
famous wharf, they see adjoining it on their right a
rambling, gabled building, with a pleasant lawn and a tall
flagstaff in front of it, looking out, from a position of great
advantage, over the noble harbour. This is the Yacht Club,
one of the chief centres of social life in Bombay; and
(except servants) no one of Indian birth, not even the
Rajput prince or the Parsi millionaire, may set foot across
its threshold. The same rule obtains at the Byculla Club;
an Indian who was appointed to a post which had always
carried with it an almost *ex-officio* membership of the club,
was nevertheless excluded. On the other hand, as you drive
round the Back Bay to Malabar Hill, you pass the unpre-
tending but commodious home of the Orient Club, which has
recently been founded for the express purpose of bringing
Indians and Europeans together. Many European officials
frequent it as a point of duty, and meet on equal terms
their Indian colleagues, and the leaders of the commercial
world of Bombay, Parsi, Hindu and Muhammadan. It is,
I understand, a fairly successful institution;* but it is not

---

* Some one has called it the true Byculla (bi-colour) Club of Bombay.
Mr. Price Collier dined at the Orient Club in a mixed company of Indians
and Europeans, almost equally divided; and he records that "problems
of government and politics were discussed as freely as they would have
been in New York or London."

[110]

as a point of duty that all official Bombay crowds to the Yacht Club on the afternoon of mail-day.

There you have a picture in little of social conditions in India—of the great gulf fixed between the races, and of the strenuous efforts that are being made to bridge it.

The natural tendency of the liberal-minded, stay-at-home Briton is to exclaim upon the racial exclusiveness which makes the Yacht Club forbidden ground even to princes and potentates of the most ancient lineage and the most cultivated manners. But we must take human nature as it is, and not harshly blame the instinct which makes Englishmen, who are day by day immersed to the eyes in Indian interests and affairs, hunger for one little spot where they can, for an hour or two, entirely shut out the obsession of the Orient. Every club in India is a little England, reproducing exactly the interests, the comforts and the vulgarities of an English club;* and it is, I repeat, only human nature to desire that it should remain a little England, and not become a little India. Moreover—and here lies the most serious difficulty—all, or almost all, Indian clubs admit ladies as well as men, and are common ground to the two sexes. Is it desirable that ladies should be brought into frequent contact with men whose own womenfolk are jealously secluded, and who in their hearts despise the unveiled Western woman? No doubt there are many Indian (especially Parsi) ladies in Bombay who are not "purdah"; but it would be ridiculous, and it would not help matters, to make a rule to the effect that "Indian gentlemen may be admitted to clubs on condition that they are accompanied by their wives." Let us own, then, that it is no mere insensate arrogance which draws the colour line at the threshold of the Yacht Club and other institutions of a like nature.

* The lowest sporting papers must owe to India a large part of their circulation.

But let us own, too, that such a drawing of the colour line must be inexpressibly galling to a proud and sensitive people, who see their alien rulers, when the business of "running the country" is over, withdraw into impregnable caste-strongholds, with the almost openly-confessed design of washing their hands of India, and returning in spirit to their island home. The club is a far more irritating mark of subjection than the cantonment.

The better sort of British official feels the drawbacks of the situation acutely, and is unwearied in his efforts to diminish them. Aided sometimes (not always) by his womenfolk, he tries to establish some reasonable system of social intercourse with his Indian colleagues and sub-ordinates. Now and then he succeeds in a certain measure; but he has two great difficulties to encounter: obstinate prejudice among the stupider members of his own race, and the domestic arrangements and traditions of the other race. Very often the personal relations between British officials and their Indian assistants are excellent—relations of sin-cere mutual respect and friendship. But the attempt to carry these relations from official into social life is generally a laborious failure.* It is almost impossible for the average memsahib to get upon human terms with the average un-educated purdah woman. Even if the language difficulty be overcome, the three common topics—dress, jewels and babies—are soon exhausted. A few Western women have no doubt a genius for getting "behind the Indian veil;" but

* Let it be noted, however, that if our attempts at social intercourse are not brilliantly successful, between the different sections of Indian society no such attempts are made at all. "There is less social inter-course," writes H. H. the Aga Khan, "between Muhammadan and Hindu or between Rajput and Parsi than between any of these races and the English in India. . . . Englishmen, and Englishmen alone, receive and have friends among all classes and races." *National Review*, February, 1907.

they are rare at best, and they seldom happen to be the
wives of collectors or commissioners.

Two little experiences of my own may be cited in illustration of these social difficulties. A high-caste Hindu
gentleman, well up in the Government service, invited me
to visit his house—thereby showing, of course, great liberal-
ity of spirit. He even introduced me to his wife, a pleasant-
featured lady, no longer young, wearing in her left nostril
a sort of little aigrette of rubies and emeralds. It would
ill become me to repay his kindness by a detailed criticism
of his "interior"; but every moment of the half-hour I spent
in it brought home to me the world-wide difference of standards—in ventilation, freshness, decoration, comfort, things
material and things spiritual—between this civilization and
ours. How impossible it was to imagine any Englishwoman,
not violently prepossessed, like "Sister Nivedita," in favour
of everything Indian, getting into comfortable social relations with the mistress of this mansion! It is not a question
of superiority or inferiority, but simply (as I have said)
of world-wide difference. Very likely the devotions done by
the Brahmin lady at the altar in her back yard, with its
little pot of basil, may have more of spiritual quality than
whatever exercises of a like nature the collector's or the
colonel's wife may indulge in. The decorations of her
salon—a frieze of garish German colour-prints of Siva, and
Parvati, and Rama and Sita, and other divine personages,
all elaborately "tinselled" by the ladies of the family—may
perhaps express as much artistic feeling as the Tottenham
Court Road photogravures that adorn most of the bunga-
lows of the neighbouring civil station. For my part, I have
no overpowering admiration for Western culture as it commonly manifests itself in India. But whether it be higher
or lower, it is irreconcilably different from the culture
of the East. I could not but feel in this high-caste house-

hold that any attempt at social intercourse between it and the European households of the station must be an elaborate and laborious hypocrisy, however admirable might be the spirit prompting it.

There are, in Calcutta, Bombay and elsewhere, a certain number of emancipated and highly cultivated Indian families with whom social intercourse is a privilege and a pleasure. The difficulty in their case is that one is apt to feel like a semi-barbarian intruder upon an abode of ancient, fine-spun, aristocratic culture. One begins to realize the force of Arnold's lines:

> "The brooding East with awe beheld
>   Its impious younger world—"

—only that "awe" is perhaps not quite the emotion with which these grave Orientals regard our Western crudities. But such households are as drops in the ocean of Indian life. They show what might be and may be; but they are immeasurably removed from the general level of what is.

My second little experience may be more briefly narrated. I had the pleasure of spending some days with a British official of high rank who makes it a rule to exclude from his kitchen all pork, bacon and other products of the pig, in order that his Muhammadan subordinates may be able at any time to lunch or dine with him, without fear of partaking of any forbidden dish. As a matter of fact, I met at his table two Muhammadan members of his staff, who were evidently quite at their ease among their European colleagues. Here was an admirable instance of real, unforced, social intercourse. But two things have to be noted. First, it was Muslims, not Hindus, who joined in the pleasant repast; second, our host was a bachelor.

There has been a great improvement, beyond a doubt, in the manners of Europeans towards servants and lower-

[114]

class Indians in geneal. The days are long past when the memsahib could send a khitmutgar to the cantonment magistrate with a chit: "Please give bearer a dozen"—lashes understood—knowing that the order would be executed without inquiry. I have heard an official—a civilian, I am sorry to say—cite admiringly John Nicholson's (alleged) exploit of tying a tehsildar to a well and making him turn the wheel for twenty-four hours, an orderly with a cat-o'-nine-tails standing over him the while. But this was narrated with fond regret, as a trait of the good old days never to return: "You couldn't do such a thing now—you'd be broke." Outrageous domineering and brutality are now very rare.

In the course of six months' pretty constant travelling, I came across only two mild cases of bad manners. The offender in one instance was a Scotch commercial-traveller or insurance-agent. At tiffin at a Madras hotel, he took it into his head that the waiter had brought him too small a plate for his salad, though, for my part, I could see nothing wrong with the crockery. After angrily ordering the man—who was twice his age and three times as dignified in appearance and bearing—to bring him another plate, he fell to badgering him in this strain: "Now, why couldn't you have done that at first, boy? * Just because you were too lazy, hey?"—and so on till he was tired. The waiter listened with imperturbable calm, and was, for the moment at any rate, immeasurably the better man of the two. On the other occasion, a dyspeptic officer lost his temper, very foolishly, because of the failure of a refreshment-room

---

* The habit of addressing waiters as "boy" is greatly to be deprecated. It is not originally Indian, I believe, but has crept in from China, where it is much less offensive. I heard an American woman address a cashier in Cook's office at Calcutta as "boy"; but this, I think, was a mere slip of the tongue. She was hurried and "rattled."

[115]

attendant to understand his order—of course a frequent cause of friction.* These were the only instances of bad manners that came to my notice.† On the other hand, I heard on unquestionable authority of several cases in which low-class unofficial Europeans, or (unfortunately) young subalterns fresh from England, had treated even high-caste Indians with monstrous bumptiousness, scarcely stopping short of violence. There is a general feeling among civilians that the military authorities do not show sufficient sense of the enormity of such conduct on the part of young officers. A gross manifestation of ignorant arrogance will be visited, perhaps, with a little stoppage of leave. It is greatly to be desired that, before they come to India at all, officers should go through a brief course of instruction as to the country entrusted (in part) to their guardianship, and should have it impressed upon them that in order to be sahibs they need not, and indeed must not, cease to be gentlemen.‡ I have read an earnest and admirable circular addressed by the Government of India to the Civil Service, urging the cultivation of a scrupulously "courteous and considerate demeanour towards all with whom they are brought in contact."§

* "There goes my lord the Feringhee, who talks so civil and bland,
 Till he raves like a soul in Jehannum if I don't quite understand."
 Lyall: *The Old Pindaree.*

† I once heard, in England, a young man in the Indian police speaking of the "natives" in brutal and indefensible terms. He took a very pessimistic view of our position in India; as well he might, if there were many officers of his stamp in the services.

‡ It is agreed on all hands that the relations between British officers and the Indian officers and men of Indian regiments are generally excellent. Many people hold, indeed, that it is a great advantage to members of the "political" (as distinct from the civil) service that they should have passed through the Indian army, and thus acquired a special understanding and appreciation of the Indian character.

§ In an article published in 1914 Mrs. Besant gave many instances of gross rudeness and violence on the part of Europeans towards In-

But however we may deplore the bad manners of the past, and survivals in the present of a bad tradition, it is only fair to remember that in our worst excesses of arrogance we were only "doing at Rome as the Romans did." When Burke inveighed against "the despotic style, the extreme insolence of language and demeanour used" by Warren Hastings "to a person of great condition among the politest people in the world," he was indulging beyond all measure his gift of idealization. "Polite," in his day, had a wider meaning than in ours; but, in this context at any rate, it must be taken as including our narrow meaning. It would seem that nothing less than a frenzy of partisanship could make that people the politest in the world which had, in the caste system, elaborated arrogance into a science and elevated it into a religion. On the inhuman insolence of

dians, some of the cases of rudeness (but not of violence) having come within the writer's own observation. It makes one's blood boil to read of such incidents as the following: "Lately in Madras an Indian nobleman, fearing to miss his train, drove his car swiftly past an Englishman's. The Englishman followed him to the station, insulted him, struck him and kicked him so seriously that the Indian was lifted helpless into the train; he summoned the Englishman and a paltry fine was inflicted. The ex-sheriff of Bombay was assaulted as he approached a ladies' carriage to speak to his wife; he summoned his assailant; and the man apologised and was let off. Such cases are innumerable. Sentences of whipping for trivial thefts are constantly inflicted on coolies, and in one case recently, where a little tobacco was stolen by a railway coolie, he was sentenced to be flogged, and was flogged in the magistrate's office by the magistrate himself, according to the testimony of several respectable Indians. He was 'severely reprimanded,' but remains on the Bench. A coolie, struck by his master, died; a fine was inflicted, as 'there was only one blow, and it was not meant to kill.'" If Mrs. Besant can substantiate these accusations, and others, she would do a great service by giving them such prominence that the Government of India should be forced to take cognisance of them. The situation is complicated by the fact that young Indians are sometimes guilty of deliberately provocative behaviour; but that is all the more reason why European brutality should be sternly checked.

caste what need is there to dwell? Something has been said of it in the foregoing chapter. I take, almost at random, from the report of the 1901 Census, the following quatrain, expressive, it is said, of the contempt of the up-country Brahmins for men of their own caste who had migrated to Chhattisgarh:

"This is Chhattisgarh, where the Gond is king of the jungle,
 Under his bed is a fire, for he cannot pay for a blanket,
 Nor for a hookah indeed—a leaf-pipe holds his tobacco:
 Kick him soundly first, and then he will do what you tell him."

One would say that the whole spirit of the swashbuckling white ruffian toward the lowest African "nigger" breathed in these lines; yet Sir Herbert Risley's comment is undoubtedly just, that they "reflect the intolerant and domineering attitude of the Indo-Aryan towards the Dravidian, of the high-caste man towards the low, that has been characteristic of Indian society from the earliest times down to the present day." Where such a spirit prevailed between Indian and Indian, is it wonderful that the relations between the European and the Oriental were not always regulated by the most scrupulous courtesy?

Perhaps it may be said that when impoliteness becomes a religion it ceases to be impolite: in the spirit of that atrocious line of Dante's:

E cortesia fù lui esser villano.

I have not actually come across this plea, but should not be at all surprised to find it in the works of the India-worshippers.* It must not be supposed, however, that caste

---

* In *The Web of Indian Life* (p. 46) "Sister Nivedita" enlarges on Indian courtesy: no doubt justly, as regards the domestic life of certain castes. A man, she admits, will always take precedence of a woman passing through a door; but this is because they "maintain the tradition of

is responsible for the whole of the mannerlessness of Indian life. It is at the root of a good deal of it, no doubt; but I think it may be taken as a general rule that the amenities of social behaviour do not greatly flourish anywhere among low-class Orientals. I am doubtful whether an exception should be made for the Japanese. When they exist, Oriental manners are magnificent: but in the intercourse of the masses of the people, they are apt not to exist. I am not assuming that they are always conspicuous among the masses of Europe. I am making no comparison, but simply stating what I take to be a fact. Beside the two instances I have mentioned of objectionable conduct on the part of Europeans, I could place numberless instances of over-bearing rudeness and hustling aggressiveness on the part of Indians towards Indians. These are, indeed, the everyday incidents of travel. Mr. Price Collier bears witness to the same effect. He says that in the course of all his wander-ings he saw no cases of rudeness, except on the part of minor railway officials towards travellers of their own race. "Once," he says, "sometime after midnight, I saw an English officer pile out of his carriage in his pyjamas and slippers, and soundly berate a native official who was bullying a third-class native woman passenger."

I shall not, I hope, be suspected of palliating bad manners and brutality. I merely recall to mind a fact which is sometimes forgotten—namely, that the domineering ten-dencies of the past, which to some extent survive in the present, were indigenous rather than imported. The trouble was that the British official and soldier became too much Orientalized. So far as I can discover, after pretty dili-

the path-breaker in the jungle." I do not pretend that there is any importance in our conventional rule of "ladies first"—I merely note this as an amusing example of the ingenuity which has been applied to the ennoblement of every slightest trait of Indian manners.

gent inquiry, they found in the Indian languages no forms of politeness ready to hand—no "please" or "thank you," or "I beg your pardon." Formulas of servility and adulation existed in plenty, but of ordinary courtesy, none. This may seem a very trifling matter, but it is not. These little phrases are invaluable lubricants of social intercourse, whether between equals or between superior and inferior. Some languages are better supplied with them than English; and one misses them sadly on returning to England from a country—I have Norway specially in mind—in which they are more abundant. In the country where they are absolutely lacking, there is no such thing as a request—there are only orders. What wonder if "Jo hookum,"—"As ordered,"—is the constant burden of the intercourse between Indians and Europeans? And what wonder if the awakening national spirit of India resents it?

Here again I suggest that a vast improvement would be effected if we could rid our minds of the superstition that British rule is and must be a failure if it aims at anything short of an adamantine eternity. Not the least of the evil results ensuing from that habit of thought is the notion that we must constantly pose as conquerors among a conquered people—a notion peculiarly prevalent, it is only fair to say, among bagmen, and shipping-clerks, and other haughty spirits of the type of my Madras compatriot. I have seen traces of it, too, among very young men of a better class. Once, in an out-of-the-way region, I encountered a young civil-engineer, the only European for many miles around, who invited me to his bungalow and treated me most hospitably, like the nice boy he was. But, perhaps because I did not take my fair share of the bottle of hock he produced in my honour, he became, certainly not drunk, but a little loquacious; and I shall never forget the comedy of his conversation with the station-master, as I

[120]

BRAHUI, SHEPHERD CLASS

waited for my midnight train. No Viceroy could have been more condescending, or could have imposed his commands on the official with a loftier superiority. I remember, too, that he gravely remonstrated with me for carrying a small handbag, instead of giving it to my servant—thereby lowering the prestige of the ruling race. It was a case of *in vino veritas*—without at all impairing his self-control, the hock had simply released the instinct of racial masterdom which he had brought with him from England, only a year before, and which had no doubt been fostered by the tone he found prevalent among other young men of his class. His fresh rapture of autocracy was innocent enough, so far as it went that night; and it would very likely wear off as he advanced in years and discretion. But there are too many irresponsible (and some responsible) Anglo-Indians in whom it does not wear off.

Such an Anglo-Indian is the author of a letter which appeared in the *Civil and Military Gazette* (the leading paper of the Punjab) on September 5, 1906—a letter signed, I regret to say, "Sagittarius."

I take no alarmist view (says the writer), but regard the whole subject calmly and rationally. Not only myself but many others must surely see daily the increasing impertinence, disrespect, officiousness (!) and disloyalty of the subject race. I wish to lay special emphasis on the words *subject race,* for the native of India, be his position and salary what it may, should and must understand that British blood has conquered India and rules it, and respect and deference must be shown to it at all times and in all places.

This is only one of a number of similar utterances which appeared in the *Civil and Military* about the same time, and did incalculable harm—as the conductors of the paper have realized and tacitly admitted. Here are one or two more specimens: "Let the Babus clearly understand that we have admitted them into the administration as our servants, not as our partners. A partnership between Europeans and natives there must inevitably be," but it must be "with the ruling classes, not with the servile classes." Again: "Already discerning people in England must be beginning to see that even half-a-dozen princely Counsellors of the intellectual type of the Maharaja of Bikanir would be worth a whole parliament of babbling B.A.'s." Yet again—from a letter signed "Fifty Years in India": "When *Swadeshism* degenerates into ruffianism, unveiled disloyalty and racial antagonism, I say again, '*Sjambok!*'" Pretty sort of writing this to mitigate "racial antagonism!"*

---

* Perhaps the worst, or at any rate the silliest of these effusions, was the following jibe at the extremely popular national song of Bengal, "Hail to the Motherland":

"BANDE MATARAM"

(By Autolycus).

I love my Aryan brother,
  And I love to see him gay—
It's nice to watch him hard at work,
  And nicer still at play:
As David danced before the Ark
  (While thinking out a psalm),
So doth Bengal
Nautch at the call
  Of "Bande Mataram."

Why should the "Raj" attempt to stay
  Such pure innocuous folly?
A puny thing of froth and fat
  (Half "dhoti"—quarter "brolly")
No more accords the ruling race
  An obsolete "Salaam,"
But—better still—
With organ shrill
  Cries "Bande Mataram."

The senseless swagger of such utterances is directly due to the idea that we have some sort of providential mandate to rule India for ever and a day, and that our right is founded, not on administrative capacity, but on an inborn genius for despotism, in which every white-skinned shop-boy has his share. If we were encouraged by those who set the tone of Anglo-Indian thought to take a saner view of our position and responsibilities, this pitiful and mischievous racial snobbery would soon die out. The fact that it is in some measure due to the contagion of our Oriental environment does not at all excuse it. If we are to justify our existence in India, it must be by our resistance to this contagion, to which all former invaders succumbed.*

Moreover, if we could realize and admit that our relation to India was temporary, not eternal, we should be less discouraged by the scant success of our heroic efforts to lower existing social barriers. It is the false ideal of our status that makes our isolation seem inhuman. Those of us who

> Our English topsy-turvy rule
>   Possesses humorous charms;
> Behold a race that bares its legs,
>   But never, sure, its arms!
> How can such children bother MEN?
>   It really takes the palm
> To think that we
> Should care a D
>   For "Bande Mataram."

* The following passage from an article in the *Asiatic Quarterly* by Shaikh Abdul Qadir (April, 1906), is much to the point: "The European official in India, in the interests of the Empire, and in order to win the confidence of the people, should so act as not to show any assumption of a Divine right to rule, or any air of conscious superiority, which, without strengthening his position, jars upon the susceptibilities of the people. I can quite imagine somebody objecting to the view I have expressed, and saying: 'This must be some new sensitiveness that the Indians have developed, as their fathers rejoiced in honouring the rulers.' Yes, it is new, but it is there, and it has to be taken into account."

give any thought to the matter know that two races cannot be locally intermingled in perpetuity without the smallest social or spiritual intermingling; so we strive to invent some form of social intercourse which shall make the situation a little less manifestly impossible. But in all such efforts there is a tacit "Thus far and no further" which renders them artificial and in great measure abortive. The real amalgamation which springs from inter-marriage is, by common consent, out of the question; and it is only in the rarest cases that anything like intimate equality of friendship is possible. Nor would it, if possible, be altogether desirable; for the strength of British administration lies in its superiority, not merely to pecuniary, but to personal influences. Another difficulty arises from the fact that those Indians who show themselves most accessible to social advances from the British side, are not always the best or the most respected members of their own community. This view is stated, with some exaggeration, in a letter from a "Mussulman" which appeared in the *Civil and Military Gazette* at the time when racial relations were being discussed in such an unfortunate tone by the correspondents of that paper.

"Those Indians," he wrote, "who claim and crave admission to Anglo-Indian society are 'knaves' and 'fools;' but I submit to Anglo-Indians—these knaves and fools are *your* creation. They are a detestable set; we Indians abhor them and call them degenerate. . . . They are the biggest snobs we have. They decry you when they come strutting to us, and they denounce us when they go cringing before you."

This is clearly a somewhat intemperate, partisan outburst; but it points to a real difficulty. No Indian, and especially no Hindu, can enter upon social relations with Europeans without in some degree derogating from the

[124]

ideals of his race; and though he may be sincerely convinced that the ideals he renounces are false and noxious, he none the less lays himself open to suspicion of currying favour with the ruling caste.

I am far from suggesting that the efforts to place the two races on a better social footing should cease. I think they are of great educational value to both parties. But let us not fail to bear this in mind: if these efforts should ever meet with any large measure of success, it would mean that India no longer stood in need of alien tutelage. So soon as there is a large class of educated, emancipated Indians, fitted to take part on equal terms in European society, India will be fitted to take part on equal terms in the fellowship of the nations. I do not mean that fitness for self-government is necessarily to be tested by Europeanization of manners. It is quite possible that, when India awakens to the need for civilization,* she may take a line of her own, very different from that marked out for her by Europe. But if she does elect to make Europe her model, and succeeds in assimilating European manners and ideals, her success will constitute a conspicuous proof of her ability to work out her own salvation.

Meanwhile, if we realize and admit that the two races are not handcuffed together for all eternity, but only associated for a particular purpose, the problem of their social relations loses much of its importance. It is when we take up the "Whom God hath joined, let no man put asunder" attitude that our failure to get into sympathetic

* "When she awakens!" some readers may exclaim. "Is not her civilization the most ancient and the noblest in the world?" It is precisely because so many even of her educated men are deceived by this juggling with the term "civilization" that I hold her to be very imperfectly awakened to her most urgent needs. Rightly or wrongly (as readers who have followed me so far must realise) this is one of the cardinal points of my whole contention.

personal relations with our Indian fellow-citizens seems like failure in a crucial point of policy, if not of duty. One thinks of old Mrs. Baird's pity for "the chiel that's chained to oor Davie;" had that union been indissoluble, it would indeed have been of the first importance that the parties should get into some sort of human relation to each other. If, on the other hand, there is no question of eternity in the juxtaposition, we may without any sense of failure "admit impediment" to "the marriage of true minds." If we would but see ourselves in a realistic light, as persons called in to perform for certain other persons a set of services which, if honestly and capably rendered, must, in the nature of things, work themselves out and become unnecessary, we should find ourselves relieved, not, indeed, of social duties, but of the oppressive sense of their momentous importance and insurmountable difficulty. Here, in England, doctors, lawyers, architects, bankers, stockbrokers do not feel themselves bound to become the personal cronies of their clients. It is only in a small minority of cases that professional relations lead to social intimacy; nor does any professional man measure his success by the number of such cases in his own experience. We are, in India, simply professional men exercising certain protective, administrative, educative, constructive functions; and it is only when, forgetting this, we pose as heaven-appointed affable archangels that we have any need to reproach ourselves with the incomplete success of our attempts at affability.

VII

THE Abbé Dubois, that shrewd observer from whom I have already made several quotations, placed his finger, a century ago, upon the great difficulty of British rule in India. Though a Frenchman, writing at a time when the defeat of French ambitions in the East was still comparatively recent, he was in every way friendly to an administration which, as he said, "had freed the Indian people from the iron yoke of a long series of arbitrary rulers under whose oppression they groaned during so many centuries." But he added, with admirable insight or foresight: "It is the poverty of the country which, in my opinion, gives most cause for apprehension—a poverty which is accompanied by the most extraordinary supineness on the part of the people themselves. The question is, will a government which is rightly determined to be neither unjust nor oppressive be able always to find within the borders of this immense empire sufficient to enable it to meet the heavy expenses of its administration." This may seem to imply that good administration is necessarily more expensive than bad; but the seeming paradox is easily resolved.

Under a system of oppression and corruption, the cost of government is enormous, but undefined. The people suffer as long as they can, and die when they can suffer no more. Even if the cost in money were ascertainable, who could reckon the cost in misery, enervation and general lowering of vitality? As there is no assumption, open or

[127]

tacit, that government exists for the good of the people, no one collects statistics of popular well-being or ill-being. The blight of misrule seems to be part of the natural order of things; and, if the sufferers complain at all, it is just as they might complain of any natural calamity, such as drought or pestilence. Among more energetic races, intolerable suffering may seek relief in rebellion; but popular risings, as distinct from dynastic revolts and military mutinies, are almost unknown to Indian history. Misrule, in short, goes unaudited and unchecked. It sins against no ideal because it owns none; and its victims are too inarticulate to protest.

But good administration starts from the principle that it exists for the benefit of the people; and, moreover, it collects statistics and submits its accounts to criticism. If, then, its necessary expenses are heavy in proportion to the wealth, or the poverty, of the country, its practice seems to conflict with its professions, and discontent, aided by education, becomes vocal and importunate. Peace and security encourage the growth of population; and unless a similar increase in the means of subsistence can be effected, the strain on the resources of the country is by so much the more severe. It is possible, of course, that an honest and well-meaning administration may be extravagant in its finance, and may claim too high a remuneration for its services. That, as a matter of fact, is one of the chief counts in the Indian indictment of British rule. But it is also quite possible—as the Abbé Dubois foresaw—that a country may be so situated as to require for its administration and defence, even on the most economical terms, such sums as to involve a considerable draft upon the scant subsistence of its poorer classes. That this is the condition of India there can be no doubt. It may be that she is to some extent overcharged for the advantages of British

rule; but even if that overcharge, on any reasonable estimate, were to cease to-morrow, the country would be scarce
the less bitterly poor. No conceivable relief of taxation
would make the ryot prosperous, or place him beyond the
reach of starvation in time of drought. If his poverty is
to be remedied, it must be by different methods of agriculture, different credit facilities, different social habits, and,
above all, by the maintenance of a fair equation between
mouths and food.

I have spoken of the Indian "indictment" of British rule,
and the word is not too strong for the attacks made upon
the system and its results, not by fanatical extremists, but
by moderate and sensible men. Mr. G. K. Gokhale, for instance, was a man of fine character and high ability, justly
respected both by Indians and by Englishmen. He was a
member of the Viceroy's Legislative Council, an admirable
speaker, and much less addicted than most of his countrymen to the vices of the rhetorical temperament. In a formal
profession of faith, made on behalf of the brotherhood of
Servants of India which he founded, he "frankly accepted
the British connection, as ordained, in the inscrutable dis-
pensation of Providence, for India's good." This declaration (which must not be taken as ironic) he was ready
enough to repeat; and yet, almost in the next breath, he
would launch such accusations at the British rule as to make
one wonder what worse fate Providence could have allotted
to India had it been evilly instead of kindly disposed. Here
are some extracts from a speech delivered at the National
Liberal Club, on November 15, 1905:

It is necessary to consider how far the best interests—material
and moral—of the people of India have been promoted by your
administration during the last hundred years. If the results,
judged by this test, were satisfactory, however much one might

object on principle to the present form of government maintained in India, there would be something (!) to be said in its favour. . . . Let us first consider the moral results. These, it will be found, are of a mixed character. There is a great deal in them which you may regard with satisfaction and even pride. . . . On the other hand there are great evils too. . . . Our rigorous exclusion from all power and all positions of trust and responsibility . . . is leading to a steady deterioration of our race, and this, I venture to think, is a cruel and iniquitous wrong you are inflicting upon us. . . . Let us now turn to the material results, and here, I am sorry to say, the verdict is even more emphatic against your rule. . . . The economic results of British rule in India have been absolutely disastrous.

Read literally, this invective is surely inconsistent with even the most guarded acceptance of "the British connection." If it causes "steady moral deterioration" and "absolute economic disaster," what worse results could ensue from its overthrow, and a return to the chaos of the eighteenth century, with perhaps, a Japanese or Russian *raj* to follow?

Mr. Gokhale, of course, was not to be understood literally when he used such language. He spoke, no doubt, with sincerity, but it was the sincerity of the Leader of the Opposition denouncing a flagitious Treasury Bench. It should never be forgotten that this is, and must be, the nature of a great deal of Indian criticism of British rule. The Government of India is a Ministry which never goes out, and the Indian Nationalists are an Opposition which never comes in, and is consequently unrestrained by any sense of responsibility, by any anticipation of having to make good its words when its turn comes. From such an Opposition, scrupulous fairness is not to be expected. Everything that goes wrong is laid to the charge of the Government, and it is assumed that but for the stupidity and arrogance and

[130]

cupidity of the Government, everything would go right.
This is, indeed, the nemesis of autocracy; but most autocracies have a short way of dealing with an inconvenient
Opposition. In India the Opposition, far from being suppressed, is allowed not only the utmost liberty of speech
that any constitutional party could possibly claim, but is
given a clear and honourable official standing. It might
even be said, I think, that the existence of such a man as
Mr. Gokhale, and his freedom to utter such charges as
those above quoted, carries in itself the confutation of one
of the charges—that of stunting and depressing the Indian
genius.

There are, then, two groups of grievances currently
alleged against the British rule: grievances material and
grievances moral. Let us look into them in this order.

The material grievances all reduce themselves to one:
the alleged impoverishment of the country. But this fact, if
it be a fact, is viewed from different aspects and attributed
to three main causes:

(1) The "drain" of wealth due to heavy payments for
the services of an alien administration, a large part of whose
earnings is spent outside the country.

(2) Excessive military expenditure.

(3) Commercial subjection.

Material Grievances—I. "The Drain."

Most of the Indian arguments upon the "drain"—or,
as it is sometimes called, the annual "tribute" paid by
India to England—would lead one to imagine that the proverbial lore of India lacks an equivalent for the wise old saw:
"You cannot both eat your cake and have it." No doubt it
would be better for India if peace, order and security from

invasion were products of her own soil, and had not to be imported. But as this is, for the present, not so—by the admission of all thinking men—it is futile to talk of the payment for these imported commodities as a dead loss. The metaphor is neither fantastic nor sophistical. It would be perfectly fair to enter in the balance-sheet, under the heading of "Imports":

Peace	.	.	.	.	£x,000,000
Order	.	.	.	.	£y,000,000
Security	.	.	.	.	£z,000,000

Items in the detailed account may be open to criticism; but even if an overcharge be detected here, an ungenerous exaction there, the main result—a large surplus on the import side—will be very slightly affected. It is true (and this is what we are all apt to forget) that even peace, order and security are not absolute and unmixed blessings, but are good only in so far as a nation is capable of using them wisely. It is no special reproach to India to say that she has not made the wisest use of them; for no people on earth has yet discovered the art of so ordering its social economy as to beget the highest measure of common weal. But India is at least as far as any other nation from knowing how to reap the advantages of peace without its drawbacks: and her thinkers would perhaps be better employed in studying this art than in making fantastic calculations (under English guidance, it must be owned) of the sums of which she is annually despoiled by ravenous England.

In his *Economic Transition in India*, Sir Theodore Morison examines the theory of the so-called "drain." He analyses the "Home Charges Budget" of 1910-11 and shows (to my sense, convincingly) that its total of nearly £20,000,000 reduces itself to a sum of a little less than £7,000,000 which may not unreasonably be called a pay-

[132]

ment "due to the political connection with England."* He then asks: "If India stood outside the Empire, as Japan does, would she be saved the expenditure of these £7,000,-000?" and his answer is that she would not. On the analogy of Japan, he points out, she would have to pay between four and five millions a year for a navy: and this is surely an under-estimate, inasmuch as India offers a much more tempting field than Japan for foreign aggression. Further, she has not to maintain a diplomatic and consular service; and he might have added that the £24,000 a year paid to her Viceroy is a trifle compared to the salaries and civil lists of monarchs, whether European or Oriental. But, he continues, "The greatest saving of all arises directly from India's political connection with England. It is this: England's credit enables India to borrow money much more cheaply than she could otherwise do." Japan pays on an average 5½ per cent. on her loans; India borrows at 3½ per cent. "An additional 2 per cent. on India's total debt of £267,000,000 would represent an additional charge of £5,340,000 a year. This in itself is not very far from being enough to wipe out the whole of the 'political drain.' " But Sir Theodore goes on to point out that the present gain is not all that has to be taken into account. In the course of India's development, she will have to borrow some hundreds of millions "in the near future," and for every £100,000,000 she will pay £2,000,000 a year less interest than if she were Japan.† This, one may remark in paren-

---

* The other items are: Interest on Capital Invested, £8,869,900; Interest on Ordinary Debt (with cost of management), £2,238,900; Stores and Goods (simply imports), £1,046,900.

† The Indian politician reckons among his grievances all payment of interest on imported capital; but since India admittedly does not possess sufficient capital for her development, and is extremely chary of investing what capital she has, this complaint is, in other words, a plea for economic stagnation. See *post*, pp. 148-151.

thesis, assumes that the credit of an independent India would be as good as that of Japan—a tolerably large assumption. "The answer, then," says Sir Theodore, "which I give to the question 'What economic equivalent does India get for foreign payments?' is this: India gets the equipment of modern industry, and she gets an administration favourable to economic evolution, cheaper than she could provide it herself."

It seems to me, I confess, that this is an extremely moderate statement of the case. If we take a larger view of the whole question and compare what the Indian people pay for peace, order and security with the sums paid for these advantages by any similar number of people in other organized communities, we shall see, I think, that India profits quite enormously by the unity imposed on her by British rule, and the security she gains from her participation in the defensive establishment of the British Empire. We have seen that the area of India is equal to that of Europe, minus Russia; and, oddly enough, the population of Europe minus Russia is roughly equivalent to the population of India.* To compare the cost of government of all Western Europe with the cost of government of India would of course show a gigantic disproportion; but in order to do this we should have to include all the budgets of the native states, which, so far as I know, are not available. It is more to the point to take British India alone, with its population of 244,000,000, which exceeds by about 9,000,000 the united populations of Great Britain and Ireland, France, Germany, Austria-Hungary, and Italy. Here, again, a comparison of the whole budgets would not be instructive, the discrepancy of conditions being so enormous. It is sufficient to put the tax revenue of the

* I take the figures from the *International Whitaker* for 1913. They work out thus: Europe, minus Russia, 312,104,000: India, 315,132,537.

United Kingdom alone—about £155,000,000—beside the tax-revenue of India—about £45,000,000:* the incidence per head of population being about £3 8s. in the United Kingdom, as compared with 3s. 8d. in India. It is more to the point to see what the defence of 235,000,000 people in Europe costs, in comparison with the defence of 244,000,000 in India. This, I submit, is a legitimate and really instructive comparison: for defence is a function that depends not so much upon what a country *ought to afford*, in consideration of its wealth, as upon what a country *must provide*, in consideration of the dangers to which it is exposed. I shall try to put my meaning more clearly after having stated the figures.

Defence now ranks in the Indian budget at about £21,000,000 per annum, and the Indian Opposition is never tired of denouncing the reckless extravagance of this expenditure. But the defence of a smaller number of people in Europe costs more than ten times as much, namely £235,500,000—to say nothing of the economic loss involved in conscription. Western Europe (United Kingdom, France, Germany, Austria, Italy) pays just about £1 per head of population for defence: British India pays less than 1s. 8d. per head. Further, as the whole of India benefits by the security it enjoys, it is quite fair to include the whole population in reckoning the incidence of defensive expenditure: in which case it works out at less than 1s. 4d. per head.† The defence of Russia costs the people of the Russian Empire about 7s. 9d. each; the defence of Japan

* The total revenue and expenditure of British India are now between £75,000,000 and £80,000,000 a year.

† The inclusion of the expenses of the Imperial Service Corps might infinitesimally affect this figure. The armies of the Native States may be disregarded, as contributing, not to the defensive strength of the Empire, but to the necessity for maintaining in high efficiency the forces which guarantee the Imperial bond.

[155]

costs the people of Japan alone 7s. 5d. each; if we include the population of her dependencies, the figure is reduced to about 5s. 7d.—more than four times as much as the cost per head of the defence of India.

Now this, I say, is no unfair comparison, since the needs of defence are not to be measured by the wealth or poverty of the people, but by the dangers which threaten it. Why does defence cost Western Europeans, per head, fifteen times as much as it costs to Indians? Because Western Europe is broken up into hostile communities, jealous of one another's prosperity, afraid of one another's power, and with more than one old score to be wiped out at the first opportunity. Why is India not similarly broken up into hostile communities with apparently conflicting interests, with territorial disputes unsettled, with mutual jealousies and rancours necessitating a constant readiness to repel aggression? Simply because British rule imposes unity and peace upon races and religions more diverse than those of Western Europe—peoples which, in the past, have shown a tragic inability to live at peace with each other. It is true that, as we have seen in Chapter III., British rule has begotten a certain sense of solidarity, which will doubtless grow and strengthen if present conditions remain undisturbed; but the unifying process is as yet very incomplete, and it is scarcely to be doubted that, were the external pressure now withdrawn, India would break up again into numerous potentially hostile states, which would proceed to arm against each other with all the ruinous apparatus of modern warfare. How long, in such an event, could the requirements of defence be kept down to one rupee per head, or even to one rupee, four annas?[*]

* "I do not think the comparison with European expenditure a good one," writes a friendly critic, familiar with India, "because I do not believe that, were we to leave India, the separate races would ever arm

Let us imagine, however, that India, outside the British Empire, remained an empire at peace with itself, or a confederation of united states, requiring no force for what may be called inter-state defence. It would in that case present a marvellous and unprecedented spectacle to the world: that of a huge congeries of heterogeneous races, tribes and tongues, falling into a condition of stable equilibrium without any external pressure: a triumphant proof, by the way, of the beneficence of the alien rule which, in a single century, had worked such a miracle. But would the admiration which this spectacle ought to command render the India of the future any more inviolable from without than the India of the past? Would the country which has tempted invasion after invasion since the very dawn of history be exempt from the need of fortifying her frontiers, patrolling her coasts, and being prepared to hurl back from her soil any invaders who broke through her lines of defence? In the present state of the world, the answer must be: certainly not. There are several nations which, rightly or wrongly, wisely or unwisely, would be only too glad to step into England's shoes in India; and if India's weakness invited them, they would not long lack a pretext for aggression. India outside the British Empire, in short, even if she continued to present a united front to the world, would be forced to strengthen that front at enormous cost. Even

on such a stupendous scale against each other: they would soon submit to some control either from within or from without." As to the probability of the latter contingency, I agree; but I am putting it aside for the moment to consider the other alternative. If it be true that India would "soon" and peacefully submit to "control from within," then she is already ripe for self-government. I wish I could believe it! That her different sections would not arm against each other on the "stupendous" European scale is no doubt true: their poverty would render it impossible. But they would strain their resources to make their armaments as formidable as possible.

[137]

supposing she could save on her army estimates (and the probability is all the other way) she would certainly have to create a powerful navy; and a rupee per head would leave very little margin for that.

I believe, then, that the theory of the "drain" is absolutely and ludicrously unfounded. I believe that not only does India receive a full equivalent for the sums withdrawn from her, but that she gets her administration and defence quite amazingly cheap—incomparably cheaper than any other region in the world of similar extent and population.* It is always possible to argue that, in a metaphorical sense, she "pays too dear" for these benefits: that it would be better for her soul if she were thrown back upon war and rapine, and left to work out her salvation for herself. But, in the first place, this is not the argument advanced by any responsible politician; in the second place, she would almost certainly not be "left to work out her salvation," but would merely exchange the British for some other foreign *raj*. I do not think even the wildest extremist imagines that there would be any great gain in that.

MATERIAL GRIEVANCES—II. MILITARY EXPENDITURE.

We now come to the second count of the indictment on the material side—that of excessive military expenditure. It may appear that I have already dealt with this subject; but that is not so. I have tried to show that the burden of defence is very small in comparison with that borne

---

* I cannot find any data which would enable us to bring China into the comparison. But, however it might work out in figures, two considerations would have to be borne in mind: first, that China has a very much more homogeneous population, and that the tradition of unity is there as strong as the tradition of political disunion in India: second, that the peace of China is very much less secure than the peace of India under British rule.

by other nations, and in proportion to the temptations which India has always offered to foreign invaders. But it does not follow from this that the military expenditure is not higher than it need be. If equal security could be attained at less cost—if, say, it could be bought for one shilling per head instead of 1s. 4d.—then India has, in so far, a just grievance.

This is, of course, a question for experts, on which it is difficult for a layman to form a decided opinion. Indian politicians have not the least hesitation in condemning the "forward" frontier policy which has added so largely to the military budget. It is an article of faith to them that we should have ensconced ourselves behind the inmost line of defence* and not gone out to meet a possible invader. This opinion may conceivably be right in itself; but it is held in India, not because it is right, but because it is the opposite opinion to that of the Government. I do not mean that the politicians have not studied the question; I mean that they have accepted the arguments which appealed to them in their character of a permanent Opposition, and which made for immediate, if not ultimate, economy. For my part, I do not attempt to decide. All governments are fallible; and if the Government of India has made a mistake in its frontier policy, it has at least not been for lack of earnest thought and deliberation. It is useless to talk as if it had been animated by insane acquisitiveness or reckless and wanton extravagance.

One argument frequently advanced on the side of the Opposition I hold to be clearly fallacious. In his evidence

* "British Baluchistan and the Gilgit Protectorate are beyond the line of our impregnable defences, and India has no concern with them except as Imperial charges." Mr. Gokhale, Evidence before the Welby Commission 1897. It is a little surprising to find Mr. Gokhale speaking of the "impregnable defences" of the most invaded country in the world.

before the Welby Commission (1897), Mr. Gokhale said: "If England thinks that a certain number of European officers and a certain strength of the European army must always be maintained in India, she must be prepared to pay a fair share of the cost . . . the maintenance of British supremacy in India being a matter affecting the most vital interests of England." And in his Budget Speech of 1905, in the Imperial Legislative Council, Mr. Gokhale repeated the same argument: "It is said that India is the strategic frontier of the British Empire. If so, the defence of such frontiers is clearly an Imperial responsibility, and India ought to be relieved of part of her present military burdens." In sum, England ought not merely to organize the defence of India, devoting much of her best brain and muscle to the task, and paying enormous sums to keep her communications clear: she ought also to bear part of the actual military expenses incurred within the country, or on the frontier. What part she ought to bear Mr. Gokhale did not say, nor did he suggest any principle on which the proportion should be determined.

This contention can be not obscurely traced back to the idea that India is a source of vast profit to England, or in other words to the theory of the "drain." With its implications stated at length, the argument would run something like this: "Since the peace and security of India are of direct value to England, in order that she may devote herself undisturbed to her work of exploitation, she ought in common decency to contribute to the cost of keeping intruders out of her preserves. Why should the people who are robbing us from within throw upon us the whole cost of frightening off those who would rob us from without?" Such views find a certain amount of sanction in the loose talk of the Imperialists who regard the British Empire as an asset

and not as a responsibility. But if it be not true that we
get from India any more than a very reasonable equivalent
for the services we render her,* what becomes of the argument that we ought to pay heavily for the privilege of rendering these services? We do pay heavily for it, outside
India. Our interest in "the Eastern Question" arises mainly,
if not solely, from our responsibilities in India; and what
has not that interest cost us? We assume the entire charge
of India's maritime defence except a little over £400,000 a
year.† It would be rather hard if we had to pay for the
defence of her land frontier as well.

It does not appear from whom Mr. Gokhale quoted the
saying that India is "the strategic frontier of the British
Empire"; nor is it quite clear what the phrase means, unless
that it is the most vulnerable point in the frontier. Mr.
Dadabhai Naoroji, in his Presidential Address to the Indian
National Congress at Lahore in 1898, put the plea more
definitely, in quoting from Lord Roberts two statements to
the effect that "the retention of our Eastern Empire is essential to the greatness and prosperity of the United Kingdom,"
and then asking why, if this be so, the cost of defence should
be "to the last farthing thrown on the wretched Indians."
That this is far from being the case we have just seen; but

* If we go back to the eighteenth century, we must of course plead
guilty to much "shaking of the pagoda tree." We robbed the native
robbers who were bleeding the country to death; and here and there
we took up and carried on their work. But to quote as applicable to the
present day, a phrase of Ruskin's about "our native desire to live on
the loot of India," is not, I think, to promote lucidity of thought. Still
less is it helpful to endorse without reserve the phrases of Indian agitators who talk of the British as being "day and night engaged in the
exploitation of our country and the spoliation of our people."

† The average of ten years' "marine expenditure," 1900-10. This is
less than a quarter of the cost of a single battleship, less than one-twen-
tieth of the naval expenditure of Japan, and less than one hundredth
part of the naval expenditure of England.

[141]

even if it were the case, what country can justly claim to
be relieved of the cost of its own defence? It is not our
fault that India is poor.* It is not our fault that she
invites invasion. It is not our fault that she has never been
able, by her own organization and resources, to offer any
sustained resistance to invasion. We place her in a strong
defensive position by means of an army of 225,000 men,
one third of whom are Europeans. That this force, and the
constructions and operations undertaken for securing the
frontier, should cost a little over £20,000,000† a year is no
doubt to be regretted, when we consider the poverty of the
country; and the Opposition has every right to urge
economy and object to unfair charges. Especially may it
with reason protest against the throwing upon India of
expenses incurred in the service of the Empire in general
and not of India in particular. But that is a quite different
thing from claiming exemption from expenses incurred in the
direct interest of her security. Some of them may have
been unwisely incurred; but that is not the point here at
issue. The point is whether England ought to relieve India
of a proportion of the outlay necessary for her land
defence; and in that contention I can see no reason.

"But," it may be urged, "the 75,000 British soldiers in India are not really—at any rate not primarily—a force hired
to protect the country against menace from without. They
are the garrison required to consolidate British rule within
the country—to give strength, when necessary, to the 'civil
arm.'" No doubt that is so; no doubt India (by the admission of all reasonable Indians) requires, as yet, protection
against internal no less than against external dangers. But

* Mr. Naoroji and Mr. Gokhale maintain that it *is* our fault—a contention we have already examined, and shall return to later.

† Note that at least three-fourths of this sum is expended in India,
and can by no manner of reckoning be docketed as "drain."

is that the fault of England? Can England be rightly debited with the cost of maintaining peace and order in a country which would certainly never have come under her control had it been able to perform that duty for itself?

This brings us round again to the suggestion that, on the evidence of Lord Roberts and many other authorities, India is "essential to the greatness and prosperity of England," which therefore ought to pay for her defence. Now it is perfectly true that the prestige and (for a time at any rate) the prosperity of England would suffer considerably by a catastrophic end of her rule in India, whether due to invasion from without or rebellion from within. An unsuccessful war is necessarily a calamity, at any rate in its immediate results; and as the expulsion of the British from India would probably mean the installation of a government (whether native or foreign) hostile to British trade, the blow would doubtless be severely felt in the industrial world. But because the violent overthrow of an existing arrangement would be disastrous, it does not follow that the arrangement in itself is particularly profitable. Apart from the question of trade, it is very doubtful whether we make any clear profit at all out of our connection with India. She is a huge addition to our responsibilities, and she "drains" us year by year of many of our best intellects, returning them to us when their vigour is declining, and when (in many cases) they have formed habits of thought and feeling of doubtful advantage to their British citizenship. Whatever we gain by the connection, except in the way of commerce, is probably a very poor compensation for what we sacrifice. If we are not in India for India's good, still less are we there for our own. There is a certain stimulus, no doubt, in the romance of the adventure, and a certain satisfaction in the sense of work well done, which, on the whole, and despite our critics, we may justly feel. But one need not be a Little

Englander to hold that India has tended to check rather than to promote the course of sound development in our national life.

There remains the commercial advantage of the connection: is it so huge, and of such vital importance to us, that we ought, as it were, to tax our profits in order to relieve India of part of the burden of her military defence? Before the war—that is to say, under normal conditions—our trade with India was about 8 per cent. of our total trade; our exports to India were less than 10 per cent. of our total exports. If we were entirely excluded from the Indian market—and, even in the worst event, that would scarcely be the case—the blow to our commerce would be considerable, indeed, but by no means crushing. Our total trade with the United States and our total trade with Germany —protectionist countries both—were in each case greater by many millions than our total trade with India. In the scale of our exports alone, India came well below both these countries. If, then, we are bound to contribute to the military charges of countries whose trade is valuable to us, we ought to begin with the United States and Germany. With reference to these countries, the suggestion cannot be taken seriously; has it any greater validity with reference to India?

There is some evidence, I think, that the Home Government treats India in a niggardly spirit on certain points of sheer accountancy, debiting her with charges which ought, if not in justice, at any rate in generosity, to be borne by England. A prominent case in point is that of the India Office, of which the charges, something like £175,000 * a

* I take this figure from the *Statistical Abstract of British India*, 1900-10, p. 71. Mr. Gokhale, in his evidence before the Welby Commission, placed it at £273,000. "The salary of the Colonial Secretary," he said, "together with his official charges, is borne on the Imperial Estimates. . . . I am aware, however, that . . . under present arrange-

[144]

year, are borne by India. This cannot, I think, be called positively unjust, but it has the appearance of being ungenerous, and I believe it would be a measure of wise economy to do away with the small but rankling grievance. An excellent rule in Anglo-Indian finance would be, "When in doubt, charge England." *

MATERIAL GRIEVANCES—III. COMMERCIAL SUBJECTION.

The third grievance, on the material side, is that of commercial subjection or exploitation. It is very clearly formulated by Mr. Gokhale in his evidence before the Welby Commission: "The resources of our Empire," he said, "are really vast; but the great difficulty in India is about capital, and we are unable at present to take advantage of these resources ourselves, but our hope is that in course of time we might be better able to spend money in that direction, and then we should be able to utilize our resources for ourselves. At present, owing to the vigorous manner in which railways are constructed, and the way in which foreign capitalists are encouraged to invest their money in India, the result is that we get only the wages of labour, while all the profits that are made are taken out of the country, and our resources are being utilized by others." Mr. Naoroji, who was a member of the Commission, then proceeded to question Mr. Gokhale as to the reason why India was

ments, the India Office has to do much directive and executive work ... which the Colonial Office is not called upon to do, and I should, therefore, be satisfied if the charges were divided half and half between India and England."

* I do not remember to have seen any protest against the item of "Ecclesiastical Expenditure," running to over £190,000 a year. The European community ought surely to pay for its own spiritual luxuries. This item comes under "Salaries and Expenses of Civil Departments." The "Ecclesiastical" expenses of the army, which may fairly be reckoned as necessary, are very much lower.

so ill-provided with capital: "Is it not because our capital is carried away from the country?" "Yes, that is so." "Is not that at the root of the whole thing?" "Yes, it is at the root of the whole thing." Once more the famous "drain"!

Mr. Gokhale further said that, while he admitted the benefit of the trunk lines of railway, he would have had no further development of the railway system, except such as could be executed out of surplus revenue: that, in a word, he would have had "India make her own railroads." In his Budget speeches of ten to fifteen years later, he criticizes very severely the system of "budgeting for surpluses" and of paying extraordinary expenses (such as those of military re-organization) out of revenue, instead of by way of loan. There is, to my mind, a great deal of force in his objection to any system of finance which takes from the Indian tax-payer more than is strictly needful for the time being; but it is hard to see how, on this principle, the Indian railroads would ever have got themselves built.

I have read criticisms on details (and important details) of Indian railway finance which seemed, to my inexpert judgment, distinctly damaging. That the Government has now and then entered into disadvantageous bargains, and allowed itself to be "put upon," seems probable enough. But the Indian railways now bring into the exchequer the substantial annual revenue of from £12,000,000 to £14,000,000 —far more than half the total of the so-much-denounced military expenditure. It would seem as though the system had not been, on the whole, absolutely ruinous to the country.

But the railways are only a particular instance of the exploitation of which Mr. Gokhale and Mr. Naoroji complain—the exploitation which, to use their own favourite phrase, is reducing them to nothing but "hewers of wood and drawers of water." The real question is whether they are right in arguing that India's assumed inability to provide the capital for her own development is due to the malign influence of foreign rule, and whether, realizing that inability, a wise statesmanship ought to have checked development until such time as India could have paid for it out of her own resources?

The second half of the question raises an economic problem of great interest. Where it is a matter of choosing between comparatively slow development by (so to speak) home-grown capital, and rapid development by foreign capital, it is very probable that far-sighted statesmanship would choose the former alternative. But this choice would presuppose two conditions: first, that the country could afford to develop slowly: secondly, that, given reasonable time, its people had the energy and the thrift to furnish for themselves the means of development. Were those conditions present in India? Would not the policy now advocated by the Indian Opposition—the deliberate exclusion of foreign capital—have left the country exposed to far greater evils than those now complained of? Effective measures of famine relief would have remained impossible; education would have been enormously retarded; the sense of national unity would have grown very slowly, if at all. I think it may safely be said that the Indian Opposition would never have existed, or at any rate would have remained in the far future, if the Government, fifty years ago, had acted upon the economic principles which it is now reproached with ignoring. It is not accused of having recklessly or corruptly given away valuable rights and concessions to foreign capitalists, or alienated what ought to be regarded as the property of the nation. It is not accused of blindly pandering—after the manner of Porfirio Diaz—to capitalistic greed. All it has done is not to interfere artificially with the natural influx of capital for the development of resources

[147]

which the Indian people lacked the means, and more particularly the energy, to develop for themselves. The view that it should, or could, have acted otherwise, does not seem seriously tenable.

If, on the other hand, India's lack of capital was due to impoverishment consequent upon British rule, that is a serious, even a terrible, grievance. We have already seen some reason for doubting whether this fundamental theory of the Indian Opposition tallies with the facts of the case; but it may be well, at this point, to look a little more closely into the whole question of Indian wealth and poverty.

In the first place: is it true that the resources of the country are being exploited exclusively, or nearly so, by Europeans? When one has seen the palaces of merchants and manufacturers around Bombay and Ahmedabad, and the Calcutta mansions of the zemindars, or landlords, enriched by the "permanent settlement" of Bengal, one has a little difficulty in compassionating these "hewers of wood and drawers of water." Almost all of the 200 to 250 cotton mills (mostly in Bombay Presidency) have been built by Indian capital, and if the 60 to 70 jute mills of Bengal are mainly in European hands, that is not, certainly, because the Bengalis have no money to embark in such enterprises. It is true that coal mines, tea plantations and gold mines are for the most part owned by Europeans; but Indian capital and enterprise are largely employed in the production of silk, paper, timber, flour, in oil-pressing and in carpet-weaving. It is not the fact that European enterprise has elbowed Indian enterprise aside; it may rather be said to have flowed in where the lack of Indian enterprise (far more than the lack of Indian capital) left gaps for it to fill; and it is the fact that Indians are, year by year, securing a larger share of the import and export trade of the country. The Parsis, Bhathias and Banias of Bombay, being born traders, have

[148]

all along known how to avail themselves of their opportunities. It is not our fault if the Bengali prefers to live on the income of his lands, and let the European carry on the jute, coal and tea industries. There is an impression abroad that the merchant princes of Bombay Presidency are almost all Parsis. This is scarcely the fact: there are many Hindus and Muhammadans among them: but even if it were the fact, what would it prove? Not that the British rule prevented Hindus and Muhammadans from profiting by the resources of their country, but that the Parsis, by reason of their greater intelligence and energy, were quicker than their neighbours in seizing opportunities. The Parsi has no special privileges or immunities as compared with other Indians. What a Parsi can do, a Hindu can do—if he has it in him. If he is not in general an alert and enterprising man of business, the fault lies, not with the British rule, but with influences operating through ages before the British rule was dreamt of.

Again, even as to railways, is it the case that India could not, if it would, have provided the capital for their construction? It did provide the capital for a certain part of them, in the form of loans from three or four Indian princes, on terms said to be not wholly advantageous to the Indian tax-payer. As to the general mass of railway stock, I am not aware of any statistics to show how much of it is held in India; but if it is a small proportion, the reason must lie in the Indian character. There is no doubt that the hoarded, or, at any rate, the uninvested wealth of India is great, and that rich men, from princes downwards, might do a great deal more than they actually do towards developing the resources of the country. If they lack the enterprise or the intelligence to invest judiciously in joint stock concerns, is that the fault of the British rule? To say that development ought to have been suspended because India had not the capital to undertake it for herself, is not, at best, very practical; but what becomes of the suggestion should it appear that she had the capital, and forbore to use it?

One of the proofs of poverty which the Indian Opposition is fond of adducing is the small amount of the deposits in the Post Office Savings Bank. "The total deposits in your Postal Savings Bank," said Mr. Gokhale at the National Liberal Club in 1905, "amount to 148 million sterling, and you have, in addition, in the Trustee Savings Bank, about 52 million sterling. Our Postal Savings Bank deposits, with a population seven times as large as yours, are only about seven million sterling, and even of this a little over one tenth is held by Europeans." * This is certainly a striking contrast; but Mr. Gokhale makes no allowance for his countrywomen's habit of carrying the family savings about their persons in the shape of gold and silver ornaments and jewellery. The European who has not visited India can scarcely believe how universal is this practice, or what a weight of precious metals the Indian woman will suspend at her ears and string upon her wrists and ankles. If India would capitalize her nose-rings alone, her Savings Bank total would go up at a bound.†

After all deductions and qualifications, however, we come at last to the hard fact that the peasantry of India—four-fifths of the population—are as a whole extremely poor, and that many millions live habitually on the brink

---

* On March 31, 1912, there were in the Post Office Savings Bank 1,500,834 accounts representing over £12,500,000. Government promissory notes to the amount of £517,153 had been issued; and Postal Life Insurance had been effected to an aggregate sum of £2,022,532. For further figures showing the steady increase of savings, see *Lord Curzon in India*, pp. 132, 281.

† As to the sums lavished on mendicant "ascetics" see Chapter IV., p. 82.

of starvation. It is time that we should get at the true and ultimate reason of this fact.

THE CAUSES OF INDIAN POVERTY.

The reason alleged by the Indian Opposition is that the ryot has been ruthlessly taxed for a century past in order to pay the "tribute" demanded by his foreign rulers, so that he has all the time grown poorer and poorer, less able to lay by against a rainless day—in other words, against times of famine—and, by reason of impaired vitality, more apt to fall a victim to plague, cholera, malaria and other forms of disease. Nor is this a theory held by Indians alone. It is repeated and worked out by Englishmen in such fantastic figures that one wonders why the whole Indian people is not dead of starvation years ago.

Even when more sanely stated, this argument presents serious difficulties on the very threshold. There is, as we have seen, ample evidence that the Indian peasant was very poor a century ago.* If, now, you keep on steadily making a poor man poorer year by year, you must come ultimately to the point at which he has nothing left at all; and the fact that that point has not been reached in a hundred years is of itself sufficient to throw doubt on the theory. Again, it is quite certain that in the eighteenth century, not only was the country tormented by war and brigandage, but many princes and their deputies ground the people most inhumanly in order to meet the costs of their ambition and their luxury. Is it not, indeed, the standing and just reproach against the East India Company, that, before it awoke to its responsibilities, some of its agents connived

---

* "The indebtedness of the ryot is no new thing. Munro in Madras and Elphinstone in Bombay showed at the beginning of the nineteenth century how utterly sunk in debt the ryot was." Morison, *Economic Transition in India*, p. 79.

at, profited by, and even participated in, gross tyrannies
of this nature? If this be so, who can believe that, under
a reign of peace and order, legitimate taxation, even if
somewhat burdensome, can have such a depressing and im-
poverishing effect as rapine, pillage, and arbitrary exaction?
If, as a matter of fact, people are not much richer than
they were at the end of that chaotic period—much poorer
they could not possibly be—must we not suspect some other
cause or causes at work, besides the pressure of taxation?

Going still further back, to the great days of the Mogul
Empire, we know that the land revenue exacted by Akbar,
Shah Jahan, and Aurungzeb was very much larger than
that which has at any time been demanded under British
rule.* "Allowing for difference in area and purchasing
power of silver," writes Sir William Hunter, "Akbar's tax
was about three times the amount which the British take"
(in 1893). The land revenue of Aurungzeb after his an-
nexations in Southern India was nearly 38 millions, exclusive
of what he drew from Kashmir and Kabul. The land revenue
of 1910-11 was less than 21 millions, probably (though of
this I am not quite sure) drawn from a larger area than
Aurungzeb controlled. Aurungzeb's total revenue from all
sources was estimated in 1695 at 80 millions sterling, and in
1697 at 77½ millions. The total revenue of recent years
ranges somewhere around the same figures; but from this 20
to 25 millions have to be written off as arising from sources
unknown to Aurungzeb, such as railways, post-office, telegraphs and the opium excise, which is paid by the Chinese
consumer.

Even in the absence of precise data, who could doubt
that the country was squeezed by the Moguls to a degree
unimaginable in these pusillanimous times? They kept large
armies afoot. We know that Shah Jahan and Aurungzeb

* See Hunter's *Brief History of the Indian Peoples*, pp. 139, 144, 150.

[152]

maintained 200,000 horse and a considerable force of artillery. The infantry, it is true, were weak, but on the other
hand there were enormous hosts of camp-followers. Bernier
says that they exceeded 200,000 "in the army alone which is
with the king." "Delhy and Agra," he added, "liveth of
almost nothing but of the soldiery." * The military expenses were partly met by *jagirs*, or grants of land to leaders who provided contingents—a system which certainly led
to great abuses, and cannot at best have been to the advantage of the cultivator. Expenses of fortification were not
slight—witness the vast citadels of Lahore, Delhi, Agra,
Allahabad and other places. Court life was lavishly luxurious. Akbar never had fewer than 5,000 elephants and
12,000 stable horses, besides great hawking and hunting
establishments. On festival days "the king was seated on his
throne in a marble palace surrounded by nobles wearing high
heron plumes and sparkling with diamonds like the firma-
ment.† Many hundred elephants passed before him in com-
panies, all most richly adorned, and the leading elephant of
each company with gold plates on its head and breast set
with rubies and emeralds. Trains of caparisoned horses
followed, and after them rhinoceroses, lions, tigers, and
panthers, hunting leopards, hounds and hawks; the whole
concluding with an innumerable host of cavalry glittering
with cloth of gold." ‡ But pageantry probably cost less

* In another place, Bernier says, "Many wonder, considering the huge
number of persons living of pay (which amounts to millions), whence
such vast revenues can be had for such excessive charges; although
this need not be so much wondered at considering the riches of the Empire, the peculiar government of the State, and the said universal pro-
priety of the Sovereign." He means that the Emperor was the universal
landlord.

† "I own I never saw such inestimable wealth." Sir Thomas Roe.

‡ Elphinstone: *History of India*, p. 586. Those who have seen the
Langar parade at Hyderabad, Deccan, can form some conception of the
gorgeousness of Mogul pageantry.

than the seraglio, to the "incredible expenses" of which, under Aurungzeb, Bernier bears explicit witness. Nor need we search old records for testimonies of Mogul prodigality. The face of the land is covered with their palaces, mosques and tombs, which must have cost huge sums of money, even if the cash payments were somewhat reduced by the employment of forced labour. Go to Fatehpur-Sikri and see the magnificent city which Akbar built only to be abandoned, nobody quite knows why. Return to Agra and view the marble miracle which Shah Jahan dedicated to the memory of the chief lady of his harem. Wander through the exquisite marble palaces of Agra, Delhi, Lahore. Mark the giant plinths upon which such splendid structures as Humayun's Tomb and the Jumma Musjid at Delhi are elevated. Then ask where the price of all these high-piled glories came from, and you will find that it was, for the most part, wrung from the red soil of India. The proportion which arose from mines or manufactures or commerce must have been comparatively small; and if some of it came from the loot of conquered provinces, even that must have sprung ultimately from the soil. Any neglect of economy that could ever be laid to the charge of the British Government shrinks into insignificance when compared with the imperial exorbitancies of the Moguls.* "But at least," it may be said, "the wealth which they extracted from their subjects remained in India, and was not 'drained' away." It did, no doubt; but how much of it came back to the ryot? The theory of the "drain" is relevant to a discussion of the gen-

* Shah Jahan, says Elphinstone, "was the most magnificent prince that ever appeared in India. . . . His expenses can only be palliated by the fact that they neither occasioned any increase to his exactions nor any embarrassment of his finances." But if his exactions were not increased, this could only mean that they were from the first enormous. His famous "Peacock Throne" was valued at £6,500,000.

eral riches of the country: scarcely, if at all, to the question of the well-being of the peasant class.

Observe, too, that throughout the Mogul period, though some parts of India enjoyed a fair measure of exemption from actual war, there was never any approach to the universal pacification of to-day. The Moguls were often fighting among themselves, and almost always either trying to extend their territory or to crush rebellious vassals. There was no efficient system of police, and life and property were everywhere insecure. William Hawkins, who visited Delhi in the early years of Jahangir's reign, writes: "The Great Mogul is severe enough, but all helpeth not, for his poore Riots or Clownes complaine of Injustice done them, and cry for Justice at the King's hands. . . . At first coming to the Crowne, he was more severe than now he is, which is the cause that the country is so full of outlawes and theeves, that almost a man cannot stirre out of doores throughout all his Dominions, without great forces." Often, if not always, the land revenue was exacted with unscrupulous rapacity. Bernier, who was in India from 1655 to 1661, notes that there appears "little money in trade among the people: partly because much of it is consumed in melting over and over all those nose and ear-rings, chains and finger-rings, bracelets of hands and feet, which the women wear"; partly because "Governors and [tax] farmers have an absolute authority over the countrymen, and even a very great one over the tradesmen and merchants of the towns, so that . . . there is not any person to whom a countryman, tradesman or merchant can make his complaint in cases of extortion and tyranny often practised upon them by the soldiery and the governors. . . . Whence is it that ordinarily they affect to appear poor and moneyless . . . and at last they find no other remedy to secure their wealth than to hide and dig their money deep underground . . . infatuated with the

[155]

belief that the gold and silver which they hide in their life-time shall serve them after death." The last sentences evidently apply rather to the urban middle-class than to the peasantry. But the same acute observer goes on: "Tyranny often grows to that excess that it takes away what is necessary to the life of a peasant or tradesman, who is starved for hunger and misery. . . . The land is not tilled but almost by force, consequently very ill, and much of it is quite spoiled and ruined." It is true that in this passage Bernier is speaking rather of Oriental countries in general than of India in particular; but it is the condition of India which suggests his remarks, and he makes no exception in her favour.

We see, then, that, under the Moguls, an enormous revenue was raised, often by very oppressive methods and under conditions far less favourable to the peaceful cultivation of the soil than those of to-day. It may be added that plague and famine were by no means unknown,* though people paid much less attention to them than they do at present. Is it for a moment credible that the ryot was better off then than now? He was not: he suffered, then as now, apathetically and uncomplainingly; and it was nobody's business either to relieve his hardships or to bewail his fate. To this day it is only the class which has come under the influence of European humanitarianism that is greatly concerned about the sufferings of the peasant. European officials engaged in famine work are frequently startled by the fatalistic indifference of their Indian subordinates. "Why trouble about this carrion?" they will say: "It is the will of the gods."

Assuredly the lot of the peasant is not worse to-day than it was in the brave days of old; but the fact remains that

* For plague, see Sir Thomas Roe (Ed. Hakluyt Society), pp. 307, 375, 505. For famine, see Sir Theodore Morison, *Economic Transition*, pp. 105-116.

it ought to be very conspicuously better, and that somehow it is not. Taking India all round, it cannot be said that the position of the cultivator is satisfactory. There is conflict of evidence as to details. The official view seems to be that in some parts of the country, at any rate, the ryot shows greater recuperative power after a bad season than he formerly did: * the Opposition view is just the reverse. Some people hold poverty to be systematically exaggerated (as Bernier says it was in the seventeenth century) and talk, with Mr. Kipling's philosopher, of the "bloomin' *garib admi* swindle." But the main fact is only too evident, namely, that large masses of the agricultural population are in a condition of stagnant indigence and indebtedness, and that the failure of a single season's crops deprives them even of the handful of pulse which is all they require to keep body and soul together. Why is it that vastly improved external conditions have not brought with them a striking advance in prosperity?

The reason, in my view, is simple: namely, that the benefit of good government is, in part at any rate, nullified, when the people take advantage of it, not to save and raise their standard of living, but to breed to the very margin of subsistence. Henry George used to point out that every mouth that came into the world brought two hands along with it; but though the physiological fact is undeniable, the economic deduction suggested will not hold good except in conditions that permit of the profitable employment of the two hands. Can they, by increasing the efficiency of cultivation, increase, in the necessary ratio, the productivity of a given portion of soil? Or is there fresh soil for them to till? Or can they

---

* Speaking from their own observation, many British officials of long experience assert unhesitatingly that the peasantry in general are now better clothed, better fed, and better able to afford the small conveniences of modern life, than they were thirty years ago.

be applied to the production of commodities exchangeable for food? Under present conditions in India, taking it all round, the answer to these questions can only be a qualified affirmative. The study of intensive cultivation has not yet yielded great results, and the peasantry lack the intelligence, the energy and the capital to profit by such methods as have been devised. In many parts there is no new land to be taken under cultivation; and, where expansion is possible, it is to be presumed that, except where irrigation comes into play, the new land is of inferior quality.* As for manufactures, though they do in some measure relieve the strain upon the soil, they are as yet so little developed that the effect is scarcely felt.† When India first came under British control she was already well-populated. She had not, like the United States at the same period, or Canada to-day, enormous powers of expansion. She had not immense mineral resources to supplement the resources of the soil. She had not an eager, energetic, provident breed of agriculturists, quick to seize upon every method of saving labour and increasing produce. What she had was a multitudinous peasantry, frugal, indeed, inasmuch as its daily wants were small, and industrious in a languid, mechanical way, but wasteful in its social habits, incapable of foresight or rational thrift, preyed upon by usurers and parasites, and regarding procreation as the most sacred of all duties. It is true that its marriage customs did not really make for

* "In 1880," said Lord Curzon in 1901, "there were only 194 millions of acres under cultivation in India. There are now 217 millions, or an increase in virtually the same ratio as the increase in population." The average quality of the additional 23 million acres does not appear. If it was better than that of the 194 millions the result would be a real addition to the resources of the country. But the chances are that the average quality was poorer, in which case the ratio between population and subsistence was altered for the worse.

† In 1911, the total number of persons employed in factories fell something short of 850,000.

[158]

healthy fecundity, and that there were many checks upon increase which would not have been operative in a more enlightened community. Still, peace and order did their work, and the population steadily grew. Though every million mouths was accompanied by two million hands, that was far from meaning that production increased twice as fast as consumption. There must have come a point after which the hands failed even to keep pace with the mouths; and, as the utmost margin of productivity was approached, each new pair of hands meant a relatively diminished return. This being so, what wonder that the mass of the people remained poor? The root of Indian poverty lies in the fact that the people at large have no will to be rich, or even well-to-do. Not till they yearn to "want more wants" will they learn to take thought how to supply them.

The argument of the foregoing paragraph may be thus summed up: The productivity of a given portion of soil is a function of three factors: natural quality (including climatic conditions), artificial methods, and the labour required to apply these methods. The first two factors remaining constant, there is a limit to the amount of the third which can profitably come into action. If ten pairs of hands are sufficient to extract from a field all that its natural quality and the prevailing methods will enable it to produce, fifteen pairs of hands will reap no richer harvest, but will reduce by a third the quantity of grain assignable to each mouth.* If the additional five pairs of hands can break new soil, so far good; but, under Indian conditions, the chances are that the new soil will be poorer, and the share of each of the fifteen will still be less, perhaps very much less, than the shares of the original ten. This, I suggest, is a picture in

* I am told that this is an inaccurate representation of the Law of Diminishing Returns; but I do not think it substantially misrepresents the facts of the case.

little of what is constantly going on in India—the population is constantly tending to outpass the limit of profitable employment upon the soil.*

Mr. Dadabhai Naoroji, in his presidential address to the Indian National Congress of 1893, quoted this passage from Macaulay: "To trade with civilized man is infinitely more profitable than to govern savages; that would indeed be a doting wisdom which, in order that India might remain a dependency, would . . . keep a hundred millions of men from being our customers, in order that they might continue to be our slaves." After the words "a hundred millions" Mr. Naoroji inserted in parenthesis "now really 221,000,000;" but it does not seem to have occurred to him that in this vast increase, unaccompanied by a commensurate increase of productivity, whether of food or of commodities exchangeable for food, he had found the key to the poverty which he and his fellow-congressmen were always

---

* The land-revenue statistics of the past fifty years may seem, at first sight, to conflict with this theory, showing, as they do, an increase proportionally greater than the increase of population. From this it would seem to follow, either that the share of produce claimed by the Government has greatly increased, or that the additional population has found means to make more than a proportional addition to the produce of the land. Now the share exacted in taxation has certainly increased very little, if at all; wherefore we would seem to be thrown back on the other alternative. But the surface meaning of the figures proves, on examination, to be wholly misleading. To interpret them aright we have to take into account, firstly, the fall in the value of the rupee, secondly, the rise in prices. "The total increase in the gross land revenues during the past fifty years," says a Government memorandum of 1909, "has been 60 per cent., measured in rupees; but, as the gold value of the rupee has fallen from 24d. to 16d., the increase, if measured in gold, is less than six per cent." And again, "As wheat has risen in value by 100 per cent., a given money assessment now represents a very much smaller portion of the produce than in 1858." I do not know that exact figures are available, but there is little doubt that the increase of land revenue, measured in produce, is smaller in proportion than the increase either of population or of cultivated soil.

THE TAJ MAHAL

(and rightly) bewailing. It is probable that Macaulay's rough estimate of 100,000,000 was under the mark, and that the population had not actually increased by 120 per cent. But even if we reduce that figure by one-sixth and assume an increase of 100 per cent., is it not manifest that this must mean a terrible strain upon resources at no time over-abundant?

And, spite of famine, plague, malaria, child-marriages, and all the ills that Indian life is heir to, the increase still goes on. After deduction of the figures for areas not previously enumerated, the increase of the thirty years between 1881 and 1911 works out at a little under 50,000,000 —just about the whole population of over-populated Japan.* The decade 1901-1911 witnessed an increase of over 19,000,000; twelve and a half millions in British territory, six and a half millions in States and Agencies. The potency of the check exercised by famine and disease is apparent in the extraordinary fluctuations of the rate of growth. Mr. E. A. Gait, director of the Census of 1911, after eliminating all causes of error, estimates the real increase between 1872 and 1911 as follows:

1872-1881	.	.	.	.	3,000,000
1881-1891	.	.	.	.	25,000,000
1891-1901	.	.	.	.	4,300,000
1901-1911	.	.	.	.	19,000,000

Referring to the assertion that Indian fecundity is less than "normal," Mr. Gait points out that "there is no such thing as a normal rate of increase. All that can be said is that

* This means that, assuming the India of 1881 to have been just able to support herself, with very little over, a development of her resources, equivalent to the whole resources of Japan, ought to have taken place in thirty years, if she was not to find herself sensibly poorer per head of population.

since 1872 * the average increment has been about 5 per cent. per decade"—which is less than that of the Teutonic races and greater than that of the Latin races. It is obvious that a country subject, as India is, to pestilence and calamitous drought, is not likely, other things being equal, to show so large a rate of increase as countries in which better climatic and hygienic conditions prevail. But such comparisons are irrelevant to the present question. We are not discussing the relative prosperity of India and other countries, but simply considering the fundamental equation between mouths and food. If mouths increase in a higher ratio than food, the tendency must be towards greater poverty, no matter what may happen in other parts of the world.†

We have seen above that, both in area and in population, India is practically equal to the whole of Europe minus Russia. If, now, we consider what an immense proportion of the people of Western Europe are concentrated in towns, and are occupied in manufacture and trade—drawing their sustenance, that is to say, largely from other portions of the world—is it not evident that the strain upon the soil must be incalculably greater in India than in Europe? India imports food-stuffs (mainly sugar) to the value of some ten millions a year; but she exports food-stuffs (mainly rice and wheat) to more than double that value; which means that she feeds not only herself, but a considerable number of other people, from her soil alone. Here, no doubt, is a real

* Up to which date no exact statistics were available.

† The views expressed in the above paragraphs are in general borne out in a singularly able book, entitled *The Population Problem in India,* by Mr. P. K. Wattal, of the Indian Finance Department (Bombay: Bennett, Coleman & Co., 1916). I cannot too strongly commend to all who are interested in the subject this intelligent, lucid and thoroughly well-informed study.

"drain," * a symptom of unsatisfactory economic conditions, to which over-taxation may possibly contribute; but this is not the same thing as the alleged "drain" in payment or over-payment for services.

I am not denying that if such over-payment exists—if security, stability and good administration could be bought at a cheaper rate—the over-payment must help to impoverish the country. If my argument in preceding sections holds good, India buys her defence and administration far cheaper than most other countries; and the fact that these benefits have, for the present, to be in some measure purchased from abroad, is her misfortune, not our fault. This does not prove, however, that good government might not be bought on even more advantageous terms; and still less does it prove that the government for which India pays might not be a better, wiser, more far-seeing government. In pleading for economy, and in urging measures conducive to general well-being, the Indian Opposition is performing a natural and laudable function; nor would one quarrel with it because its arguments are sometimes one-sided and its recommenda- tions not always practicable. But I suggest that its remonstrances would be far more telling (and perhaps a little less querulous) if it did not close its eyes to the fundamental fact that over-population lies at the root of Indian poverty, and that Government is not to blame for this, except in so far as good government removes the checks upon fecundity which bad government incidentally imposes. Roughly speaking, the population of India has doubled under British rule: could there be a more conclusive testimony to its general

* Many people hold that it ought to be checked by restrictions on the export of grain; but economic experience seems to show that this is an illusory remedy, inasmuch as "any enactment which artificially lowers the price reduces the quantity of grain raised in a country." See Morison, *Economic Transition*, Chap. V.

beneficence in all matters which government can control? That the thrift, the prudence, the energy, the intelligence of the mass of the people have not similarly increased may, indeed, be partly attributable to government, which may not have done all that was ideally possible for education and economic progress. But every reasonable Indian must surely. admit that no government can remake a people; they must do that for themselves. So long as the Indian people, remaining dependent on the soil, continue to breed up to the margin of subsistence in good seasons, they will continue to suffer in bad seasons.* Here is a very significant passage from Baden-Powell's great work upon *The Land Systems of British India* (Vol. I., p. 346):

"Nothing can be more curious than the result of a low assessment, whether fixed for ever or not. In one large district at least, where a low assessment was secured for thirty years, the result has been, not that a wealthy class has arisen, but simply that all restraint has vanished and the poor population has multiplied to such an extent that the wealth accumulated is not more able to support the increased mass of people than the former resources were to feed the then existing numbers. Under native custom properties become sub-divided and again sub-divided till their value is frittered away; the money-lender steps in, and land begins to aggregate in the hands of a class alien to agricultural knowledge and interests. . . . I must add the notorious fact that in well-managed Native States, where the revenue is double, per-

* The true meaning of famine is thus clearly stated by Sir Theodore Morison: "When the monsoon rains fail, Nature pronounces a lock-out in the agricultural industry that throws ninety per cent. of the population of the district affected out of work for the whole year." Famine relief, now admirably organized and administered, may minimize the actual mortality; but famine relief can only mean, of course, a sort of national insurance against the effects of drought—a spreading of the loss over the whole land, those parts which do not directly suffer being taxed for the benefit of those which do.

[164]

haps four times, as high as in British districts, the people are apparently as prosperous."

Need we look any further for the main reason of the poverty in India? In the face of these facts, can we plausibly attribute it to over-taxation? Mr. Gokhale would make Government further responsible for two subsidiary facts: the decreasing fertility of the soil and the increasing death-rate. He tells us that "over the greater part of India agriculture is, as Sir James Caird pointed out more than twenty years ago, only a process of exhaustion of the soil," and he declares that in the twenty years from 1885 to 1905, the average annual death-rate increased by "no less than ten per thousand." Assuming the facts to be as stated, where does the responsibility of England come in? Is it the fault of the Government that from time immemorial the people of India have used cow-dung for fuel instead of for manure—have flushed their floors with it instead of fertilizing their fields—and have multiplied to such a point as to render it almost impossible to give the land its necessary periods of rest? It may be said that a far-seeing Government would have taken steps to provide other sorts of fuel, and perhaps other sorts of manure as well. But I have not seen this point urged by the Opposition: I have not seen any positive and constructive remedial measures proposed. It is so much easier to cry out upon the rapacious settlement-officer, and to assume that all would be well if peace, order and material development could be had for nothing. As for the high death-rate, poverty no doubt contributes to it by rendering the people less able to resist the ravages of plague, malaria and other diseases. If Britain is responsible for India's poverty, then she is responsible for whatever part of the death-rate is fairly attributable to poverty; but it is unreasonable to bring this forward as a separate charge, an additional subject of reproach. If, on the other hand, the responsibility for Indian poverty rests, not with Britain, but with the Indian people themselves, it is not merely unreasonable but unjust to lay the high death-rate at the door of the Government. British rule has brought with it medical science, the rudiments, at any rate, of sanitation, and a network of hospitals and dispensaries at which from twenty-five to thirty million patients are annually treated. It may, indeed, be argued that Government has not done all that was possible in the way of forcing sanitation upon a very recalcitrant people; but sanitation costs money, and any extra expenditure would have meant either additional taxation or the diversion of funds from other purposes. "Why not from defence?" the Opposition cries—and so the endless wrangle goes on. It is, of course, impossible to prove that Government estimates rightly the relative urgency of the different objects to which it devotes its resources; but it is hard to imagine any apportionment at which no one should be found to cavil.

EMIGRATION.

In the question of emigration we find a long-smouldering grievance which has recently become acute. Here we must carefully distinguish between two very different points at issue.

India has every right to insist upon fair and humane treatment for those of her people who have already been induced or allowed to emigrate; and the Government of India, though placed in a difficult and delicate position, has not been slow to take up their cause. But when Indians interpret the word "Empire" as implying the right of unrestricted immigration into any country under the British flag, the reply must be, in the first place, that "Empire"

[166]

does not connote any such right, and, secondly, that it would not be to India's advantage if it did.

Can India reasonably look to emigration as one of the remedies for the evils from which she suffers? I submit that, in the present condition of the world, the remedy is impossible, and that, if it were possible, it would be illusory. Why is it impossible? Because there is no part of the habitable globe where India can spill her overflow in such numbers as sensibly to relieve the congestion at home, unless she is prepared to conquer territory and subdue or exterminate the existing occupants. Why is the remedy illusory? Because it would merely postpone the facing of her population-problem, which India must assuredly undertake before she can claim her due place among the civilized nations of the world.

Is it conceivable that South Africa, Australia, or Canada should permit, except at the sword's point, the invasion of their territory by such hordes of Indians as should appreciably alter the proportion between mouths and food in India? There are, between Kashmir and Cape Comorin, over three hundred million people. Suppose 4 per cent. of them, or 12,000,000, were to emigrate, what difference would that make in India? In a single decade (supposing no very grave calamity to intervene) the population would have risen at least to its former level. But 12,000,000 is very little short of the whole white population of South Africa, Australia, and Canada. Is it for a moment to be imagined that these countries would submit to having their whole policy, their conditions of life and course of development, altered by such a huge influx of an alien and unassimilable race? Of course, this is a flagrantly impossible contingency; but that only makes it all the clearer that no emigration which is practically conceivable would sensibly ameliorate Indian conditions. Any outflow that should be at all perceptible

[167]

in India would mean, in other countries, an inflow amounting to a cataclysm. But suppose emigration on a large scale were possible—suppose, say, that a new India could be set apart in Africa, capable of absorbing a million immigrants a year for the next half century—would that be a real and permanent benefit to the Motherland? On the contrary, it would be a misfortune. It would indefinitely adjourn the day when India shall realize that life is to be valued by its quality, not its quantity, and that a country which would be master of its fate must first be master of its instincts. Of course, this is a lesson that many other peoples are far from having taken to heart; but India has not even begun to learn it. She is still unquestioningly devoted to that religion of fecundity which she must one day modify unless she is prepared to conquer the world.

Let it be realized that this is no mere rhetorical phrase. The world, indeed, is not yet overfilled; but the limits of possible expansion are being rapidly approached; and practically all desirable territory is staked-out by people who naturally propose to reserve it for development along the lines of their own racial traditions. It is quite certain that only by force of arms can this right of reservation be infringed; and its successful infringement, in a series of "folk-wanderings," would mean a relapse into chaos.

No member of the Indian Opposition (so far as I am aware) has manifested any clear insight into the importance of the population question in its bearings upon the true welfare of the country. Nor can it be said that European observers have shown themselves keenly alive to it. Sir Valentine Chirol, in his book on Indian Unrest, lays it down without the least hesitation that "her inexhaustible supplies of cheap labour are India's greatest asset." In almost the same words a Bombay manufacturer (Muhammadan) remarked to me, "The greatest asset of India is her three

[168]

hundred millions." But how is it possible that cheap labour can be a real "asset" to a country? To her capitalists, no doubt, it may be, though India forms no exception to the rule that cheap labour is bad labour. A vast proletariat, with a low standard of living, will doubtless help to swell those imposing battalions of figures which prove what may be called the statistical prosperity of a country. But statistical prosperity has very little to do with real well-being. To say that cheap labour is India's asset is practically the same as saying that poverty is India's wealth. And while the ryot does not mind how poor he is, so long as he can be prolific, it is certain that he, at any rate, will know no other form of wealth.

But emigration, on any considerable scale, being fortunately impossible, a time must one day come when (with the help of vernacular education) the peasant will learn that, beyond a certain point, every additional pair of hands mean a diminishing return, whether in produce of soil or in wages, and will gradually adjust the equation between labour and remunerative opportunity. He will learn to "want more wants," and will rise above that extreme of frugality which may rather be called apathy. Then India will be on the high road to real wealth—not that wealth which consists in the exploitation of her "greatest asset."

"But what about irrigation?" it may be asked. "Might not she still add indefinitely to her 300,000,000 if the Government did not culpably neglect irrigation in order to multiply railways?" Unfortunately—or, in my view, fortunately—there is a limit to the potentialities of irrigation, and experts declare it to be well within sight. Redistribution of population might no doubt permit of a certain amount of increase without any further pressure on the margin of subsistence; but in a country where local attachments are so strong, and differences of race, caste and language so many, redistribution is no easy matter. Sooner or later, at all events, the pinch must come, and India must learn that her salvation lies, not in numerical expansion, whether within or without her boundaries, but in the intensification and ennoblement of life.

The moral grievances on which the Indian Opposition is in the habit of dwelling may be classed, like the material grievances, under three heads:

(1) Neglect of education.
(2) Exclusion from civil employment.
(3) Denial of opportunity for military training.

MORAL GRIEVANCES—I. NEGLECT OF EDUCATION.

The first and second complaints I shall not here discuss at length. On the question of education there is a good deal to be said in another chapter. For the moment, it may be sufficient to point out that when Indian extremists accuse the Government (as they sometimes do) of deliberately keeping India in darkness, for its own oppressive ends, they are talking very wildly. As regards Western education, with English as its medium, the Government is open only to the reproach of having supplied, with perhaps inconsiderate lavishness, an article which, though not very satisfactory, was the best it had to give. In the face of numberless warnings that it was thereby sapping its own position,* it deliberately set about the creation of that educated class, to which, as the prophets foretold, we owe "the unrest" of the present day. It might easily have satisfied its conscience by promoting only Oriental education—a course which many people urged upon it, as its one clear duty.

* See the views on this point of Elphinstone, Metcalfe and Lyall, pp. 304-306. These are only specimens of a host of similar utterances.

[170]

By this means it would have saved itself a great deal of trouble, and indefinitely retarded the development of India, both intellectual and material. But it chose the other course, and called into existence the many excellent Government servants of to-day, as well as the less fortunate multitude who bitterly complain because, having invested so-and-so many rupees in the attainment of a B.A. degree, or in the failure to attain one, they find that the lucrative posts to which they thereby consider themselves entitled are not unlimited in number. The educational system established some sixty years ago might no doubt have been very much better; but its defects were those of English education in general, which the Government of India could scarcely be expected to reform. In this department, in short, whatever criticisms of detail may be admissible, the Government cannot reasonably be charged with any lack either of diligence or of good will.

In vernacular education, on the other hand, it is true that little has been done in proportion to the vast work that remains to be done. Here it is that the Indian Opposition has a plausible case. It may be argued that, in spite of the poverty of the country, in spite of the indifference, if not hostility, to education displayed by the people themselves, the Government ought to have done more to combat the general illiteracy.* To this end, either fresh taxation would have had to be imposed, or large sums must have been diverted to education from defence, public works, and other heads of expenditure. The latter is, of course, the policy urged by the Opposition; and it is clearly impossible to prove them wrong. At the same time, one would be more willing to accept their judgment, if it were not evident in many other ways that they are unduly, if not unnaturally,

* For statistics, see p. 261.

jealous of any and every expenditure incurred by Government in the interests of its own security and prestige. When one regards a given institution as a necessary evil, one is apt, without desiring its overthrow, to scrutinize with a grudging eye every halfpenny of the sums allotted to its maintenance. This being so, it is scarcely possible that the Opposition and the Government should agree in their estimate of the relative importance of the various objects of public expenditure. The Government, at all events, is now definitely committed to a large and liberal policy in regard to vernacular education; and such is the difficulty of the problem that, for my part, I would urge a slow, cautious and thoroughly well-prepared advance, rather than a hasty multiplication of ill-provided schools and incompetent teachers.

MORAL GRIEVANCES—II. EXCLUSION FROM CIVIL EMPLOYMENT.

Perhaps the bitterest complaint of the Opposition is that, according to them, the Government has made a dead letter of the following clause in Queen Victoria's Proclamation of 1858, often called the Magna Charta of India:

It is our will that, so far as may be, our subjects, of whatever race or creed, be freely and impartially admitted to offices in our service, the duties of which they may be qualified, by their education, ability and integrity, duly to discharge.

This mandate has certainly not been made a dead letter; but there may have been a tendency to take a narrow and prejudiced view of that fitness for the discharge of official duties on which the Proclamation naturally insists.

Again and again I have put to British officials the question, "Do you know any Indians whom you consider to be

[172]

capable of more important employment than they actually hold—employment of high responsibility?" The answer has almost always been, "Yeŝ, I know two or three." The inference seems to be that the Government has, at any rate, not proceeded with any undue rapidity in the promotion of Indians to places of trust. On the other hand, there is no reason to doubt the sincerity of its often-repeated desire to advance in this direction as far as prudence will permit. Many of the most distinguished administrators have expressed themselves, both in private and in public, strongly in favour of the policy of the open door. Sir Alfred Lyall, for instance, writes in 1882: "I have just appointed a native judge to the Allahabad High Court, the first who has ever been sent there. I want to push on the native wherever I can—our only chance of placing Government here on a broad and permanent basis." Some of the highest judicial appointments are, and have long been, held by Indians, and that with great distinction. There is a pretty general opinion that Indians are better fitted, as yet, for judicial than for executive functions; and one can easily understand that this may be true.

The question at issue, in any case, is not one of principle, but only of rate of progress. It is certainly at first sight a grave injustice that admission to the higher branches of the Civil Service should be impossible to Indians who have not the means to present themselves for examination in London. The objection to simultaneous examinations in England and India which is commonly alleged by Anglo-Indians is in a sense flattering to Indian self-esteem. "The Hindu has such a prodigious memory," it is said, "and is so clever at examinations, that the Englishman cannot stand up against him. But the ability to shine in a competitive examination is not in itself a proof of either the character or the talent required in administrative work; and an English candidate who may be defeated by a few marks is much more likely than his Hindu rival to develop these qualities." As matters stand at present, there is something in this argument. It may be maintained that the voyage to England is in itself a valuable part of the test of fitness to which Indian candidates ought to be subjected. The poor, no doubt, are thereby absolutely excluded; but they could scarcely qualify even for simultaneous examinations. If young men of the wealthy and well-to-do classes have not sufficient will and energy to undertake the journey, the inference is (it may be said) that their character does not fit them for responsible positions. It is certainly hard to conceive that an Indian who, was prevented by religious scruples from crossing the *kala pani* could be an efficient administrator.

On the whole, and with all sympathy for the natural impatience of educated Indians, I do not find it proven that Government could, with advantage to the common weal, have gone much faster and farther in this matter than it has actually done. The report of the recent Public Services Commission, however, does not recommend any very drastic changes. As regards the Civil Service, the proposal of the Commissioners is that "roughly three-quarters of the superior posts be recruited for in England, and one quarter in India." In the public works and railway (engineering) departments, they propose that "provision be made for obtaining half the staff from India." I cannot find that materials are given for a very exact comparison between the results to be produced by these proposals and the existing state of things. It appears, however, that in 1913, of officials drawing salaries of £400 a year and upwards, 19 per cent. were Indians, while of officials drawing (roughly) £600 a year and upwards, 10 per cent. were Indians. As most, if not all, the "superior posts" alluded to will probably fall within the latter class, it appears that the pro-

[174]

posal is to raise the proportion of such posts held by Indians from 10 per cent. to 25 per cent. of the whole. This will scarcely be regarded, even by moderate Indian opinion, as more than an installment of the desired reform; but because such an installment is now due, it does not follow that it has been long overdue, or that it could with advantage be greatly increased at the present moment.

It seems abundantly clear, however, that henceforward every effort should be made to educate, and to employ in responsible posts, a large class of efficient Indian civil servants. This is evidently an indispensable preliminary to that fitness for self-government which, in my view, both principle and policy should urge us to promote. So long as the opposite ideal is dominant—so long as our rule is supposed to be justified by an incurable incapacity for self-direction on the part of the Indian people—it is clear that every official of Indian race labours under a very severe disadvantage. He is handicapped even in the eyes of his own people, who are apt to criticize his proceedings as those of an amateur, admitted by some fluke to the heaven-born ruling caste. There is no reason to doubt the anecdotes one frequently hears of the preference for "sahib" officials, sometimes amusingly manifested by Indian villagers. But this is a state of things which is probably changing of its own accord, and which, in any case, we should make it our business to alter. The encouragement, and not the depression, of every legitimate form of Indian energy should be the constant aim of a wise government. We should try to abridge, not to protract, the term of our trusteeship. But one proviso should perhaps be suggested—namely, that the growth of a class of competent Government servants would not necessarily imply the fitness of the country for independence. It is possible, and even probable, that such a class may have come into existence long before national unity is firmly established and the mass of the people is sufficiently civilized to dispense entirely with external influence and guidance.

MORAL GRIEVANCES—III. DENIAL OF OPPORTUNITY FOR MILITARY TRAINING.

For an official statement of the third grievance, I turn once more to Mr. Gokhale. In his Budget speech of 1906 he said:

Japan's ordinary Budget for the army is only about 37.3 millions yen * or a little under six crores of rupees. And for so small an expenditure it has a standing army of 167,000 men, with reserves which can raise it to over 600,000 men in time of war. We spend nearly six times as much money a year, and yet in return for it we have only an inexpansive force of about 230,000 men, with about 25,000 native reservists, and about 30,000 European volunteers! Both on financial and on political grounds, therefore, our present unnational system of military defence is open to the gravest objection. My Lord, I respectfully submit that it is a cruel wrong to a whole people—one-fifth of the entire population of the world—to exclude them from all honourable participation in the defence of their hearths and homes, to keep them permanently disarmed, and to subject them to a process of demartialization such as has never before been witnessed in the history of the world.†

* If this figure was correct in 1906, Japan's military expenditure must have doubled in six years. In the Budget of 1912-13 it stands at 76,790,-438 yen, while an additional 17½ millions are put down as "extraordinary" expenditure.

† "Japan," Mr. Gokhale continued, "came under the influence of Western ideas only forty years ago, and yet already under the fostering care of its Government, that nation has taken its place by the side of the proudest Nations of the West. We have been under England's rule longer than forty years, and yet we continue to be mere hewers of wood and drawers of water in our own country, and, of course, we have no position anywhere else."

[176]

Again, in his Budget speech of the following year (1907), Mr. Gokhale said, "The wrong inflicted on all classes of the Indian community indiscriminately by keeping them compulsorily disarmed—thereby slowly crushing all manhood out of the whole race—must be cautiously but steadily set right."

In this argument we have a typical example of three habitual practices of the Indian Opposition: (1) Appealing to the experience of Japan, while ignoring the heaven-wide difference between the conditions of Japan and those of India. (2) Assuming, in defiance of all the evidence, a general superiority of the past over the present. (3) Admitting, in one breath, the necessity, for an indefinite time at any rate, of British rule, and in the next breath complaining bitterly of measures plainly indispensable to its continuance.

Japan is, of all countries, the most unlike to India. The Japanese are more nearly homogeneous than any other nation on earth. They have inhabited their islands since the dawn of history. Though they themselves were doubtless invaders in the first instance, no other invader has ever set foot on the soil of Nippon. They have always been in theory, and generally in practice, a single nation, united under one ruler, who is at present the object of universal and passionate loyalty. The two religions they profess are not mutually exclusive, but subsist together in unbroken harmony. Japan, in short, is, both historically and actually, the most perfect example in the world of national unity, while its power of self-protection and self-direction is conspicuous and indubitable. In all these points—and they are fundamental—India presents the most glaring contrast. I need not recapitulate the differences; let me only say that it is impossible to name a single resemblance or analogy, historical or actual. Why, then, attempt to argue from the

one country to the other, and reproach the Government of
India for not imitating the Government of Japan? If the
racial, geographical and historical conditions of the two
countries were in the least alike, the English would not be in
India at all. Since they are there, they must act in accordance with the conditions of India, and not of Japan.

What, now, of the "demartialization of India," the
"crushing of its manhood?" One would naturally conclude from such language, that England had found in India
a highly-developed system of citizen service, and had deliberately put it down. As a matter of fact, India is as
"martial" to-day as she ever was, except in so far as she
no longer offers a happy hunting-ground for armies of
robbers and marauders. She has 150,000 Indian regular
troops, 20,000 Imperial Service troops and nearly 40,000
reservists—an army practically equal to the estimated hosts
of the Mogul Emperors, and far superior to them in discipline, appointments and every essential of soldiership.
True, there were other armies in India in the Mogul period;
but so there are to-day. The troops of the Indian princes
may not be very efficient, but at least they are not denied
the advantages (such as they are) of military training.
Again, there is an army in India to-day of which the Moguls
knew nothing—I mean the police-force of nearly 200,000.
It is not altogether a satisfactory body, but at all events it
cannot be said that the police are having the manhood
crushed out of them. In brief, there are in India something
like half-a-million men under some sort of military training,
and more than 150,000 of them very highly trained. The
statistics of former periods are too vague to permit of an
exact numerical comparison. The plain fact is—and it
cannot be seriously contested—that if India was ever more
"martial" than to-day, it was only in so far as large num-
[178]

bers were employed in purely noxious military occupations, whether intestine war or undisguised brigandage.

We have not "demartialized" India; but have we done her a wrong in not taking pains to "martialize" her? Ought we to have established a system of citizen service, or a strong and well-trained Indian volunteer-force? Who can rationally demand that a government situated as is the British Government of India should deliberately call into being "a nation in arms?" To do so would be not only a suicidal folly, but a gross betrayal of trust. The very foundations of our rule in India lie in the fact that India requires protection, not only against external, but against internal dangers—in other words, protection against herself. He who does not admit this, ought clearly to make no terms with the British *raj*. To accept its employment or to enter its councils, even as one of a permanent Opposition, is implicitly to own that India is not yet ripe for self-government, and that, for the present at any rate, the overthrow of the British rule would be a disaster. And this the Indian Opposition does freely admit, not only implicitly but explicitly, and (one cannot doubt) sincerely. Where is the sense, then, in making it a grievance that we do not arm India to her own undoing? In the best-governed country there are always ample subjects of discontent, and always politicians to make the most and the worst of them. When the wisest of Indians, like Mr. Gokhale, can talk of our inflicting "cruel and iniquitous wrongs" upon his country, what wonder if unwise and hot-headed agitators should use even stronger language, and should find thousands of people to listen to them? Painful experience proves that such agitators abound—men who are unbalanced enough to believe that independent anarchy would be preferable to dependent law and order. If, then, these men could appeal

[179]

to a vast populace in arms, one of two things would be inevitable: either the violent end of the British rule, or such an enormous addition to the British garrison as would in very truth crush the country to ruin under the load of militarism. The latter alternative is quite unthinkable. Those who demand the arming of the people are so clearly making for the former alternative, that it is hard to see what meaning they attach to their protestations of loyalty.*

Is it for a moment to be expected, or, in the interests of India, to be desired, that England should deliberately face another and a greater Mutiny? The Mutiny, according to Mr. Gokhale himself,† was a "serious disaster. . . . The cloud of distrust, suspicion and prejudice then raised still hangs over the country, and casts its blighting shadow over, more or less, the whole of our Indian finance." Whether this is true of finance in particular, we need not inquire; but it is undeniable that the Mutiny gave us a stern warning against the policy of fatuous trustfulness in which it confessedly originated. Mr. Gokhale, in a very curious passage of the document above cited, makes it a point of complaint that India had to pay the whole cost of the suppression of the Mutiny. "England," he says, "contributed absolutely nothing, though her responsibility was possibly greater than ours, in consequence of the withdrawal of European regiments from the country, despite the protest of the Government of India, for service in the Crimea and Persia." This means, in effect, that England, in blind over-con-

---

* Mr. Gokhale, as we have seen, admits that the arming of the people must be gone about "cautiously." But unless and until immense numbers are armed, the manhood which is being "crushed out of the whole race" cannot, in terms of his argument, be restored. It might perhaps be suggested to him that manhood can be attained and proved in other ways than by the bearing of arms.

† See his evidence before the Welby Commission of 1897.

fidence,* upset the balance of military power in India, and ought therefore to have paid the price of her folly in hard cash, as well as in the lives of men, women and children. The contention is an odd one at best; but it is doubly strange as proceeding from a politician who calls it a "cruel wrong" that we do not permanently destroy any possibility of a balance of power by creating a nation in arms.

A CHOSEN PEOPLE.

I am far from suggesting that the Indian Opposition has no legitimate functions, or even that, on the whole, it mistakes its function and does no good. My point is that there is a fundamental inconsistency in its attitude towards the British rule; that while it wills the end, it grumbles at the means; and that it constantly lays to the charge of Government evils rooted in the history of the country and character of the people—evils which Government does not cause, and can cure, if at all, only by aid of the people themselves, and of Time.

Especially must one regret that the wisest of Indians cannot get over the inveterate habit of admitting in one breath that India's past is her disaster, and asserting in the next that it is her glory and her pride. The two propositions are not absolutely irreconcilable; but the first alone is of any practical moment. If only the Indian politician would cling fast to that, and give up talking as though British rule had involved a decline from some high estate of splendour and felicity, he would do much to hasten the advent of a brighter future.

* The withdrawal of British troops was not the only or the main symptom of over-confidence. There are few things in history more pathetically ludicrous than the infatuated belief of many British officers in the loyalty of their Sepoys.

Here is the admirable peroration of a speech by Mr. Gokhale on Lord Curzon's Indian Universities Act:

> To my mind, the greatest work of Western education in the present state of India is not so much the encouragement of learning, as the liberation of the Indian mind from the thraldom of old-world ideas, and the assimilation of all that is highest and best in the life and thought and character of the West. For this purpose, not only the 'highest, but *all* Western education is useful. I think Englishmen should have more faith in the influence of their history and their literature. And whenever they are inclined to feel annoyed at the utterances of a discontented B.A., let them realise that he is but an accident in the present period of transition in India, and that they should no more lose faith in the results of Western education on this account than should my countrymen question the ultimate aim of British rule in this land, because not every Englishman who comes out to India realises the true character of England's mission there.

Whatever we may think of the opposition to Lord Curzon's Act, there is no question that this particular passage is wisely and generously inspired. But the same speaker, addressing the National Congress at Benares two years later, said of Lord Curzon:

> Thus the man who professed in all sincerity, before he assumed the reins of office, his great anxiety to show the utmost deference to the feelings and even the prejudices of those over whom he was set to rule, ended by denouncing in unmeasured terms not only the present generation of Indians, but also their remote ancestors, and even the ideals of their race which they cherish above everything else.*

Now it may be admitted that Lord Curzon's Convocation

---

* Again, at the New Reform Club in London, Mr. Gokhale reproached Lord Curzon with "attacking not only the educated classes of to-day, but also their ancestors, of whom he knows nothing, and the ideals of their race, of which every Indian is justly proud."

speech of 1905 was more conspicuous for candour than for
tact, but it is hard to discover in it any denunciation of
Indian ideals, old or new. Supposing, however, that the
Viceroy had denounced certain "ideals of the race," why
should Mr. Gokhale have been so bitterly resentful? How
could he join in the clamour of outraged racial suscepti-
bility, he, who had admitted, and even insisted, that the
work of education is to "liberate the Indian mind from
the thraldom of old-world ideas"? It may be said that
ideas and ideals are not the same thing; but if an ideal
is not an idea, and a dominant idea, what is it? Ideas, as
such, do not enthral the mind; even a false idea (the idea,
for instance, of a flat earth resting on an elephant) does
no particular harm; it is only when false, barbarous or
imbecile ideas take on the semblance of ideals that they
establish a "thraldom" from which the mind has to be
"liberated." No wire-drawn verbal distinctions will explain
away the radical inconsistency between Mr. Gokhale's two
utterances. In the one he was speaking as a man of sense
and enlightenment, in the other as an Indian "patriot" who
cannot endure to hear an unpopular Viceroy say of his
people what he perfectly well knows to be true, and what,
on occasion, he is prepared to say himself. This is a not
unamiable human weakness; we are all willing to say of our
country things that we should resent if foreigners repeated
them; but the Indian Opposition can only create friction
and retard progress by identifying patriotism with racial
vanity.

Towards the close of the speech which caused so much
exasperation, Lord Curzon, addressing the graduating
students of Calcutta University, spoke as follows:

"To all of you who have the ambition to rise, I would say—
Use your student days to study the history and circumstances of

your race. Study its literature and the literature of Europe.
. . . Compare the two; see what are their lessons or their warnings. Then equip yourselves with a genuine and manly love for
your own people. . . . Avoid the tyranny of faction and the poison of racial bitterness. Do not arm yourselves against phan-
tasms, but fight against the real enemies to the welfare of your
people, which are backwardness and ignorance, and antiquated
social prescriptions. Look for your ideals, not in the air of
heaven, but in the lives and duties of men. Learn that the true
salvation of India will not come from without, but must be created from within."

This may fairly be called the gist of the speech, and it
is hard to see why it should have been received with fury.*
It differed only in one important particular from the following passage from a speech by a very distinguished Indian
patriot, the late Mr. Justice Ranade, of whom Mr. Gokhale
is proud to call himself a disciple: "The true end of your
work," said Mr. Ranade, "is to renovate, to purify, and also
to perfect the whole man by liberating his intellect, elevating
his standard of duty, and developing to the full all his
powers. Till so renovated, purified and perfected, we can
never hope to be what our ancestors once were—a chosen
people, to whom great tasks were allotted, and by whom
great deeds were performed." Lord Curzon's admonition
is very much the same as Mr. Ranade's, except for his
omission to assure his hearers that their ancestors were "a

* The main cause of offence lay in the following passage: "I hope
I am making no false or arrogant claim when I say that the highest
ideal of truth is to a large extent a Western conception. I do not thereby
mean to claim that Europeans are universally or even generally truthful,
still less do I mean that Asiatics deliberately or habitually deviate from
the truth. . . . But undoubtedly truth took a high place in the moral
code of the West before it had been similarly honoured in the East, where
craftiness and diplomatic wile have always been held in much repute."
The point of historic priority may be disputable; not so the substantial
justice of the remark.

chosen people." If only the Indian Opposition would understand, once for all, that "chosen peoples" are an illusion,
and that there are few peoples who have less excuse than
themselves for yielding to the illusion, they would shorten
by years, and perhaps by centuries, the period of their
tutelage.

But, when all is said and done, we must not wonder over
much at the captiousness of the Indian Opposition. It is
not for a moment to be expected that they should accept
British rule with effusive gratitude, as a good in itself. In
itself it is at best a reminder of India's failure to shape
her own destinies: a testimony to her lack of internal unity,
of self-assertive vigour, and of political capacity. The
utmost that the Opposition can sincerely admit is that the
present state of things is the least of several evils:* a less
evil than anarchy; a less evil than subjection to any other
people, whether European or Asiatic. Nor is it to be
expected that his citizenship of the British Empire can do
much to restore the Indian's self-esteem. India's relation to
the Empire is that of a customer rather than a partner.
She buys peace, order and security; and I have tried to
show that she gets them on very reasonable terms. But
men who hold the contrary opinion are not likely to think
that bargain a better one because they have the honour
and glory of Imperial citizenship thrown in.

Is there no other commodity that we can cast into the
scale to make the bargain advantageous beyond all doubt,
and to silence, or at any rate mitigate, the grumblings of
our customers? Certainly there is such a commodity; we
are all the time heaping it into the scale; but we perversely

---

* "India suffers from two evils," said a Nationalist orator at Oxford
the other day: "First English education, second English rule." To
which the obvious answer is that, but for English rule, the numeration
of her ills would not be so short and easy.

insist on keeping up an official pretence that we are not. We are giving India what she has never had before—unity, cohesion, in a word, nationality. We are endowing her with political ideals and ambitions, and are laboriously qualifying her to take her place among the great nations of the future. These things we are doing, whether we like it or no; and many of us have always realized it and gloried in it. But officially we must needs deny it; officially we must denounce as disloyal any suggestion that our rule in India is destined to serve a great purpose, and that, when once that purpose is achieved, it may naturally and rightly end. If we could only unlearn this short-sighted habit, we might count upon a welcome change in the attitude of all Indian politicians, except the fanatics of anarchy. And even they would be largely disarmed.

The moment our rule becomes confessedly a means to an end, and that end the creation of an enlightened, prosperous, autonomous India, it ceases to be in any true sense humiliating. The disciple is not humiliated before his teacher, the patient before his physician. All rational Indians admit that, whatever may have been her spiritual glories, India, as a whole, has hitherto shown no great political capacity. "God," says Mr. Gokhale, "does not give everything to every people, and India in the past was not known for that love of liberty and that appreciation of free institutions, which one finds to be so striking a characteristic of the West." The same authority, and with him all his thinking fellow-countrymen, confesses the "enormous difficulties of enabling the Indian people to govern themselves according to the higher standards of the West." * These obvious truths admitted, there can be no shame in accepting instruction in self-government at the hands of a

* Address to the New Reform Club, London, November 15, 1905.

country which has undoubtedly set the standard for the world in that art; and it follows from the very terms of the case that the process of instruction must be slow. But when the *guru* turns upon his *chela* and says, "You can never master this art, and it is not intended that you should: on the contrary, my personal welfare and glory are bound up in keeping you in a state of perpetual subjection"—what wonder if the *chela* grows sullen and resentful, and accuses his preceptor of avarice and base self-interest in everything he does? Once let the Indian Opposition feel that we sincerely and cordially invite their co-operation towards the one great end we both have in view—the building-up of a united, self-sufficing, self-controlled Indian nation—and the whole tone of their criticism will alter for the better. There will still be plenty of room for discussion, especially, one can foresee, as to the rate at which progress is being made, and the amount of acceleration that can safely be attempted. But the sting of subjection will be removed when it is recognized as an apprenticeship, and not as an unalterable status. Both parties will approach the common task in a much better temper; and the ideal of deliberative efficiency— the generation of light without heat—will perhaps be within measurable distance of achievement.

VIII

ART AND CULTURE

INDIAN art may be regarded in two aspects: as a reflection of the soul of the people in the past, and as one of the influences which must shape the soul of the future. In other words, it is at once a key to the national psychology and a factor in the problem of education.

The term "art" is here understood as covering all æsthetic activities: not only architecture, sculpture, painting and music, but all literature that is not primarily religious or philosophical. The Vedic hymns are ruled out, for two reasons. In the first place, though scholars assure us that they contain some great lyric poetry, they are primarily religious rather than æsthetic utterances. In the second place, the emotions they express cannot fairly be called those of Indians, but rather of an invading race not yet subdued to the climatic and ethnic influences which have made the Indian people as they emerge into the light of history. Even if we suppose all the hymns to have originated on Indian soil (and this is denied by good authorities) they remain the work of an external and as yet unamalgamated race.

I propose to speak first of Hindu (as distinct from Muhammadan) art; then of Hindu literature down to the coming of the Muhammadans; then of the influence of Islam on the arts of India. Finally, I shall attempt an estimate of the evidence offered by Indian art as to the capacities and limitations of Indian character.

[188]

Hindu and Buddhist Sculpture.

European writers, in dealing with Indian art, have gone to wild extremes of depreciation and idealization. We have on the one hand Sir George Birdwood's dictum that "sculpture and painting are unknown as fine arts in India." In estimating the value of this pronouncement we must remember that Sir George Birdwood's definition of fine art, "the unfettered and impassioned realization of the ideals kindled within us by the things without us," would exclude a great deal of the most highly-esteemed religious art of Europe. But with whatever qualifications we read it, the statement remains excessive. India has certainly not been lacking in artistic talent, and abounds in very noteworthy works of art, which it is impossible to attribute entirely either to foreign influences or to the mechanical reproduction of fixed types. On the other hand, we have Mr. E. B. Havell as the chief spokesman of a group of critics who glorify Indian art as a supremely great expression of the spirit of man, equal, if not superior, to the art of any European people, ancient or modern, and owing little or nothing to influences from without. This opinion is in my view just as excessive as Sir George Birdwood's. It may be said, indeed, to follow with a certain plausibility from the initial definitions and assumptions of the Havell school of criticism. But these definitions and assumptions are rather hard to accept.

The apotheosis of Indian art is clearly allied to the general revolt against Renaissance ideals and conventions, which has given birth to Post-Impressionism, Futurism, and other kindred movements. But there is more in it than this. Its mainspring is not really æsthetic but theosophical. I do not mean that it proceeds specially from the body calling themselves Theosophists, but that it is based on religio-philosophic dogmas to which the term theosophy, in its widest sense, may fitly be applied. Whether its leading champions would acknowledge themselves Theosophists in the narrower sense of the word, I do not know.

Mr. E. B. Havell is a writer of wide knowledge and no small literary power. If whole-hearted, uncompromising conviction be a merit in advocacy, then Indian art is indeed fortunate in its champion. Let us turn to his *Ideals of Indian Art** for a few characteristic utterances:

When we consider (he writes) the esoteric and exclusive character of early Aryan culture, we shall begin to realise that what seems to be an abnormally slow development in the technic arts in Indian civilisation was deliberately willed as a part of the extraordinary precautions taken by the early Aryan immigrants in India, and their allies, to prevent what they believed to be their divinely-inspired wisdom being perverted by popular superstition. . . .

If the intellectual aristocracy of the Aryan tribes refrained from committing their thoughts of the Divinity to writing, and strictly observed the Mosaic law, "thou shalt not make to thyself any graven image, or likeness of anything which is in heaven or earth," it was certainly on account of the peculiar conditions in which they found themselves placed, and because they stood on a much higher spiritual plane than the races by which they were surrounded, not from any lack of artistic genius † (p. 7).

* London, John Murray, 1911.

† A little further on, Mr. Havell tells us that "The *devas* themselves came down from heaven to take part in the sacrificial feast," and that "the correct recitation of appropriate hymns" transported the soul of the sacrificer to the abode of the gods. Then he proceeds, "When they saw the *devas* themselves sitting at the feast, and when men could transport themselves at will to the abode of the Shining Ones, what need had they of gods of stone or wood?" If this does not mean that Mr. Havell literally believes in these *devas* and their manifestations, what does it mean? If he is speaking of hallucinations, he must know that the prevalence of hallucinations in other religions never prevented the production of images and pictures.

[190]

Already in this Vedic period, centuries before Hellenic culture began to exert its influence upon Asia, India had conceived the whole philosophy of her art. . . . The Vedic period, though it produced no immediate development in what we are accustomed to call the fine arts, must nevertheless be regarded as an age of wonderful artistic richness (p. 9).

These passages afford a good example of the intensity of faith with which Mr. Havell contrives to turn everything to the advantage of the Indian genius, even extracting from the absence of all art at a given period a testimony to the wealth of its artistic endowment. I do not know what is the evidence for the abstention of the Vedic Aryans from making graven images or likenesses of anything in heaven or earth. One would suppose it probable that they might have exercised their graphic and plastic faculties upon perishable materials which had left no trace. At a later point (p. 18) Mr. Havell says, "Nearly all Indian sculpture previous to the Buddhist epoch was in wood or other impermanent materials." Given two periods, A and B, if it is admitted that in period B sculpture existed, but has perished, one does not see why it should be asserted that in period A no sculpture existed at all. Probabilities, however, must curtsey to evidence; and it is possible that Mr. Havell may have evidence (to me unknown) for the artistic barrenness of the Vedic period.* It is when he finds in that barrenness a proof of consummate genius that reason falters and protests. He may be able to prove that the primitive Aryans would not if they could have made

* From the mere non-existence of monuments or documents, nothing, surely, can be concluded. The Aryans were certainly surrounded by Dravidian and other tribes, who cannot possibly be supposed to have had any conscientious scruples about image-making. If, then, no sculpture at all has come down to us from the Vedic period, we can only conclude that the sculpture of the Dravidian peoples has perished—and why not that of the Aryans with it?

images or pictures; but how can he possibly arrive at the
knowledge that "they could an' if they would"? It is surely
a masterpiece of paradox to assert that an age which produced no art "must nevertheless be regarded as an age of
wonderful artistic richness."

The point is of no importance except as a symptom of
Mr. Havell's mental habit. He cannot endure that there
should be any period, from the dawn of history until the
blight of South Kensington fell upon the land, when India
did not possess a marvellous genius for art. If, then, there
was a period in which she produced no art, it can only have
been because, for good and sufficient reasons, she deliberately suppressed her genius. She had "conceived the whole
philosophy of her art," though as yet no art existed within
her bounds, at any rate within the limits of Aryavarta.
It is very true that India has an unrivalled gift of aprior-
ism; but one can as well imagine a blind man conceiving
the whole philosophy of light as an artless people conceiving
a valid philosophy of art. Does not Mr. Havell really
mean that already in the Vedic period the philosophy was
more or less developed which was destined in after ages
to influence Indian art? That is a rational proposition;
but the value to art of a philosophy which knew not art is
perhaps open to doubt.

Not, however, for Mr. Havell. Here is another group
of extracts in which he definitely discloses the basis of his
doctrine:

Indian art was conceived when that wonderful intuition flashed
upon the Indian mind that the soul of man is eternal and one with
the Supreme Soul, the Lord and Cause of all things. . . . The
creative force generated from those great philosophical conceptions has not ceased to stimulate the whole art of Asia from that
time to the present day (p. 6).

It was about the beginning of the Christian era that the great universities of Northern India, in which the many schools of philosophy were combined with schools of painting and sculpture . . . provided Asiatic art once and for ever with a philosophic basis, and created the Indian divine ideal in art (p. 22).

It was by *Yoga* also—by spiritual insight or intuition—rather than by observation and analysis of physical form and facts, that the sculptor or the painter must attain to the highest power of artistic expression (p. 32).

Art thus becomes less the pursuit of beauty than an attempt to realise the life which is without and beyond by the life which is within us—life in all its fullness and mystery, which is, and was, and is to come (p. 40).

The West, surfeited with the materialism of the Renaissance, is already slowly turning again to the East for spiritual instruction (p. 41).

Is it not evident that we have here to deal primarily, not with artistic, but with the theologico-philosophical, or, more briefly, with theosophical, doctrine? And is it not clear that Mr. Havell is setting forth to interpret art in the light of a principle which, carried to its logical issue, would destroy art, or reduce it to a purely conventional symbolism? One can accept a figure with three heads and eight arms as a type of omniscience, or omnipotence, or creative energy, or, in short, anything that may be agreed upon; but why, in that case, seek to make out that it is beautiful in the ordinary, non-symbolic sense of the word? Why praise it in terms of that very *maya*, that illusion, which, we are told, it is the business of art to dissipate and dispel?

There are, I submit, two fundamental flaws in Mr. Havell's doctrine. In the first place, it assumes the positive, objective, one might almost say the historic truth of certain metaphysical tenets which are, in the nature of things, incapable of verification, and which, at best, belong to a region inaccessible to art, in any reasonable sense of the word. In the second place, it proceeds on principles which ought, if consistently applied, to place any savage Mumbo-Jumbo on a level with, or above, the so-called Zeus of Phidias; since the Zeus is an attempt to subject the idea of godhead to the bonds of material illusion, while the Mumbo-Jumbo rises superior to illusion, and expresses in its quiddity, so to speak, the savage's conception of the power behind the veil. Of course Mr. Havell does not begin to apply his principles consistently. He seizes with avidity on any trace of naturalistic grace, beauty, realism, that he can find in Indian art. It is only when these qualities are hopelessly undiscoverable that he falls back on spiritual significance, on contempt for the outward shows of things, in order to justify monstrosity, mannerism and grotesque convention.

To illustrate what I mean by the acceptance of metaphysical concepts as though they were verified truths, I cannot do better than quote a quotation made by Mr. Havell, with unquestioning approval, from an essay by his kindred spirit, Dr. A. K. Coomaraswamy. It runs thus:

What, after all, is the secret of Indian greatness? . . . The secret of the infinite superiority of intuition, the method of direct perception, over intellect . . . [Intuition] came to Sir Isaac Newton when he saw the apple fall and there flashed across his brain the law of gravity. It came to Buddha as he sat through the silent nights in meditation, and hour by hour all things became apparent to him.

Just consider the difference between the two phenomena so airily bracketed together! We need not inquire whether the anecdote of the apple be authentic or not. No doubt there did come to Newton, whether in an orchard or elsewhere, a flash of insight in which he divined the universality of a law towards which he, and other physicists for centuries before him, had been feeling their way by dint of patient experiment, measurement, calculation, reflection. The precise magnitude of the advance made in that moment of insight, it must be left to specialists to estimate. Probably, if we could follow all the mental processes that led up to it, we should find that the leap was not a very great one. But supposing it to be—as it may have been—the greatest single achievement recorded of any human mind, can we possibly call it an effort of "intuition" as distinguished from "intellect"? No, surely. It was the last step in a long intellectual process; and (mark this) it consisted in the formulation of a hypothesis to be experimentally verified or disproved. Verified it has been, a million-fold, and it is continually being verified in mechanical calculation and astronomical prediction. Those of us who are neither physicists nor astronomers have, indeed, to take it on trust; but to suppose it untrue is to suppose ourselves the victims of an utterly incredible conspiracy of fraud. Now compare this daily and hourly verified law with the "intuitions," not only of the Buddha, but of all the Indian sages put together. What characteristic have they in common? In place of generalization based on a patient study of phenomena, we have a logical exercise resulting in a denial of the reality of phenomena, and then a fantastication at large as to the noumena conjectured to lie behind the world of illusion. It may be mentioned in passing that the fantasies of individual sages constantly contradict one another. For instance, the Buddha, cited by Dr. Coomaraswamy, would not have accepted the "wonderful intuition" which Mr. Havell regards as the root principle of Indian art, "that the soul of man is eternal and one with the Supreme Soul, the Lord and Cause of all things." But the contradictions are of minor moment. The one plain fact is that these Indian speculations are in the nature of things unverifiable, and would remain so even if they could be reduced to mutual consistency or unanimity. I am not denying the subtlety or the profundity of Indian metaphysics. I am not denying the historical importance of Indian thought. It was inevitable that the constitution of mind should be investigated as well as the constitution of matter; and I am perfectly ready to admit that matter is only "a name for the unknown and hypothetical cause of states of our own consciousness." Granted certain definitions, there is no doubt that the universe must be admitted to be illusion—*maya*. So far we can all go along with Mr. Havell. It is when he assumes the positive, scientific validity of this or that attempt to penetrate the illusion and see behind the veil—when he places such attempts on an equal footing with a verified hypothesis like the law of gravitation—then it is that I, for my part, must regretfully part company with him. Such speculations may be extremely ingenious. They may even be incontrovertible conclusions from the stated premises. But they are all efforts to know the unknowable, and think about the unthinkable. To the soul that finds solace in them, who shall grudge it? But when such a speculation is set up as a—or rather the—basic principle of art, one cannot but cry out. Nor is there anything in Mr. Havell's critical applications of this principle that tends to reconcile one to it. On the contrary, his very able treatises merely confirm one in the belief that the domain of art is precisely the phenomenal world, and that, if it can ever get at noumena at all, it will not be by distorting and denaturalizing phenomena. Nature may be (or, if you prefer it, must be) an illusion; but it is an illusion kept up with such admirable consistency that we are all constrained to act as if it were real. In what else

[196]

does sanity consist? And ought not sanity to be the basis
of art as well as of life?

Before attempting a rational estimate of Indian art, as
an index to the soul of the people, I thought it well to show
clearly the anti-rational basis of the unqualified and unmeasured eulogies of the Indian genius which have lately
been loud in the land. This done, I go on to state my
personal impressions for what they are worth. They may
possibly be coloured by the chance that I entered India
from the south, and that Hindu art first confronted me in
some of its most exaggerated forms, at Madura, Trichinopoly and Tanjore. But I have done my best to supplement
my own observations by careful study of the lavishly illustrated works of Mr. Havell, Dr. Coomaraswamy, Mr.
Vincent Smith and others; and I can at all events say that
I approached the whole subject without any prejudice.

On a broad general survey, and putting aside for the
moment all question of individual exceptions, I do not see
how it is possible to argue away the palpable and glaring
fact that Hindu (as distinct from Muhammadan) art habitually tends to extravagance and excess. It is the art of a
swarming, pullulating people in a country where Nature
itself scorns the very idea of moderation. Remember—
it is certainly not irrelevant—that India is the most tropical
country that ever possessed any art of importance. China
is another region of multitudinous humanity, but only a
small portion of China falls within the torrid zone; whereas
half of India, and that not the hotter half, lies south of the
tropic. India, then, is literally a hotbed of imagination,
which fosters all sorts of over-luxuriant and monstrous
growths. The fact that her philosophy has led her, not towards the study of Nature, but away from it, has helped her,
no doubt, to throw off all salutary checks upon her fantasy;

[197]

but her philosophy (I suggest) is not so much the cause of her art as a concurrent effect of climatic influences. Only in a hot country is it possible for a human being to spend months, years, or even a life-time, in sitting cross-legged and contemplating his own navel. Only in a hot country could the opinion arise that this was the best way of ascertaining the truth as to the nature and constitution of the universe. Whatever may be the analogies between Buddha under the bo-tree and Newton under the apple-tree, it is quite certain that Newton did not "sit through the silent nights" under the apple-tree, else he would have taken his discovery with him to an untimely grave. Indian *yoga* and Indian art are alike products of the Indian climate, and though the one has no doubt influenced the other, it cannot be regarded as its inspiring principle. Taken in the mass, Indian art does not seek to express metaphysical intuitions, but is clearly of a piece with the highly material imaginings of popular religion and popular poetry.

One need go no farther than the main staircase of the British Museum in order to study a characteristic and in some ways admirable example of Indian art. The sculptures from the Buddhist *stupa* at Amaravati, Southern India, dating from about A.D. 200, were at one time reckoned "the culmination of the art of sculpture in India" (Fergusson) and still hold a high place in the esteem of the critics. Mr. Havell tells us truly that they offer "delightful studies of animal life, combined with extremely beautiful conventionalized ornament," and Mr. Vincent Smith, though he regards some of the work as "skilled craftsmanship rather than fine art," is of opinion that the sculptures as a whole "must have formed, when perfect, one of the most splendid exhibitions of artistic skill known in the history of the world." This is high praise, and I am not concerned to discount it. I will even own it possible to pick out

[198]

scenes which more or less justify Mr. Havell's assertion
that "the most varied and difficult movements of the human
figure are drawn and modelled with great freedom and skill."
It is precisely because of the merits of these sculptures, and
because, being of Buddhist origin, they contain none of the
monstrosities characteristic of Hindu art, that I direct the
reader's attention to them.

Can any unprejudiced observer deny that even these
exceptionally favourable specimens of Indian workmanship
are marred by the gravest defects of conventionality in
form, of overcrowding in composition, of excess in ornament? In a few seated female figures, viewed from behind,
there is a certain natural grace, but most of the women who
swarm all over the reliefs are the product of a morbid
convention which gives them enormous breasts, wasp waists,
and atrophied legs,* and places them in attitudes suggestive
of a violent dislocation of the hipjoint. Whether such
figures were actually cultivated at the period, I do not know;
but even if this could be proved, the sculptures could only
be regarded as conventional exaggerations of an unhealthy
fashion. As to composition, the word is really out of place
in this context. A certain ingenuity is shown in crowding
the utmost possible number of figures into a given space; but
of order, proportion, gradation, guidance and relief for the
eye, it is hard to find a trace. In this respect, the sculptures
would rank in Europe as interesting efforts of a primitive
school, struggling towards accomplishment, but only at the
beginning of the struggle. As to excess in ornament, it may
be asked how that can be affirmed when we possess only
disjointed fragments of the whole work and cannot replace

---

* "The exaggerated thinness of the legs," says Mr. Havell, "was probably less marked when the sculptures had their finishing coat of fine
plaster;" but any even coating of plaster would leave unaffected the
truly hideous *disproportion* of legs and thighs.

[199]

them in position. It happens, however, that among the remains there are several slabs representing the great *stupa* itself, and from these we can see that it was simply crawling with ornament—there is no other word for it. Perhaps it may be said that we have no right to transfer to the East the Western ideal of temperance in decoration; but Indian profusion did not, it would seem, arise from any æsthetic principle, but from the religious notion that the more labour was expended on a pious work, the more merit was acquired.* Artistic excellence, may, indeed, be achieved in work inspired by this idea; but an æsthetic defect cannot be converted into an æsthetic merit by the fact of its being so inspired.

In order to estimate the Amaravati sculptures at their true value, we need only turn over a few pages of Mr. Havell's *Indian Sculpture and Painting*, and examine his admirable photographs of portions of the two miles of Buddhist reliefs on the vast pyramidal *stupa* at Boro-Budur in Java. This building, which dates from about the ninth century of our era, is styled by Mr. Havell "the Parthenon of Asia," and is certainly not unworthy of the name. The odd thing is that he should apparently fail to realize the gulf that separates Boro-Budur not only from Amaravati, but from Elbora, Elephanta, Vijayanagar, and all the other famous sculpture-sites of continental India. Judging entirely from photographs, one is tempted to place the Boro-Budur sculptures among the loveliest things in the world. They are crowded, yet not overcrowded, with figures of exquisite grace, in attitudes of great expressiveness, yet devoid of violence. They are perfect examples of the art of composition as applied to long relief. I concur with every word that Mr. Havell says in praise of them; it is

* For the same reason, according to Mr. Havell, sculpture was more cultivated than painting. *Ideals of Indian Art*, p. 133.

[200]

THE PALACE LAKE, UDAIPUR

only when he places them without hesitation or reservation to the credit of India, that I protest. Their themes are certainly Indian—scenes from the life of Buddha, and from Buddhist romances and *jatakas* or birth-stories. Some part of their technical method is, no doubt, Indian as well. But their physical types are quite un-Indian, and their suave and gracious humanity has nothing Indian about it—is, indeed, particularly devoid of those very qualities which Mr. Havell declares to be the supreme glory of Indian art. Certainly, these Javanese sculptors—for in the absence of evidence to the contrary, we may assume them to have been Javanese —sought no inspiration in *yoga*, and dreamt not of dissipating *maya* in order to disclose the realities which eye hath not seen and ear hath not heard. They were perfectly satisfied with what the eye sees in the phenomenal world. They loved it, studied it, and reproduced it with a rare combination of dramatic instinct and decorative tact. Devout they may have been: indeed, there is no reason to doubt it: but they were artists first and devotees second. "Nobody with the least experience," says Mr. Vincent Smith, "could mistake a Javanese relief for one executed in India. But when we compare the Boro-Budur sculptures with the seventh-century relief at Mamallapuram, or the sixth-century friezes at Badami, the difference almost amounts to that between fine art and barbarism."

Before we leave the subject of Buddhist art, it may be well to say a few words as to the numerous figures of the Buddha himself for which the Orientalizers are full of admiration. Most people are familiar with the type—a short, round, smooth face, with eyelids drooped, eyes either closed or reduced to narrow slits, full lips, huge ears, head covered with conventional snail-shell curls, broad, smooth shoulders and chest, narrow waist, legs crossed in the traditional attitude of the squatting *yogi*, and hands disposed

[201]

in one or another posture of conventional symbolism. Of the philosophy of this figure,* Mr. Havell gives the following account† :—

When the Indian artist models a representation of the Deity with an attenuated waist and abdomen, and suppresses all the smaller anatomical details, so as to obtain an extreme simplicity of contour, the European draws a mental comparison with the ideas of Phidias and Michelangelo and declares that the Indian is sadly ignorant of anatomy and incapable of imitating the higher forms of Nature. But the Indian artist, in the best period of Indian sculpture and painting, was no more ignorant of anatomy than Phidias or Praxiteles. He would create a higher and more subtle type than a Grecian athlete or a Roman senator, and suggest that spiritual beauty which, according to his philosophy, can only be reached by the surrender of worldly attachments and the suppression of worldly desires. . . .

Indian artists purposely suppressed the details of the physical body with the intention of suggesting the inner Self purified and exalted by communion with the Universal Soul. . . .

Amongst the thirty-two principal *lakshanas*, or marks of divinity, attributed to the person of Buddha—such as short, curly hair, long arms, a mark of noble birth, and golden-coloured skin— there is a very significant one: "the upper part of the body (*i.e.*, the trunk) is like that of a lion." Let us try to realise the precise meaning of this symbolism. The most prominent characteristics of the body of the Indian lion [are] the broad deep shoulders and the narrow contracted abdomen. . . . Now Buddha, as we know, attained to his Buddahood at the close of a long fast, and, according to the canons of European art, he should have been represented in a state of extreme emaciation. The Gandharan sculptors ‡ did, indeed, occasionally represent Buddha thus. But

* With slight modifications, the figure serves not only for the Buddha, but for Bodhisattvas, or saints on the verge of Buddahood, for Jain Tirthankaras, and often for Hindu gods.
† *Indian Sculpture and Painting*, pp. 25, 36, 39.
‡ Contaminated, be it observed, by Hellenic influences!

the Indian sculptors never descended to such vulgarity. . . .
They gave him a new, spiritualised body—broad-shouldered,
deep-chested, golden-coloured, smooth-skinned, supple and lithe
as a young lion.

There is no doubt that the broad shoulders and slim waist
of the typical Indian heroic figure are due to the fact that
the ideal of strength was based on the proportions of the lion
or the tiger. Such an ideal is very naturally formed by a
people in a state of semi-savagery, and adherence to it
might not unfairly be interpreted as showing that the semi-
savage state was not far outgrown. At all events, one does
not see how it can be alleged as a proof of superiority to,
or even equality with, races whose ideal of heroic manhood
is based, not on theriolatry, but on a generalization from the
highest human types. Is a people to be applauded for going
to the jungle for its ideals, instead of seeking them in the
gymnasium and the council-hall?

As for the attribution to Buddha of "a new spiritualized
body . . . supple and lithe as a young lion," we need
scarcely inquire into the appropriateness of the symbolism,
for it is more than doubtful whether the effect which Mr.
Havell declares to be aimed at is actually attained. Has
anyone, looking without preconceived theory at the cross-
legged Buddha figures, ever dreamt of seeing in them the
suppleness and litheness of the young lion? Is there any
plausible reason for crediting the sculptors with this intention? Is it not clear that the idea they sought to express
was that of contemplative immobility, and that nothing was
further from their minds than suppleness and litheness?
They adhered to the accepted type of manhood because they
had no particular reason for adopting any other; but they
did not dream of expressing qualities superfluous, and even
incongruous, in the *yogi*. As for the avoidance of emacia-

[203]

tion, what reason is there to suppose that they intended to represent the Buddha at the moment of emerging from his fast and attaining enlightenment? Asceticism was no part of his ideal; it was a phase of spiritual experience which he is represented as having lived through and put behind him. Assuming his story to be historical, we cannot doubt that, after his long ordeal was over, he recovered his normal physical condition; and it is in that condition, as conceived under the accepted canons of their craft, that the sculptors, quite naturally, chose to represent him. To seek a deep spiritual meaning in their abstention from exhibiting him as a living skeleton is to "chercher midi à quatorze heures."

It is, of course, impossible to disprove Mr. Havell's assertion that the artists who so carefully concealed their knowledge of anatomy were, in fact, as skilled in it as Phidias and Praxiteles. All that can be said is that he does not produce his evidence. And one thing is surely undeniable: namely, that when once a type was established in which all anatomical detail was suppressed, and a single hieratic pose was maintained with inconsiderable variations, it became very easy to multiply that type indefinitely, with comparatively little technical skill, and no spark of spiritual inspiration, or even understanding. This thought constantly occurs to us, not with reference to the Buddha alone, in reading Mr. Havell's impassioned eulogies of Indian art: even supposing he is right in maintaining that such-and-such types express such-and-such metaphysical and spiritual ideas, can we doubt that many of the works he so ardently admires are mere soulless reproductions, the work of clever craftsmen, wholly innocent of any desire to get behind the phenomenal world and "realize the life which is without and beyond"? He reproduces with unwearying praise about a score of divine figures (Buddhist and Hindu) from Thibet, Nepaul, Ceylon, Java, and India proper, of dates extending over something like a thousand years: can he mean that all these carvers and hammerers, deliberately and with conscious artistic-philosophic purpose, suppressed a knowledge of anatomy equal to that of Phidias?

Finally, and coming back to the Buddha-figures in particular, what are we to say of the marvellous spirituality of expression often attributed to them? It is to me, I own, far from apparent. The drooped eyelids and the immobile pose do, indeed,, express the idea of contemplation; but I am at a loss to find anything spiritual in the smooth, insipid faces. In some of the Gandharan Buddhas (found in the North-West Frontier Province) there is a certain nobility of expression; but to these Hellenistic products Mr. Havell will have nothing to say. My own preference for them will, doubtless, be set down to mere European prejudice; and I frankly confess that I see more spirituality in (for example) the ideal head of Homer, seamed by suffering and furrowed by thought, than in the whole pantheon of Buddhist-Hindu sculpture. But my preference is not founded on any general prejudice in favour of the Western as compared with the Eastern type. India to-day abounds in living men whose noble spirituality of aspect puts all the carven gods to shame. Is there a single Buddha, from Peshawar to Kamakura, that can compare in spirituality with Rabindranath Tagore? *

* I am told that in this paragraph I mistake the meaning of the "spirituality" attributed to the Buddha figures. We are not, it would seem, to look for any record or suggestion of materiality mortified and spiritual experience diligently ensued and attained. The spirituality asserted resides rather in the artist than in his work. A figure is spiritual which seems to express sincere devotion in its maker, and to have been created in an atmosphere of faith. Perhaps so; but is it not the case that sincere devotion, working in an atmosphere of faith, has often produced execrable and most unspiritual art? Moreover, qualities are often claimed for Indian sculpture which must reside in the object, and not in any in-

Hindu, as distinct from Buddhist, sculpture carries to excess all the faults which we have noted in the Amaravati reliefs, and adds to them the undesirable characteristic of constantly dealing in grotesque monstrosities. The North, indeed, is not so extravagant as the South in its abuse of the human form. No doubt the Muhammadans have destroyed more images in the regions they have more completely mastered. No doubt, too, their influence has tended to beget a certain artistic moderation, and we may, if we please, assume that there is more innate good taste in Aryavarta than in the Dravidian peninsula. But, speaking generally, the impression one carries away from the temples of India is one of oppressive confusion of ornament (often beautiful in itself) and insensate reduplication of the (more or less) human figure, almost always in attitudes of violent contortion. I have already spoken of the thousands upon thousands of figures crowded upon the *gopuras*, or gate-towers, and plastered over the walls, of the mighty temples of the South. I do not think I am exaggerating when I say that not one of these myriad figures is in an unconstrained attitude; and most of them are twisted into poses that would baffle a Russian ballet-dancer. The whole effect is that of a demon army, battalion on battalion, suddenly petrified in the midst of a furious war-dance. Within the temples, it is just the same—colossal, contorted forms, looming menacingly through the gloom—everywhere a riot of violent, often sensual, imagery, nowhere one touch of nature or one point of rest. Yes, there is one: the pot-bellied, elephant-headed Ganesh is usually quite placidly enthroned. Monster though

ference to be drawn as to the artist's soul-state. To cite one example among hundreds, Mr. Havell says of a stone figure of the Buddhist Goddess of Wisdom: "Her face has that ineffable expression of heavenly grace which Giovanni Bellini, above all other Italian masters, gave to his Madonnas." *Indian Sculpture and Painting*, p. 51.

he be, this Silenus or Falstaff of Hinduism is far less inhuman than the major gods.

What, now, is Mr. Havell's account of all this? He tells
us, in the first place, that the Indians of old had "a deep-
rooted objection to anthropomorphic representations of
the Divine," and that "the substitution of a plain stone
emblem for a statue as the principal object of worship
for most of the followers of Siva in the present day is
probably an instance of this feeling." Then he argues in a
footnote that the "plain stone emblem" was "not originally
phallic"—a point which seems rather unimportant, since
it is now admittedly understood as phallic, and has been
from time immemorial. Be this as it may, Mr. Havell has
to admit that Hinduism, as a whole, has rather successfully
got over its objection to anthropomorphic representations
of the Divine, though he still maintains that the "West
is more idolatrous than the East," inasmuch as it "often
regards the realization of form as the end of art." * The
Indian artist, on the other hand, "attempted to differentiate
the spiritual type from the human by endowing the former
with superhuman attributes, quite regardless of physiological probabilities or possibilities. Indian art has never
produced a Phidias or Praxiteles, not because an Olympian
Zeus or an Aphrodite of Cnidus was beyond its intellectual
grasp, but because it deliberately chose an imaginative
rather than an intellectual ideal. . . . A figure with three
heads and four, six or eight arms seems to a European a
barbaric conception, though it is not less (*sic*) physiologic-
ally impossible than the wings growing from the human
scapula in European representations of angels. . . . All
art is suggestion and convention, and if Indian artists, by
their conventions, can suggest divine attributes to Indian

* *Ideals of Indian Art*, p. 171.

people with Indian culture, they have fulfilled the purpose of their art."[*]

Again one can only reply that this process of reasoning would place any African or Polynesian Mumbo-Jumbo on a level with the Apollo of Phidias or the Moses of Michelangelo. It is true, of course, that many-headed, many-armed gods are not more impossible than angels. Mr. Havell might even have argued that they are less impossible: for we do hear of Two-headed Nightingales and Siamese Twins, and still more abhorrent abortions are known to physiologists; whereas I am not aware that any child has yet been born with even the rudiments of wings. But there is something graceful and ethereal in the conception of a being, otherwise human, but endowed with the glorious privilege of flight. Men have always, and very naturally, sighed for the wings of a dove, and envied the circling sea-gull and the soaring hawk. We constantly fly in our dreams, and we feel the omission of Nature to add pinions to our outfit a very regrettable oversight, which we are now doing our best to remedy. There is nothing grotesque or degrading in man's instinctive desire to assert his kinship with his wonderful cousins, the birds. But no one ever desired three or four heads; and six or eight arms would assert our kinship, not with the bird, but with the octopus. The natural, unsophisticated mind of the child loves the idea of flying, and delights in the thought of angels, fairies and beneficent genies; from many-headed, many-armed ogres, it shrinks in dread, and it sympathizes with the heroic giant-killers who go forth to slay them. Let it not be said that these are conventions of the European nursery. The monster gods of India are originally ogres, just as much as Giant Blunderbore or Giant Cormoran.

[*] *Indian, Sculpture and Painting*, pp. 56-60.

They are the figures in which cowering savages embodied their conception of the destructive powers of Nature. They have no doubt been adopted into an originally higher religion, and they have to a certain extent been used as symbols of more or less advanced conceptions of deity. But their primitive associations cling to them, and they are almost always employed to typify the destructive and terrible aspect of supernatural power. It is Siva the Destroyer, it is the grisly goddess Durga or Kali, who is characteristically represented with six arms and a necklace of skulls, in a ravening attitude like that of a barn-storming player of the good old days, tearing a passion to tatters.* Sophisticate them as you please, the monster-gods of India are survivals from a low stage of spiritual development, and it is ridiculous to suggest that their infinite reduplication throughout the country is "an attempt to realize the life which is without and beyond by the life which is within us."

"It was inevitable," Mr. Havell admits, "that Hinduism, comprising as it does so many diverse states of civilization and of intellectual development, should embrace many artistic monstrosities, the wild imaginings of primitive races, and the crude vulgarities of the uncultured. But it will never be difficult to distinguish the barbaric elements of an undeveloped state of culture from the higher ideals of Indian æsthetic philosophy." And again: "It need hardly be stated

* The attitudes of gods and heroes in Indian sculpture constantly remind one of the "penny plain, twopence coloured" prints of posturing actors which were so popular in England a hundred years ago. This resemblance suggests the possibility that Indian sculptors may have drawn their inspiration from performers in early miracle-plays. Horrwitz (*The Indian Theatre*, p. 23) tells us that the oldest Indian dramas, or rather colloquies (*sanvadas*), were, in fact, mysteries in which "either Krishna or Siva acted or danced the principal part." The attitudes so familiar in sculpture may very well have been those cultivated by a school of miracle-players, half dancers, half acrobats.

[209]

that the Indian process of artistic thought has often produced many degenerate and revolting types, just as the European process has produced a vast amount of inane and intolerable rubbish." Intentionally or not, Mr. Havell here points to a distinction which I entirely accept. Much of the art of Europe is "inane and intolerable rubbish," but it is not "degenerate and revolting"—at any rate, not in anything like the same degree as an immense amount of Indian art. I am far from denying the technical merit of a great deal of Hindu sculpture. The treatment of animals, whether on a great scale or as motives in decoration, is often superb. There is no temptation to distort and denaturalize the elephant, the bull and the antelope. Such decorative work as that in the Hoysalesvara Temple at Halebid is entirely admirable in quality, if only it were more moderate in quantity. Everywhere, indeed, there is an astounding wealth of beautiful decoration, such as could be produced only by exuberant fancy in a country where time had no existence. The Jain Temples of Mount Abu, for example, are decorated with a profusion absolutely incredible to anyone who has not seen them. Sometimes, too, there is extraordinary power and subtlety in the treatment even of monstrosities. The famous statuette of the dancing "Siva as Natesa," * for instance, is a really wonderful piece of work, especially remarkable for the skill with which the arms are so disposed that one scarcely notices their superabundance. All over the country one may find, here and there, admirable pieces of work, both early and late, in which naturalism wins a momentary victory over extravagant and unwholesome convention. But when Mr. Havell declares that it is "never difficult to distinguish the barbaric elements of an undeveloped state of culture from the higher

* This is a frequently repeated motive. The best example known to me is that in the Madras Museum, reproduced by Mr. Havell.

ideals of Indian æsthetic philosophy," he seems to me to be
asserting what his own works disprove. As soon as a piece
of sculpture, however monstrous, however barbaric, has a
certain technical quality, Mr. Havell declares it to be inspired by the higher ideals of Indian philosophy, and
imagines into it all sorts of spiritual significance. Perhaps
his greatest achievement in this way is his rhapsody over an
alto-rilievo of "Durga slaying Mahisha" now in the Leyden
Museum. To the unilluminate eye, it seems like a thick-set,
thick-lipped woman with six arms, straddling ungracefully
from head to tail of a recumbent and apparently sleeping
bull, and resting one of her half-dozen hands on the curly
head of an enormously fat boy. To Mr. Havell,* on the
contrary, it appears that in this work "Hindu sculpture
has produced a masterpiece. . . . Judged by any standard
it is a wonderful work of art, grandly composed, splendidly
thorough in technique, expressing with extraordinary power
and concentrated passion the wrath and might of the
Supreme Beneficence roused to warfare with the Spirit of
Evil. The student will find in this phase of Indian imaginative art an intensity of feeling—a wonderful suggestion of
elemental passion transcending all the feeble emotions of
humanity—a revelation of the powers of the Unseen, which
nothing in European art has ever approached, unless it be
in the creations of Michelangelo or in the music of Wagner."

It says much for the intensity of Mr. Havell's conviction
that he should actually accompany this hymn of praise
with a photograph of the masterpiece which called it forth.

Hindu Epic and Drama.

Never, perhaps, have two forms of art more completely
reflected and interpreted each other than Hindu sculpture

* *Indian Sculpture and Painting*, p. 69.

and the Hindu epics. In saying so I am not thinking of
the actual scenes from the two great poems, especially from
the Ramayana, which not infrequently occur in reliefs and
decorations. If these were entirely absent, it would remain
none the less true that in reading the epics we seem to see
the overstrained, over-elaborated, over-crowded sculptures,
and in viewing the sculptures we seem to hear the vast,
labyrinthine, multitudinous epics.

The author of *Siri Ram*, who has evidently studied Indian
character at close quarters, says: "There is a popular
fallacy that the Indian is imaginative. Nothing is further
from the truth. . . . Imagination means much the same to
him as multiplication. It is a kind of magnifying-glass
through which he sees a swollen universe. The imaginative
man is the man who thinks in crores and hecatombs and
holocausts, in Kalpas of time and vast compartments of
space. The light play of fancy does not touch him." This
is, I conceive, a far too sweeping statement, probably
founded on observation of a mediocre type of Indian mind.
It would be easy to deny imagination to the European, if
one judged (say) by the average British schoolboy. But
it is probably true—and this is perhaps what the writer
really means—that the Indian imagination suffers from
habitual and ancestral over-fatigue. The poet and the
artist have, from of old, striven to live "au-delà des forces
humaines." In a country where everything is exaggerated
—the height of the mountains, the width of the plains, the
volume of the rivers, rainfall and drought, fertility and
aridity, the luxuriance of the jungle, the size and strength
of animals, the fecundity and venomousness of reptiles and
insects, the splendour of the stars at night, and above all
the fierce prepotency of the sun by day—in such a country
it was perhaps inevitable that man should overstrain his
powers in the attempt to body forth his conceptions of

[212]

might, majesty and multitude. At all events, that is what has happened. In the Indian epics, the poets are always trying to outdo themselves and each other in their search for the marvellous, whether in virtue, prowess, gorgeousness, wickedness, demoniacal fury, or mere numerical extravagance. They are constantly creating records in exaggeration, which are as constantly broken. What wonder that a people habituated from childhood to these orgies of unbridled fancy should suffer from a certain slackening of imaginative fibre, an insensitiveness to normal and wholesome stimulation? It is that insensitiveness which seems to me to account for all that is worst in Indian art. It is that insensitiveness which will have to be corrected before India can hope to make the best of her intellectual gifts in a world in which, though all may be illusory, the God-made illusion of Nature must in the end prevail over the man-made illusions of mythology and metaphysics.

The Indian epics and Indian sculpture are, of course, co-ordinate products of the Indian mind, and must not be placed in any direct relation of cause and effect. But as the matter of the epics, at any rate (if not their extant form), is much older than most of the sculpture that has come down to us, we can fairly say that art has been influenced by literature rather than literature by art. And to this day, by all accounts, the epics continue to re-act potently on the Indian mind, and to keep it stagnant in the phase of development to which they themselves belong. It is hard to see how this can be looked upon otherwise than as a grave misfortune. Even if we could assume that the Greek and the Indian epics stood fairly on a level in point of intellectual and ethical value, would it be to the advantage of Europe if the Iliad and the Odyssey were held to be sacred revelations, were the exclusive, or at any rate by far the most desirable, mental and moral sustenance of the great

[213]

majority of the people, and were regarded with a bibliolatrous reverence, more extravagant than any that has ever been paid to the Hebrew Bible.* Would the European character be strengthened and ennobled if it were currently believed that salvation was to be attained by the mechanical repetition of the name of (say) Achilles or Ulysses? And the assumption of equality on which this comparison proceeds is really a preposterous one. The Greek epics would make ten times better Bibles than the huge accumulations of sacerdotalized folk-lore from which the Indian populace derive their notions of the heroic and the divine. "Although priests are occasionally mentioned in the Iliad and the Odyssey," says Sir M. Monier-Williams, "there is wholly wanting in the Homeric poems any recognition of a regular hierarchy or the necessity for a mediatorial caste of sacrifices. This, which may be called the sacerdotal element of the Indian epics, is more or less woven into their very tissue. Priestcraft has been at work in these poems almost as much as the imagination of the poet; and Brahminism, claiming a monopoly of all knowledge, human and divine, has appropriated this, as it has every other department of literature, and warped it to its own purposes. Its policy being to check the development of intellect, and keep the inferior castes in perpetual childhood, it encouraged an appetite for exaggeration more monstrous and absurd than would be tolerated in the most extravagant European fairy-tale." In all religions there is too much of the fairy-tale element, but it surely cannot be to the advantage of a country that its popular religion and literature should consist of extravagant fairy-tales and little else.

* "Some idea of the veneration in which it (the Ramayana) is held may be formed from the verses at the end of the introductory chapter, which declare that 'he who reads and repeats this holy life-giving Ramayana is liberated from all his sins and exalted with all his posterity to the highest heaven.'" Monier-Williams, *Indian Epic Poetry*, p. 16.

[214]

The beauties of diction, of description, of episodic narrative, in the Indian epics are acknowledged by good judges to be very great. I have no means of knowing how far the literary qualities of the original Sanskrit, or even of the Hindi transcript of the Ramayana by Tulsi Das, are reproduced in the versions of the village reciters, to whom the mass of the Indian people owes its knowledge of the epic literature. But, however skilful, however tasteful, may be their renderings, we cannot doubt that it is upon the story —the spectacular, the sensational, the passionate scenes and incidents—that the popular mind most eagerly fastens. Can we, then, regard these scenes and incidents as wholesome mental sustenance for a people which has to live and hold its own in the world of to-day and to-morrow? Let us look a little into this question.

What are the ideals, or rather, the general ideas, which disengage themselves from these poems? First, as Sir M. Monier-Williams points out, the peculiar sanctity and the insatiable appetite of the Brahmin caste is dwelt on at every turn. Such passages as these are of ludicrously frequent recurrence:

Kripa guarded wealth and treasure, gold and gems of untold price,
And with presents unto Brahmins sanctified the sacrifice.

Hungry men were fed and feasted with an ample feast of rice,
Costly gifts to holy Brahmins graced the noble sacrifice.

Ida, ajya, homa offerings pleased the "Shining Ones" on high,
Brahmins, pleased with costly presents, with their blessings filled
  the sky.

"Not so" answered him the princess, "Other boon I may not seek,
Thou art bounteous, and a woman should be modest, wise and
  meek,

Twice I asked and twice you granted, and a Kshatra asks no
    more—
Unto Brahmins it is given asking favours evermore." *

If ever there was a priesthood naïvely intent on the loaves
and fishes, it is the Brahmins, as represented in these epics.
But the glory and grandeur of Brahminhood is nowhere
so emphatically announced as in the episode of Visvamitra
(Ramayana, Book I., Cantos 52-65). This Kshattrya
prince had a contest with the Brahmin Vasishtha for the
possession of "the cow of plenty," and was beaten by
"the superior power inherent in Brahminism." Therefore,
he determined to raise himself to that dignity, and accord-
ingly subjected himself to extreme austerities for thousands
of years. "The gods," says Sir M. Monier-Williams, "who
had a hard struggle to hold their own against over-zealous
ascetics, did what they could to interrupt him, and partially succeeded. Visvamitra yielded for a time to the
seductions of the nymph Menaka. . . . However, in the
end, the obstinate old ascetic was too much for the whole
troop of deities. He obtained complete power over his
passions, and when the gods still refused to Brahminize
him, he began creating new heavens and new gods, and
had already manufactured a few stars when the celestial
host thought it prudent to give in and make him a
Brahmin." This legend shows Brahminism to be at once
the summit of earthly ambition, and a summit unattainable
to anyone not born in it, unless he be strong enough to
conquer the gods themselves.

In the story of Visvamitra, too, we come upon the second
of the general ideas which pervade the epics—to wit, the
sanctity, nobility and magical efficacy of asceticism. This
idea speaks, not to say shrieks, from every page. "The

* R. C. Dutt's extracts from the Mahabharata.

performance of penitences was like making deposits in the bank of heaven. By degrees an enormous credit was accumulated, which enabled the depositor to draw to the amount of his savings, without fear of his drafts being refused payment. The power gained in this manner by weak mortals was so enormous that gods as well as men were equally at the mercy of these all but omnipotent ascetics." No serious attempt is made to read ethical value into asceticism; it is practically admitted to be a method of pure magic. This is apparent in the fact that even *rakshasas*, or demons, can accumulate power by self-torture. The theme of the Ramayana, indeed, is nothing but the outwitting of a demon, Ravan, who had by this means rendered himself inconveniently formidable. He had extorted from the god Brahma the assurance that neither gods, genii, demons nor giants should be able to vanquish him. But he had disdained to stipulate for invulnerability at the hands of men; wherefore Vishnu, ever ready for a new avatar, consented to be born as four men, the reputed sons of King Dasaratha. One half of him became Rama, one fourth Bharata; and it needs no great skill in vulgar fractions to conjecture that the other two, Lakshman and Satrugna, each represented one-eighth of the godhead. Nevertheless, they were men within the meaning of the Brahma-Ravan compact, and were therefore able, after a gigantic struggle, to vanquish and slay the demon ascetic. This is by no means the most grotesque example of the part played by asceticism in the machinery of the epics. Ascetics are, indeed (paradoxical as it may seem), the actual fathers of most of the leading figures of the Mahabharata; and the generation-stories,* of these renowned personages, of

* In the recently-published *Myths of the Hindus and Buddhists* (London, Harrap, 1913), the birth-stories of the Mahabharata are passed over in discreet silence. This part of the work is by Sister Nivedita.

Vyasa, Dritarashtra, Pandu, and Vidura, of Yudishthira, Bhima, Arjuna, Nakula, Sahadeva, and Duryodhana, are surely among the most nauseous known to folklore. It is a characteristic of legendary asceticism that it renders its votaries insanely short-tempered and vindictive. Incalculable is the trouble wrought by the maledictions of irascible *rishis*. In short, it is not easy to think of a more unwholesome doctrine than that of the virtues of self-torture, as presented to the Indian mind in the epics.

Be it noted, however, that asceticism is a jealously-guarded privilege of the twice-born castes. The son of a Brahmin having died at the age of fourteen, it was pointed out to Rama that such a portent showed that there must be some terrible sin in progress in the world. "He found no sin in the west, or in the north, and the east was crystal clear." But in the south, beside a sacred pool, a *yogi* was standing on his head and "practising the most severe disciplines." Rama asked him to what caste he belonged, and on learning that he was a Sudra, promptly cut off his head; whereupon "the gods rained down flowers and praised the deed." The cold-blooded arrogance which inspired this legend is outdone in the story of Ekalavya, in the Mahabharata. Ekalavya was "a low-caste prince of non-Aryan birth" who aspired to be taught archery by Drona, the trainer of the Pandu princes. Rejected on account of his low birth, he retired to the forest and made a clay image of Drona, to which he paid such strenuous and ascetic devotion that he became an accomplished marksman. A dog belonging to Drona came upon the devotee, and was so alarmed by his hideous appearance that he began to bark. "Before he could close his mouth, the prince Ekalavya had shot into it no fewer than seven arrows, aiming by sound alone." This achievement attracted attention to Ekalavya, who, being interrogated, proclaimed

[218]

himself a pupil of Drona. Thereupon that hero sought him out and said, "If thou art really my pupil, give me, then, the teacher's fee. Give me the thumb of thy right hand." The low-born prince, without flinching, cut off his thumb and laid it at Drona's feet. "But when the Brahmin had gone, and he turned again to his archery, he found that his marvellous lightness of hand was for ever vanished. Thus were the royal princes left without rivals in the use of arms."

A more odious anecdote it would be hard to find in any of the Sacred Books of the world. It passes, however, without a word of protest. If David had been a Kshattrya prince, the Brahmin Nathan would have smiled upon his treatment of the Sudra Uriah, and very probably the gods would have rained down flowers.

A third general idea running through the epics, is that heroism consists in having the stronger medicine-man on your side. Especially must you be amply provided with magical weapons, like the arrow of Rama which pierced the stems of seven palm trees, penetrated a hill that stood behind them, then sped through six hells and finally returned to the hero's quiver. Similar ideas, on a less extravagant scale, are no doubt prevalent in the ballad poetry of all primitive peoples. Everywhere we hear of cloaks of darkness, blades graven with magic runes, immersion in waters of invulnerability, and so forth. But only in India do these relics and evidences of savagery pervade from end to end the sacred writings of the race. Only in India is magic the very essence both of law and gospel.

It is sometimes said that the conception of fair play is absent from the epic literature. That is true, but it is not the essential criticism. Fair play is an ideal of the assault-at-arms, not of the battlefield, of sham manœuvres, not of real war. In a boxing-match, arranged with the object of testing the skill and endurance of two competitors under equal external conditions, it would be manifestly intolerable that one of the combatants should wear spikes on his knuckles. But if a robber attacks me on a lonely road, and I happen to have a knuckle-duster, or a sword-cane, or a revolver, I do not pause to inquire whether my assailant is similarly armed before I make use of any and every advantage I can command. That is real war, and fair play has nothing to do with it. If, having disarmed my assailant, I proceed wantonly to maim him, or perhaps to blow his brains out, the law, on proof of the fact, will punish me. But in this there is no question of fair play, but simply of humanity. Even in war, unnecessary cruelties to defenceless people are, in theory, at any rate, forbidden by the common consent of mankind. If, however, England could, by recourse to magic, make her Dreadnoughts unsinkable and her torpedoes unerringly destructive—if the holy ascetics of Germany could, by uttering *mantras* over her ammunition waggons, ensure that every bullet should find its billet in a foeman's heart—would either power hesitate to make use of this advantage, because it would not be fair play? Assuredly not. Are not all nations, as a matter of fact, striving to secure for themselves the exclusive services of the magicians whom we call inventors? In bygone times, some feeble effort was made to carry the rules of the tourney into actual hostilities, and it was held unfair to strike the first blow without a formal declaration of war. But even that formality no longer obtains. It is recognized as the business of a belligerent to take every possible advantage; and if treachery, such as the abuse of the white flag, is barred, it is only because reason perceives the observance of certain conventions to be equally to the advantage of both parties.

It is not, then, because magic is unfair that its prevalence in the epics is to be regretted—it is because it is unreal. In saying this, I am not dogmatizing as to the existence or non-existence of occult powers: I am merely asserting the obvious fact that the battles of life, whether individual or national, have never been won by magic. When, by a convenient metaphor, we speak of the "magic" of science, we mean the results, not of spells or talismans, but of arduous research into the secrets of Nature, carried on by generations of tireless and devoted students. It is this recognition of the necessity for individual effort that is absent from the epics. We seldom or never feel that anyone is really brave, really strong, really skilful. Of what worth is the valour of the hero who fights with enchanted weapons, and knows that, even if he is killed, it is a hundred to one that he will be brought to life again? As for strength and skill, they are both constantly represented as so superlative, so astounding, that there is no possibility of their having been acquired by honest human effort and assiduity—they are manifestly (even where it is not stated in so many words) the results of sheer magic. Can there be anything less fortifying to character than the adoration of heroes who, while constantly extolled for their virtue, owe their prodigious powers to influences with which character has nothing to do?

Even where character can actually be said to manifest itself, it is dehumanized by gross exaggeration. The saintliness of Rama, for example—his uncomplaining, unresentful acquiescence in the banishment brought upon him by a wicked step-mother—his refusal to return to Ayodhya even when Dasaratha is dead and Bharata implores him to fulfil what both know to have been the real desire of their father —all this is too overstrained to have any true moral value. Again, his repudiation of Sita, not because he has the slightest doubt of her purity, but because "people talk," and

Rama's wife must be above suspicion, is as unedifying an act as ever hero perpetrated. This story, no doubt, occurs in the "Uttara Kanda," a late, and, one may almost say, a spurious, addition to the Ramayana proper; but do the myriad worshippers of the hero, who think to find salvation in repeating, "Ram, Ram, Sita, Ram," distinguish critically between the sacred canon and the apocrypha? Where the epic heroes perform any action that is not magical, but recognizably human, it is apt to be extremely undesirable. Such an action is Lakshman's cutting off the nose and ears of the *rakshasi* Surpanakha; such an action is the Pandus' burning alive of an unoffending low-caste woman and her five sons. Yudhishthira's gambling frenzy, upon which the plot of the Mahabharata turns, is certainly "all-too human," except in so far as it is represented that he knew he was being cheated, and played on as a point of honour. Who can say how much the Indian passion for gambling has been fortified by this episode in the life of "the Hindu ideal of excellence—a pattern of justice, integrity, calm passionless composure, chivalrous honour and cold heroism?" The same pattern of virtue, by the way, on the field of Kurukshetra, compasses the death of Drona by a particularly base equivocation. The only characters in the epics that can arouse anything like rational admiration are the long-suffering and devoted women of whom Sita is the type. Their stories are sometimes really touching, though the heroism they display is too often, like that of Alkestis or Griselda, excessive to the verge of immorality.

But in any discussion of the Indian character as manifested in, and influenced by, the national epics, the last as well as the first word must be one of regret for the self-defeating, the enervating, the exhausting extravagance of hyperbole which is their most characteristic feature. English readers probably know them best in the able, but enormously condensed, translations of Romesh Chunder Dutt,[*] in which the wildest monstrosities are very naturally and properly suppressed. Let me give a few instances culled at random from the Ramayana, which, I take it, is really the more popular of the two. Thousands of pilgrims are constantly making the round of the sacred spots where Rama and Sita abode during their exile—the stations of Rama's cross, so to speak.

Here is a passage from the battle between Vasishtha and Visvamitra for the possession of "the cow of plenty." Visvamitra has just slaughtered a mighty host of his adversaries' warriors:

> So o'er the field that host lay strewn,
> By Visvamitra's darts o'erthrown.
> Then thus Vasishtha charged the cow:
> "Create with all thy vigour now."
> Forth sprang Kambojas as she lowed;
> Bright as the sun their faces glowed.
> Forth from her udder Barbars poured,—
> Soldiers who brandished spear and sword—
> And Yavans with their shafts and darts,
> And Sakas from her hinder parts.
> And every pore upon her fell,
> And every hair-producing cell,
> With Mlechchas and Kiratas teemed,
> And forth with them Haritas streamed.
> And Visvamitra's mighty force,
> Car, elephant, and foot and horse,
> Fell in a moment's time, subdued,
> By that tremendous multitude.
> The monarch's hundred sons, whose eyes

[*] Now accessible in "Everyman's Library" (Dent), Mr. Dutt's version contains something like 8,000 lines. The Ramayana (exclusive of the "Uttara Kanda") runs to 50,000 lines, and the Mahabharata to 230,000. The Iliad and Odyssey together contain about 30,000 lines.

Beheld the rout in wild surprise.
Armed with all weapons, mad with rage,
Rushed fiercely on the holy sage:
One cry he raised, one glance he shot,
And all fell scorched upon the spot:
Burnt by the sage to ashes, they
With horse, and foot and chariot lay.

Remember that this is only one episode, in a long struggle conceived throughout in similar proportions. Visvamitra next takes to throwing a whole armoury of magical weapons:

These fearful darts in fiery rain,
He hurled upon the saint amain,
An awful miracle to view.
But, as the ceaseless tempest flew,
The sage, with wand of god-sent power,
Still swallowed up that fiery shower.

Nor could the triple world withdraw
Rapt gazes from that sight of awe:
For as he swallowed down the dart
Of Brahma, sparks from every part,
From finest pore and hair-cell, broke,
Enveloped in a veil of smoke.

The hermits, whom that sight had awed,
Extolled the saint with hymn and laud.
The king, o'erpowered and ashamed,
With many a deep-drawn sigh exclaimed,
"Ah! Warriors' strength is poor and slight:
A Brahmin's power is truly might."*

The story of the bringing down to earth of Gunga (the Ganges) is very characteristic. She was the daughter of

* Griffith's translation (Benares, 1870), Book I., Cantos 55, 56.

Himavat, lord of mountains. The sixty thousand sons of a certain king, having offended the sage, Kapila, were by him reduced to ashes. A relative, Bhagiratha, wishing to perform their funeral rites, was told that to that end he must employ the sacred waters of Gunga. Thereupon:

Bhagiratha spent a thousand years, eating only once a month, surrounded with five fires and his arms uplifted. Brahma, pleased with his austerities, granted his boon that Gunga should come down to water the ashes of his forefathers. Bhagiratha next spent a year in adoring Siva, that he might break the fall of Gunga. She fell with great fury upon Siva, thinking to sweep him down to the infernal regions. *Siva, however, compelled her to wander many years in the tresses of his hair.* By further austerities Bhagiratha forced her to flow on the earth.

Hard upon this follows the story of the Churning of the Ocean, which I shall not recount. It is admired by the thorough-going India-worshipper, and sculptures representing it are warmly praised by Mr. Havell. To me it seems (like the story of Manu, the fish, and the flood) a very interesting piece of folk-lore, but I cannot understand how it can awaken any feeling, other than scientific interest, in any civilized person, or person aspiring to civilization.

Let us now turn to the famous Hindi version of the Ramayana by Tulsi Das*—the version which brings us nearest, no doubt, to the form in which the poem now reaches the Indian masses. Here are two specimens of style:

Not Sarada himself could do justice to the noble steed on which Rama rode. Sankara was enchanted with his beauty, and congratulated himself on having fifteen eyes. When Hari affectionately gazed on Rama, he and Lakshmi were both equally charmed; while Brahma rejoiced to behold his beauty, and re-

* Translated by F. S. Growse, Allahabad, 1883.

gretted that he had only eight eyes. Kartikeya exulted greatly that in the matter of eyes he was half as well off again as Brahma. . . . All the gods broke out in Indra's praise, saying, "Today there is no one like him." [Because Indra had one thousand eyes.] All heaven was delighted at the sight of Rama. . . . The welkin resounded with multitudinous kettledrums; the gods rained down flowers and shouted in their joy, "Glory, glory, glory to Ragu's noble son" (p. 152).

From the description of Queen Kaikeyi, in the scene in which she extorts from King Dasaratha the promise to banish Rama:

So saying the wretch rose and stood erect, as it were a swollen flood of wrath that had risen in the mountains of sin, turgid with streams of passion, terrible to behold, with two boons for its banks, her stern obduracy for its current, and her voluble speech for its eddies, overflowing the king like some tree torn up by its roots, as it rushed on to the ocean of calamity.

Now let us take a characteristic battle-piece—one of a hundred similar passages scattered through the two epics:

Then Ravan * hurled forth ten spears, which struck the four horses and brought them to the ground. Rama was furious: he raised the horses and then drew his bow and let fly his arrows. The edge of Raghubir's [Rama's] shafts swept off Ravan's heads as though they had been lotuses. He smote each of his heads with ten arrows; the blood rushed forth in torrents. Streaming with gore, he rushed on in his strength; but the Lord again fitted arrows to his bow and let fly thirty shafts; his heads and arms all fell to the ground. Again Rama smote away his arms and heads; for they had grown afresh after being cut off. Time after time the Lord struck off his arms and heads, but they were no sooner smitten off than they were again renewed. . . . The

* It may be mentioned that the chariots of Ravan's host numbered 150,000,000, his elephants 300,000,000, and his horses and asses 1,900,-000,000. Griffith's Ramayana, Book VI., Canto 96.

whole heaven was full of heads and arms. . . . When Ravan saw this multiplication of his heads, he thought no more of death and waxed still more furious. He thundered aloud in his insane pride, and rushed forward with his ten bows all strung at once, raging wildly on the field of battle, and overwhelmed Rama's chariot with such a shower of arrows that, for a moment, it was quite lost to sight, as when the sun is obscured by a mist. The gods cried "Alack, alack!"—but the Lord wrathfully grasped his bow, and parrying the arrows,* smote off his enemy's heads, which flew in all directions, covering heaven and earth. Severed as they were, they flew through the sky, uttering hideous cries of "Victory, victory! Where is Lakshman, where Sugriva and Angad? Where Rama, the prince of Kosala? Where now is Rama?" cried the heads as they sped through the air. The monkeys saw and turned to flight; but the jewel of the race of Raghu, with a smile, made ready his bow, and with his arrows shot the heads through and through; as though the goddess Kali, with a rosary of skulls in her hand, and accompanied by all her attendants, had bathed in the river Blood and come to worship at the shrine of Battle (pp. 471-472).

Let it be noted that this is not a unique or exceptional nightmare; it quite fairly represents all the battle-scenes of the two poems. Indeed, there are many common circumstances of epic strife that do not occur in this passage. For instance:

Ravan mounted his own shining car and led a *rakshasa* host against the monkeys; he seemed like the Destroyer himself accompanied by ghosts and flesh-devouring monsters with burning eyes. Big-belly and Goblin and Man-destroyer and Three-heads, fighters with mountain-peaks and flaming maces, came with Ravan. . . . Then first Sugriva hurled a mountain-top at him, but

* There is nothing commoner than for the champion of the stronger magic to ward off a hail-storm of arrows by breaking them in their flight with his own arrows. Such feats are child's play to Rama, Karna, and Arjuna.

Ravan severed it with his golden shafts. . . . So Kumbhakarna ("Pot-ear") drank two thousand flasks of wine, and marched out like a moving mountain, clad in golden mail, to attack the monkeys. The monkeys fled in terror, but "Pot-ear" caught them and rushed about devouring them by handfuls; * so that the blood and fat dropped from his mouth. Then Rama with Hanuman and other brave monkeys fell on him with trees and mountain tops. . . . Despite his wounds, Jambavan, the king of the bears, spoke to Hanuman:† "Thou shalt bound over the sea, and reach Himalaya, king of mountains, and bring thence the four life-giving herbs that grow on him, and return forthwith with healing for the monkey host." Then Hanuman roared and sprang; and he passed across the sea, and over hills and woods and rivers and cities till he came to Himalaya and beheld its hermitages. He ranged the mountain, but the herbs were hidden from him; and angered and impatient Hanuman rooted up the whole mountain and sprang with it into the air and returned to Lanka [Ceylon]. And the slain and wounded monkeys rose up whole, as if from restful sleep, healed by the savour of the four medicinal herbs. . . . Sakra sent down from Heaven his car and his charioteer to aid the son of Dasaratha in his fight; and Rama went about and greeted it, and, mounting upon it, seemed to light the whole world with his splendour. But Ravan loosed at him a *rakshasa* weapon, and its golden shafts, with fiery faces vomiting flames, poured over Rama from every side, and changed to venomous serpents. . . . Then Rama took up the Brahma weapon given to him by Agastya. Blessing that shaft with Vedic *mantras*, Rama set it on his bow and loosed it, and it sped to its appointed place, and cleft the breast of Ravan and, bathed in blood, returned and entered Rama's quiver humbly.‡

* Some of them, however, escaped through his nostrils and ears.

† The monkey hero worshipped as a god all over India. There is no commoner road-side idol, unless it be the elephant-headed Ganesh. Fancy Europe bestrewn with flower-decked shrines dedicated to Puss-in-Boots!

‡ Condensed from *Myths of the Hindus and Buddhists,* pp. 84-94. (This portion by Dr. A. K. Coomaraswamy.)

The Mahabharata is in no way behind the Ramayana in crudity and extravagance. Indeed, though some critics regard it as later in point of composition,* it is in many respects the more barbarous of the two. Not to weary the reader with a piling up of extravagances, I will merely mention one characteristic trait: Arjuna is recognized as the general-in-chief of the Pandu forces because he is "capable of fighting from his chariot with sixty thousand foes at once."

Have we not, in these limitless, insensate conceptions of superhuman heroism, and of divine and demonic power expressing itself in terms of frenzied ferocity, the key to the all-pervading sense of strain and contortion that is so fatiguing in Indian sculpture? The exercise of imagination is conceived by poet and artist alike as a sort of mental epilepsy, a horrible and exhausting convulsion. As for the plea that there is a profound metaphysical or spiritual significance under these convulsions, believe it who can! I am, of course, not denying that symbolical meanings can be read into the folk-lore of the epics and the Puranas, and have been read into them, perhaps from very early ages. But that such meanings were always, or even frequently, present to the minds of the poets who sang, or the sculptors who carved, is to me incredible. Nor do I believe that the unsophisticated populace of to-day have at their command the supersubtle alchemy which can distil spiritual sustenance from the turbid flood of primitive and barbarous legendry.

If the epic heroes have, for the most part, the nine lives of a cat, this is by no means the case with the common, low-caste multitude. The carnage of the battles of Lanka, Kurukshetra and elsewhere is unparalleled in song or story; and the revival of the monkey host by Hanuman's Hima-

* One of the reasons is that suttee is not mentioned in the Ramayana, but is an established custom in the Mahabharata.

layan herbs is (I think) a unique incident. Everywhere we are conscious of a background crowded with untold multitudes of unconsidered lives; and again this characteristic is reflected in sculpture to the utmost limit of material possibility. Overstrain in individual figures, overcrowding in backgrounds and decorations: these are the besetting sins of Hindu art—both clearly traceable to ethnic and climatic influences.

The vice of hyperbole is by no means confined to the epics. It meets us on every hand. In the Harsa-Carita* of Bana, a historical romance, dating from the seventh century of our era, the epic poets are positively outdone; while with their passion for hyperbole is blended an amazing and amusing Euphuism, anticipating Euphues by a thousand years. Here is a description of the camp of Sri-Harsa:

> It seemed like a creation-ground where the Prajapatis practised their skill, or a fourth world made out of the choicest parts of the other three; its glory could not be described in hundreds of Mahabharatas—it must have been put together in a thousand golden ages, and its perfection constructed with millions of *swargas* [heavens], and it seemed watched over by crores of tutelary royal deities (p. 49).

Four pages of widely hyperbolical description of the King's favourite elephant culminate in this outburst:

> And Bana wondered, thinking to himself, "Surely in his creation mountains were used up as atoms, how else could this astonishing majesty have been produced? It is indeed a marvel—a Vindhya with tusks" (p. 56).

The Vindhyas are the dividing range between northern and peninsular India. The description of Harsa himself re-

* Translation by E. B. Cowell and F. W. Thomas.

minds one of Cleopatra's description of Antony ("His face was as the heavens," etc.) multiplied about fifty times both in length and in extravagance. Harsa hears of his father's illness while away on an expedition, and takes prompt measures for the preservation of the old king's life:

> He rinsed his mouth, and conveyed to Brahmins the whole of his regal equipage, jewels and gold and silver to a vast amount.

But his munificence is unavailing, and his father dies. The anguish of his loss, however, is assuaged by the constant attendance of

> Old Brahmins versed in *Sruti, Smriti,* and *Itihasa** . . . approved ascetics well-trained in the doctrine of the Self, sages indifferent to pain and pleasure, Vedantists skilled in expounding the nothingness of the fleeting world, mythologists expert in allaying sorrow (p. 162).

The pictures of manners, so far as they can be seen through the mists of exaggeration, are most interesting. The writer shows real art in descriptions of swarming life, in which he brings together a hundred animated groups, such as we see in Indian paintings and illuminations. Everywhere throughout the book we seem to be moving among bewildering throngs of multitudinous humanity. And this is, no doubt, mere realism on the author's part, so long as he keeps in check his passion for mythologico-metaphorical aggrandisement, after this fashion:

> The king himself was surprised at his forces, and, casting his eyes in every direction, beheld an army starting out of its encampment, in appearance like the animate world tumbling at an aeon's

---

* *Sruti*—revelations. *Smriti*—authoritative writings, not revealed. *Itihasa*—histories.

commencement from Vishnu's belly, the ocean overflooding the world in a stream from Agastya's mouth, the Narmada's flood rolling a thousand rills after being dammed and let loose again by Arjuna's thousand arms (p. 206).

Bana's most stupendous effort, however, is the statement that the Commander-in-Chief, Skandagupta, had "a nose as long as his sovereign's pedigree." This is singled out by Mr. Vincent Smith as "the most grotesque simile in all literature"—and certainly it would be hard to beat.

When we pass from epic to drama, we escape from the atmosphere of systematic inflation and contortion. Here the imagination can move healthfully and at ease, instead of passing through epilepsy to paralysis. The dramatic form imposed strict limits upon fantasy, since it was impossible to show heroes fighting with sixty thousand foemen at once, or hurling mountain peaks, or cleaving one flying arrow with another, to say nothing of performing the same feat with hundreds of shafts simultaneously. The magic of the epics so infinitely surpassed all possible magic of the stage, that playwrights made no attempt to reproduce it. But even the dialogue, in which, of course, hyperbole would have been possible, is comparatively free from it.* The drama, in fact, is a culture-product, marked, in many cases, by real grace and charm. The testimony of a cloud of witnesses proclaims Kalidasa to be a great poet; and though his *Sak-*

* There seems to have been in the dramatic period a real reaction against monstrosity, not merely due to the conditions of presentation. In the *Uttara Rama Cheritra* of Bhavabhuti, a large part of the Ramayana is summarised in a series of pictures supposed to be viewed by Rama, Sita and Lakshman. It would have been easy, in the description of these pictures, to pile up the marvels after the epic manner; but the temptation is, on the whole, resisted. So, too, in the description by "Aerial Spirits" of the fight between Lava and Chandraketu, supposed to be proceeding behind the scenes, the hyperboles, though tremendous, are judiciously vague.

untala may not seem quite to justify Goethe's ecstatic quatrain, it is undoubtedly an exquisite fairy-tale. *The Toy-
Cart,* again, is a spirited novel in dialogue, really interesting as a more or less credible picture of manners: *Malati
and Madhava* is a wild but picturesque romance, playing
around the horrors of human sacrifice; *Retnavali* is a comedy of intrigue, in which disguise and mistaken identity are
employed with a recklessness not without parallel, perhaps,
in the Spanish and Elizabethan theatre; and several other
plays are like anticipations of Lope or Calderon in their
most romantic and rhetorical moods. Of any influence proceeding from the Attic drama I can find no trace. The
mere fact that anything like tragedy is undreamed of in
India ought surely to negative that hypothesis.

But, with all its human qualities, the Hindu drama remains a curiously undeveloped art-form. In point of quantity it is meagre as compared with the dramatic literature
of either the West or the Far East, not more than three
plays being attributed to any one writer. As its heroes all
speak in Sanskrit, it can never have been understanded of
the people, but must have been mainly, if not exclusively, a
court diversion. There are traces, indeed, of a vernacular
drama in comparatively early times, but it never took literary form; and though folk-plays on epic subjects (with
wicker-work giants and demons) are common to this day,
India has never developed a theatre—I mean a form of
building adapted to her form of drama. The Greek, the
English, the Spanish, the Chinese, the Japanese dramas, all
housed themselves in appropriate edifices, in relation to
which they developed a special technic; but the Indian drama
seems never to have had even a stage of its own.* Though
critics minutely analysed and classified its devices and ef-

* The Indian theatre of to-day is frankly copied from the ordinary
European theatre.

fects, it remained fluid to the point of formlessness, accepting every possible convention, scorning all restrictions of time and place, and demanding of the playwright no skill in construction, no labour of condensation.

This might conceivably have been a merit rather than a defect. It is, perhaps, a mere Western prejudice which leads us to value the dramatist's art in proportion to its difficulty, and admire the technical skill with which he concentrates into two or three hours of time, and two or three definite points of space, the culmination of a long life-history or the disastrous on-rush of a mighty passion. Theorists are not wanting who argue that our endeavours to minimize the element of convention in drama, and limit the necessity for make-believe, are all a mistake; and even if we cannot go so far as this, we can readily grant it to be possible that a form of drama which abandoned all idea of illusion might profit by its liberty and produce remarkable effects. But I do not think that the Indian drama can be cited in support of this contention. Along with the fluidity of form goes a no less notable fluidity of spirit. The element of will, in which some critics see the very essence of drama, and which is certainly the mainspring of most of the great dramas of the world, is conspicuously absent from Indian plays. Nowhere do we find a great character at odds with destiny, or a great passion sweeping everything before it, like a glistering lava stream. Nowhere do we find energetic determination indomitably compassing its ends,* or, it may be, baffled and broken by superior cunning, or virtue, or might. The personages of Indian drama are always the

---

* One play, *Mudra rakshasa*, may perhaps be quoted as an exception to this rule. It deals with the stratagems whereby Chanakya, the Brahmin minister of Chandragupta, wins over a rival politician to his side. It is more dramatic in the European sense of the word than any other Indian play known to me.

sport of circumstances or of capricious supernatural powers. Take, for instance, the *Sakuntala*. More than a third
of the play is occupied with the idyllic love-making of hero
and heroine. Then, after their "Gandharvan" marriage,
an ascetic, irritated by some fancied neglect on Sakuntala's
part, decrees that King Dushyanta shall lose all memory
of his marriage until it is recalled to his mind by the sight
of a signet ring which he has given to Sakuntala. On her
way to Dushyanta's palace, Sakuntala chances to drop the
ring into a stream, and is consequently disowned by her
husband. Does she, then, do anything, make any effort to
counteract these unhappy chances, the angering of the *rishi*
and the loss of the ring? Or does anybody make any effort
on her behalf? Not at all. She is wafted away to some
agreeable retreat by a friendly nymph; the ring is recovered
in a fish's maw, and brought to Dushyanta; and then, either
by pure chance or by divine intervention—at any rate,
without any effort of his own—he comes upon the child
Sakuntala has borne him, recognizes him by the help of the
voix du sang and other evidences, and is finally reunited to
Sakuntala herself. This is, as I have said, a pretty fairy-
tale, but it is entirely lacking in that exercise of volition
which might have made it a drama. Compare it with Shake-
speare's *All's well that ends well*, of which the theme is not
quite dissimilar. The means which Helena takes to impose
her will on the recalcitrant Bertram are improbable and repellent, but they are dramatic. She makes a determined
struggle to obtain her ends; she is resolutely active, while
Sakuntala (like everybody else in the play) is as passive as
a leaf on a stream. The Indian poem is incomparably the
more beautiful of the two; but if it be drama at all, it is
the drama of passivity, which is, to the European mind, a
contradiction in terms. Does not "drama" mean "thing
done"?

In *Vikrama and Urvasi*, another of Kalidasa's plays, the plot again turns on a sage's curse; again the *voix du sang* contributes to the solution; and again the characters are the passive puppets of supernatural wire-pulling. The *Uttara Rama Cheritra*, which deals with Rama's repudiation of Sita because popular rumour casts suspicion on her conduct during her captivity in Lanka, offers a good instance of the Indian playwright's practice of skipping over the very crisis in which character displays itself. One would think that the interest of such a subject would lie in the struggle in Rama's soul between his love for Sita and his fancied duty to his people. But, as a matter of fact, no such struggle occurs.* The moment the popular slander is reported to him, he decides to cast her off, though a fiery ordeal has long ago removed from his own mind all doubt of her innocence.

Durmukha.   Must she . . . be banished hence
            To please a thankless and malignant people?
Rama.   Nay, blame them not . . . For who that witnessed not
            The wondrous test of purity could credit
            Such marvels in a distant region wrought?†

And this is the divine hero of the Indian people, the seventh avatar of Vishnu! It is noteworthy, too, that the playwright entirely omits to present to us Sita's discovery of the heartless stratagem whereby she has been lured away, without leave-taking, from the court of Ayodhya. It almost seems as though opportunities for the active manifestation of character were systematically avoided.

In assuming character-in-action to be the essence of

* Though there is no struggle there is plenty of lamentation. It may be noted that the Indian dramatic hero, even Rama himself, is very much given to fainting at critical moments.

† Translation by H. H. Wilson; *Theatre of the Hindus*, Vol. I., p. 309.

drama, I may appear to be insisting on an arbitrary point of æsthetic definition; but that is not really so. India has, no doubt, a perfect right to define mimetic art in her own way. She owes no deference either to the Greek word "drama," or to the European conception which it embodies. My point is psychological, not æsthetic. A people which leaves out of its drama the element of will, probably does so because the element of will plays no efficient part in its life. And is not this just the key to Indian history? Hinduism, as a popular religion, consists in the cult of a monstrous folk-lore, oppressing and paralysing the imagination, and showing human beings as the passive playthings of stupendous and multitudinous gods, demigods and demons. What avails the human will in a world which is entirely at the mercy of magical influences, in which courage is useless without an appropriate *mantra*, and resolution impotent against an inauspicious star? Hinduism, as a philosophy, preaches the unreality of the material world, detachment from terrestrial interests, and the unimportance of the life of the moment as compared with the endless chain of past and future existences—all doctrines which tend directly to the enfeeblement of volitional individuality. Is it not this passivity of mental habit, mirrored in the drama, that has, time out of mind, left India at the mercy of strong-willed races from without, until they have, in their turn, yielded to the creeping paralysis?

THE INFLUENCE OF ISLAM: ARCHITECTURE.

From the year 1000 onwards, until the coming of the sea-borne races from Western Europe, all these strong-willed invaders were of the Muslim faith. Now Muhammadanism was theoretically, and to some extent practically, inimical to art. It carried its hatred of graven images to the point of violent iconoclasm, and thus did all it could, practically as well as theoretically, to discourage sculpture. Its principles do not seem to have prohibited drama, for we hear of Muhammadan miracle-plays; but neither in India nor elsewhere did it produce anything notable in the way of dramatic literature. Perhaps its fatalism was unfavourable to the art of the struggling will; perhaps its sanction of polygamy excluded the conflicts of passion on which the European theatre so largely subsists.* A people which declines to idealize the emotions of sex cuts itself off from half the great themes of the world's drama. In narrative or lyric poetry, I cannot discover that Indian literature owes much to Muslim inspiration. But in two great arts—namely, architecture and painting—the influence of Islam was, it seems to me, conspicuous and beneficent.

Here one treads on dangerous ground. Mr. Havell and the sturdy little phalanx of India-worshippers are fiercely contemptuous of the slightest hint that India is indebted to outside influences for any of her artistic perfections. Every architectural form was independently developed in India. If anything can be proved to have come from Persia or Arabia, it had, in the first instance, been borrowed by Persia or Arabia from India, which was thus simply reclaiming its own. Hindu builders introduced the symbolism of their own creed into the details even of Muslim mosques and mausoleums. A preponderance of patently-Muhammadan names on the rolls of the craftsmen employed upon famous edifices has no terrors for Mr. Havell. He probably assumes that most of them were Muslimized Hindus; though this explanation seems hardly compatible with his tracing of the decline

---

* This would also in part account for the comparative scantiness, and nervelessness of Hindu drama. Several comedies such as *Retnavali*, *Malavikagnimitra*, and *Viddha Salabhankija* turn upon a Rani's unavailing opposition to the entrance of a new favourite into the Raja's senana.

of architecture under Aurungzeb to that emperor's dismis-
sal of all craftsmen who were not true believers.* If a Muslimized Hindu retained his racial genius under Shah Jahan,
it is not clear why he should have lost it under Aurungzeb.
I do not presume, however, to controvert Mr. Havell's eager
arguments on points on which he is learned and I very ignorant. Nor do I doubt that he is right in vindicating for
Hindu craftsmanship a very large share in the triumphs of
Muhammadan architecture and decoration. All I say is that
he does not succeed in arguing away—or, rather, that he
seems to ignore—the cardinal fact that wherever we find in
India a building of remarkable beauty or (if I may so phrase
it) of rational magnificence, it is almost certain to be distinc-
tively Muhammadan. Among religious edifices, I can think
of no exception to this rule. The exceptions that occur to
me are certain Hindu palaces, chiefly in Rajputana, from
which, however, Muslim and even European influences are
by no means excluded.

The giant temples of Southern India are no doubt marvels
of massive construction, and have often a sort of titantic
impressiveness. They seem as though they might have been
built by the *rakshasas* of the Ramayana. But of unity,
clarity, nobility of design they show no trace. Everything
is ponderous, everything is overwrought. Their most prominent features, the pyramidal *gopuras*, or gate-towers,
swarming—one might almost say writhing—with contorted
semi-human figures, are surely as senseless as anything in
architecture. Here and there some individual detail, such
as the colonnade around a sacred tank, may have a certain
beauty; but it is always a mere oasis in a desert of gigan-
tesque barbarism.

When we pass further north, to temples of more moderate
dimensions, we still find the same ponderousness of material,

* *Indian Architecture*, pp. 31 and 37.

the same absence of anything like lightness and grace, the same, or even greater, profusion of incised ornament. It has sometimes seemed to me that the tradition of the rock-cut temple must have had an unfortunate influence on temple-building in general. In the rock-cut temple, massiveness means economy, for it is clear that the more material remains, the less has to be hewn away. In constructed buildings, on the contrary, any superfluity of mass is sheer waste, both of material and of labour; yet it often seems as though Indian architects aimed at piling as many tons of stone as possible on a given plot of ground, in order to make it look as though the building were not pieced together, but carved out of the living rock. I do not state this as a definite theory, but merely to illustrate the impression left on my mind by a certain order of Indian temple. The sense of heaviness is partly due, no doubt, to the total absence of the radiating arch and dome, and the universal prevalence of the arch (if so it can be called) and dome constructed of horizontal layers of masonry, each layer projecting a little beyond that on which it rests. This system of construction is defended as eliminating the strain from the outward thrust of the true arch. So it does, no doubt; but it also eliminates the beautiful curve of the arch and the soaring majesty of the dome, while it permits of the incrustation on all constructive features of a reckless redundancy of ornament. Is it mere prejudice that prevents one from taking any pleasure in deeply-incised decoration upon columns and other portions of a building which ought to suffer no diminution of their strength, and which permit of this erosion only because they are massive out of all proportion to structural requirements?

The most prevalent external feature of Hindu temples in middle and northern India is a cluster of elongated cupolas, suggested, I suppose, by the form of the primitive reed hut

NAVIGATION ON THE GANGES. (A Raft of Inflated Nilghau Skins.)

of Bengal. Most of these excrescences correspond to no internal feature, and are in no way impressive either individually or in their grouping. They are less barbarous, perhaps, than the *gopuras* of the south, but scarcely more beautiful.

The self-defeating wastefulness of Hindu architecture is nowhere more conspicuous than in the Dilwarra Temples (Jain) at Mount Abu, dating from the eleventh and twelfth centuries. Externally they are of small account; internally they might be exquisitely beautiful if (perhaps) a twentieth part of the labour expended on chiselling and undercutting their white marble had been judiciously applied to reasonable ornament. As it is, they are almost incredible marvels of insensate over-elaboration. I should be disposed, in the face of a great array of authorities, to apply the same criticism to the famous Towers of Victory at Chitor. The labour lavished on them seems to me quite incommensurate with the effect achieved; but as I visited them hurriedly, when twilight was falling, I was perhaps unduly unimpressed.

To turn from Hindu to Muhammadan architecture is to enter another world. As chance would have it, I passed with scarcely a pause by the way from the sinister gloom of Madura to the grace and refinement of Ahmedabad. Never shall I forget the impression made upon me by the exquisite marble traceries in Sidi Sayyid's mosque and at the tomb of Shah Alam. It was my first encounter with this wonderful art of piercing thin sheets of marble in designs of inexhaustible variety; and I was scarcely more delighted with its beauty than with its appropriateness, in giving air along with jewelled light to the shady spaces of mosque and tomb. Here Mr. Havell agrees with me; but he, of course, claims all the merit for Hinduism. "In this class of window tracery," he says, "India stands alone; it is a purely Indian de-

velopment of the sculptor's craft having its origin in the
Hindu temple tradition. It owed nothing to Persian art:
the best Ahmedabad tracery shows no Persian influence."
This may very likely be so; I would not, even if I could,
argue the point, for I am in no way concerned to dispute
the artistic capacity of the Hindu as a man. All I say is
that the Hindu as a Hindu—in his temple architecture—
has produced nothing one tithe as beautiful as this marble
tracery. It is common in Muhammadan buildings: I never
saw it in a Hindu building; and as Mr. Havell cites no specimen from Hindu buildings, we may pretty safely assume
that none exists. What does it matter, then, whose hand
held the chisel, or whether certain elements in the design can
or can not be traced to extra-Indian sources? The essential and undeniable fact is that Muhammadanism begot these
things of beauty. It begot them very likely out of Hindu
craftsmanship, though there is evidence of a considerable
importation of foreign craftsmen. The one thing certain
is that, however large a part we may assign to the Hindu
genius, it was restrained, chastened, rationalized, human-
ized, by Muhammadan influence, which was thus the determining factor in the case. And in my judgment it was the
determining factor, not only in these marble traceries, but in
almost all that is truly noble and beautiful in the architecture of India.

This is to say a great deal: for India is a veritable fairyland of exquisite architecture. Wherever the Muslim has
firmly planted himself, beautiful domes and minarets have
sprung up, stately halls of sepulture, and marvellous log-
gias and arcades. The palaces of Agra, of Delhi, of Lahore, in the days of their glory, must have thrown utterly
into the shade anything that Europe had to show in the
way of sheer loveliness of material and design. To the European eye, indeed, their beauty is somewhat discounted by

the fact that, when our Western imagination wants to body
forth fairyland, on the stage or in book illustration, it generally goes to Muslim India for its motives. Thus the gardens and the fountains, the porticos, the baths and the di-
wans, of the Mogul palaces have to us an air of theatrical
unreality. We find it difficult to dissociate them from our
memories of the Arabian Nights, and to imagine them ten-
anted by real people. Their very perfection of detail is
cloying. They suggest, not only unbridled luxury, but ef-
feminacy and decadence. If, however, we put aside fortui-
tous association and moral suggestion, and are content with
visual, sensuous beauty, we cannot but admit that Alad-
din's genie could not possibly have conjured up anything
more enchanting. For grandeur, again, we may turn to the
Jumma Musjid at Delhi, to Humayun's Tomb, to the Buland
Darwaza at Fatehpur Sikri, to the great buildings of Bijapur, and a score of other famous sites. The Muslim habit
of raising mosques and tombs on magnificent plinths or
platforms gives them an extraordinary nobility of effect.
The Taj Mahal itself, that

> Fabric of enchantment, hewn
> From lucent quarries of the moon,
> Or curdled by some thaumaturge
> From lace-like foam of southern surge,
> From earliest drift of blossom-spray,
> And star-lit snows of Himalay—

—the Taj itself owes a great part of its impressiveness to
the art with which it is enthroned on the margent of the
Jumna, and sequestered by its plinth, its sentinel minarets,
its garden and its majestic gateways, from all prosaic and
commonplace contiguities.

The share of the purely Indian genius in all these wonderful achievements is an interesting question, to be deter-

mined—if it can ever be determined—by close investigation
on the part of technical experts. One would have no hesitation in accepting Mr. Havell's judgment on the point,
were he not manifestly biased by theosophical convictions.
His all-pervading note of impassioned special-pleading is
sufficient in itself to awaken scepticism. For my part, however, I readily grant that it would be absurd to look upon
Muslim architecture in India as something essentially foreign, in the glory of which India herself had no share. Hindu
influences on Muslim building are often patent to the most
cursory observer. At Fatehpur Sikri, for instance—that
unburied Pompeii of the East—the prevailing style is essentially Hindu. So, too, in that exquisite structure, Dada
Harir's well at Ahmedabad, there is nothing characteristically Muslim—except moderation and good taste. It may
even be that Mr. Havell is right in maintaining that the
Muhammadans brought with them scarcely any form or
method that had not been independently evolved in India.
That, I say, is possible, if not very probable. But were it
proved beyond all question, it would not alter the fact that
where Indians built under Muhammadan influence they built
nobly, exquisitely and rationally; where they built under the
inspiration of their own mythology, they built, often won-
derfully, but almost always heavily, gloomily, barbarously,
and irrationally. The Muslim prohibition of the human
figure in decoration, and the austere, almost puritan, simplicity of the ritual of Islam, were much-needed correctives of
Hindu over-luxuriance in ornament and monstrosity in the
conception and adumbration of the divine. I am no ardent
admirer of Islam; but the glory of its architecture—much
of it due to princes of more than doubtful orthodoxy—is a
patent, palpable fact, which proves what India can do when
it awakes from the hallucinations of *yoga* and the multitudinous nightmares of its indigenous cults.

[244]

PAINTING.

Indian painting, though discussed with the same fury of partisanship as Indian sculpture, is in truth a very much simpler matter. It is a comparatively modern art. The famous Buddhist frescoes in the caves of Ajanta, indeed, date from the sixth and seventh centuries of our era; but they are an isolated phenomenon. Judging from the copies at South Kensington, one would be inclined to see in them the beginnings of a bolder, freer, more virile art than has ever, in fact, been developed in India. They show vigour without violence, and a certain sense of composition. If their colour, in the reproductions, is not very pleasing, I presume we must allow for the effects of age, and for the peculiar conditions of light under which they were intended to be viewed. How it happens that they stand alone—that they seem to have sprung from nothing and led to nothing—historians must explain if they can. Was painting neglected because sculpture, as the more laborious, was considered the more meritorious art? I cannot tell. India is the home of arrested developments and promises unfulfilled. There are only too many analogies to the abortive impulse which has left its traces at Ajanta.

Apart from these frescoes, Indian painting is a late and post-Muhammadan development. It does not seem that anything of importance has come down to us of an earlier date than the sixteenth century. Heaven forbid that I should commit myself to any theory of foreign influence; but as a matter of historic fact, painting was mainly cultivated at the courts of the Mogul emperors, and of Rajput and other princes, during the Mogul period. It is thus not primarily a religious art, but concerns itself largely with historic scenes, martial and ceremonial, in substance not unlike the illustrations of royal progresses, investitures, marriages, reviews, drawing-rooms, etc., so familiar in the illustrated papers of to-day. There are also many episodes of princely domesticity, hunting-scenes, and the like. Where religion is touched upon, so far as I have observed, it is usually the sensual-sentimental cult of Krishna that provides the inspiration.

What, then, are the general characteristics of this whole body of work? They are wonderful illuminative richness, extraordinary delicacy of draughtsmanship in miniature, great beauty of decorative detail, a certain power of lending animation to scenes of swarming life, but withal a total inability to escape from a laborious convention, to attain freedom and breadth of design, to suggest to the imagination anything more than is presented to the eye. The absence or gross imperfection of perspective throws everything upon one plane, and forbids any gradation of tone, any play of light and shade. There are, no doubt, certain night scenes in which firelight or torchlight is employed to produce what are commonly called Rembrandtesque effects; but there is no depth, no mystery about them—at most a certain hard and limited cleverness. They are an agreeable change from the relentless glitter of military and ceremonial pageantry, and they are interesting as showing a feeling-forth towards something outside the dominant convention. But though they may be great by Indian standards, by world-standards they remain small.

Just as "monstrous" is the epithet that constantly forces itself upon us in dealing with Hindu sculpture, so "miniature" is the term from which there is no escape in the discussion of Indian painting. If Florentine art had stopped short at Pinturicchio and Benozzo Gozzoli, and if these painters had habitually worked on the scale of portfolio illuminations, then Florentine art and Indian art would have stood somewhere on the same level. The Indian paint-

er, at his best, is a consummate miniaturist. Nothing can
exceed the delicacy and beauty of the best Mogul portraiture, though even here the sitter is usually presented in flat
profile, and we feel that the painter's mastery moves within
very narrow limits. I am very far, however, from denying
the charm of this style of art. I would not even make any
large deduction from Mr. Havell's praise of certain examples of the school: "With all the sincerity, truthfulness,
and perfect finish of the old Dutch and Flemish masters,
these drawings have a delicate flavour of their own, a
subtlety and sensitiveness which suggest the music of the
Indian *vina*, or the sonnets of Hafiz or Omar Khayyam."
All I say is that Indian design has never thrown off the
shackles of a somewhat helpless convention. With what a
sense of enlargement and invigoration does one turn from
the graphic arts of India to those of China and Japan!

Though Indian painting is, as a rule, worldly rather than
other-worldly, it must not be supposed that the spiritual
genius of India fails to manifest itself in this form of art.
The Indian landscape-painter, says Mr. Havell, endeavours
"to see with the mind, not merely with the eye . . . and,
above all, to identify himself with the inner consciousness
of the Nature he portrays, and to make manifest the one
harmonious law which governs Nature in all her moods."
And again: "The difference which the European and Anglicized Indian attribute to defective technical powers or undeveloped intellect, is really due to a different intellectual
atmosphere and a different artistic temperament, created by
the different answers which East and West give to the
question—what is reality?" On this contention there are
two remarks to be made. Firstly, the arrest of development
in Indian art seems to be closely paralleled by the arrest of
development in Indian civilization, which can scarcely have
been determined by metaphysical influences, though they

may, no doubt, have contributed to it. Secondly, the Western answer to the question, "What is reality?" would appear to be the right answer from the artist's point of view, if from no other, since it has begotten the superbly vigorous and various painting of Europe, as opposed to the elaborate miniature-work of India. I have seen in a private collection one unfinished painting—I think it represented Aurungzeb with a hunting-party crossing a river by night—which seemed to me a real picture, largely-conceived, imaginative, suggestive. All other Indian paintings that I have come across are more or less elaborate and beautiful illuminations and illustrations.

Art and Character.

There is no more ungracious or unpopular task than the attempt to restore things to reasonable proportions, after they have been exaggerated and distorted by enthusiasm. It is because I think the Hinduizers do a very ill service to India that I have throughout this chapter assumed the part of the devil's-advocate. No nation in the world will ever qualify itself for facing the complexities of the future by idealizing and idolizing its past. No nation will ever make itself valid and self-sufficing by fancying that it is peculiarly favoured by Heaven, an elect people, the depository of inspirations and intuitions not vouchsafed to the rest of mankind. Such illusions may produce a temporary intoxication, and lead to apparent success in some particular crisis. But permanent well-being cannot be founded on illusion.

There is no question whatever that India has splendid artistic capacities. They are manifest even in her worst excesses of architecture, sculpture and epic poetry. Nowhere is it faculty that is lacking: it is restraint, self-criticism, sanity. Where feebleness appears, it is the feebleness

[248]

of exhaustion, the reaction following upon violent overstrain. I see no reason to think (though the question is
really unimportant) that any considerable measure of stimulation reached India from without. It was not stimulation she wanted, it was restraint; and that she received,
often very much to her advantage, from Islamic puritanism.
From Greece, if she can be said to have learned anything,
she did not learn nearly enough. Self-satisfaction was from
the first her besetting sin. As it led to the stereotyping
and sanctifying of all sorts of social abuses, so it led to the
arrest and petrifaction of art, in rudimentary, or at any
rate very undeveloped, stages. We find, therefore, many
powerful and promising artistic beginnings, but (except in
Muhammadan architecture and architectural decoration)
no consummate and perfectly accomplished art. What is
entirely lacking in the art history of India is "der nie zu-
friedene Geist der stets auf Neues sinnt." In other countries artistic movements germinate, ripen, culminate and
decay; in India they do not ripen, but are checked before
they have even approached maturity.

All this, of course, is shocking heresy in the eyes of the
enthusiasts. And why? Because they have fallen under
India's illusion, and have persuaded themselves that art inspired by transcendental Truth must be the greatest art
in the world.* But India's truth, if it were true—and it is
neither more nor less true than any other expression of the
inexpressible—would be destructive to art. It is only in so
far as India ignores her own truth, and accepts, provision-
ally, the real existence of the visible universe, that she pos-
sesses any art at all. Nor is it probable that her artists,

* "If India took this from here, that from there, so did Greece, so
did Italy; but out of what she took came higher ideals than Greece
ever dreamt of, and things of beauty that Italy never realised." E. B.
Havell, *Indian Sculpture and Painting*, p. 169.

as a class, troubled themselves about transcendental Truth. They seem to have been highly contented with the surface aspects of the tropical jungle of folk-lore which they regarded as revelation.

The apotheosis of Indian art has aptly coincided with a tendency to depreciate the accepted values of the West. Europe is a little tired of her own accomplishment, and oppressed, it may be, by the very mass of her achievement. But though this transient weariness is natural enough, and is, indeed, only a symptom of that divine discontent which saves Western art from stagnant self-complacency, it must not be suffered entirely to upset our sense of proportion. The plain truth is that if all the great masterpieces of European sculpture, painting, epic and dramatic literature, were destroyed, Europe would, still, in virtue of its works of the second and third order, be incomparably richer than India in products of artistic genius. In architecture alone can India put forward a really plausible claim to equality, and then not with Europe as a whole, but rather with a single region or a single school. If it be said that the confrontation is not fair, inasmuch as it pits a country against a continent, I reply, firstly, that it is not I, but the India-worshippers who challenge the comparison, secondly, that India is as large and populous as all Western Europe, and is never tired of asserting the greater antiquity of her civilization.

What is the inmost secret, when all is said and done, of the radical inferiority of Indian art? Does it not lie in the almost total lack of strong and individual human character? Why have the Indian epics taken no hold upon the imagination of the world at large? Simply because Rama and Sita and Lakshman, Arjuna and Yudishthira, Drona and Karna, Kunti and Draupadi, are not human beings, but clockwork idols, moving in an atmosphere of magic. It is by devotion that they are endowed with a semblance of life for their

[250]

Indian worshippers. For those who cannot approach them with devotion, they do not live at all. And this lack of human individuality is curiously manifest in the types assigned to them in painting and sculpture. Nothing can be more insipid and characterless than the epic heroes as represented whether in ancient or in modern art.* It is wonderful, as I have already remarked, how hieratic convention has succeeded in blinding Indian·artists to the splendid types of humanity they see every day around them.

If we compare classic antiquity with Indian antiquity, is it not manifest that the fundamental difference lies in the wealth of the one, the poverty of the other, in individual human character, mythic and historical? Greek epic and drama is one glorious pageant of strong individualities; Greek and Roman history is so obviously a battleground of great men, that historians have often neglected to look behind the protagonists, and study the social and economic forces they represented; Greek and Roman sculpture, even in its ideal aspects, pre-supposes a profound knowledge of reality, and has, moreover, left us such abundant treasures of consummate portraiture that the statesmen and generals of antiquity, from Pericles to the Antonines, are almost as familiar to us as the celebrities of our own age. What a contrast is presented by the corresponding period in India! The heroes of epic and drama are shadowy and conventional when they are not monstrous; and as for the leading figures of real life, only a few of them are known to us even by name, not one by portraiture. To the splendid procession of Greek and Roman worthies, we can only oppose a sha-

---

* Note, for instance, the smooth pretti-prettiness of the heroic types in the otherwise charming illustrations provided by the Tagore school of art for the *Myths of the Hindus and Buddhists*. Abanindro Nath Tagore himself gives his "Buddha as Mendicant" great nobility of character—but the type is European.

dowy Chandragupta, an Asoka to be laboriously reconstruc-
ted from his graven edicts, a vague Kanishka and Vikramaditya. It may be said that there must have been strong
men in India, as elsewhere, but that it was not the habit of
the people to write histories or carve portraits. They are
empty names to us, "carent quia vate sacro." But why was
history not written? Why was portraiture neglected?

A complete answer to these questions would be a complete
psychology of the Indian people. Briefly, I think we must
attribute the facts to the general undervaluing in religion
and philosophy of will and endeavour. Life was conceived
as a shoreless expanse in which generations rose and fell as
helplessly and purposely as waves in mid-ocean. Passivity, detachment, the inhibition of will, was the summit alike
of wisdom and virtue. Men had to be argued into activity,
as Krishna, in the Bhagavat-Gita, exhorts Arjuna not to
take the doctrine of detachment too literally. Virtue, much
talked of, consisted in ceremonial observances and obedience
to the rules of caste. Energy, strenuousness, were of no
avail; for since life, by hypothesis, was not worth living, to
labour for its betterment was futile, if not impious. Kings,
indeed, were flattered and adulated; but even a king was
only, as it were, a foam-fleck on the crest of a wave, conspicuous for a moment, but with many obscure existences behind
him, and many others, no doubt, awaiting him in the future.
Thus the individual life was in every way dwarfed and de-
preciated, the cultivation of individual character discouraged, and its recognition impeded. Something like this, I
conceive, must be our explanation of the amazing lack of
character in Indian history and art. It may almost be said
that, down to the coming of the Moguls, India had contributed only one great character, Gautama Buddha, to the
world's pantheon—and he, perhaps, never existed. If a

claim be put in for Asoka, it may possibly be allowed; but, after all, how featureless he is!

And when we pass from antiquity to medieval and modern times, is not the contrast almost as striking? European history, literature and art swarm, above everything, with great characters. Where are the Indian Charlemagne and Alfred, Columbus and Luther, Cromwell, Richelieu and Napoleon? Against a score of such master spirits, India may advance one figure who certainly stands in the front rank of historic rulers: the great, the enlightened, the truly heroic Akbar—grandson of a Tartar conqueror. After him came a few individualities of the second rank—the romantic voluptuary Shah Jahan, the tragic zealot Aurungzeb, Sivaji, the typical Maratha chief, Hyder Ali, the daring adventurer, and perhaps a dozen other men of notable political or military talent. But when we have named the Buddha and the Akbar, we have exhausted the list of supreme personalities whom India has given to history.

As for fictitious characters—and they indicate the genius of a race almost as clearly as real personages—where are we to look for the Indian Hamlet or Falstaff, Shylock or Lear, the Indian Quixote, the Indian Alceste or Tartuffe, Don Juan, Mephistopheles or Peer Gynt? Or if, again, we turn to the portrayal of character in colour, is it possible for a moment to compare the charming miniature portraits of the Mogul period with the superb records of commanding personalities left by Raphael, Titian, Velasquez, Holbein, Rembrandt, Vandyke, Reynolds and a host of other European artists? At whatever point we institute a comparison, we find India deficient in the record, at any rate, of strong, energetic, dominant personality. However imperfect may be our analysis of the causes of this depression of will and energy, the fact can scarcely be contested; and India would do well to realize and reflect upon it.

[253]

Music.

There remains one art of which nothing has yet been said, and of which, in the absence of technical knowledge, I can at best speak vaguely. There is an undeniable and penetrating charm about Indian music. The fine artists, whom I have been so fortunate as to hear, can produce delightful effects from their very picturesque stringed instruments— *cithar, sarangi* and *vina*. I was especially struck with the way in which they could make the strings almost literally speak, coaxing from them plaintive utterances which, with one's eyes shut, one could almost believe to proceed from the human voice. The pieces I heard appeared to me to be composed of fragments of melody akin to the folk-songs of Europe, but developed on wholly different rhythmic principles. I have not the least doubt that Indian music is a most interesting, highly-subtilized and elaborated science, though on some of the claims put forward on its behalf—such as the power of painting landscapes, which can be quite definitely visualized by the initiated—one may beg leave to maintain an attitude of suspended judgment. I very sincerely take on trust a great many refinements and excellences which cannot be fully apprehended without a special education: just as I take on trust the verbal beauties both of Sanskrit and of vernacular poetry. Yet in music, it seems to me, we have the final, irrefragable proof that the Western mind has decisively outgrown the Eastern, has embraced a wider range of experience, and touched greater heights and—I do not hesitate to say—deeper depths of thought. Once more, it is a mere denial of all sense of proportion to institute any serious comparison between the two forms of art—to place the delicate tinklings of Indian melody beside the titanic harmonies of Handel and Haydn, Beethoven and Wagner. The triumphs of imagination

[254]

which the epic poets sought to attain by force of hyperbolical arithmetic; the miracles of intuition which the sages hoped to achieve by *yoga*; these, and far greater triumphs and miracles, are nightly compassed in the European concert-room, by the mightiest *rishis* the world ever saw, through the medium of that divinest of human inventions, the modern orchestra. It is very possible that Indian music has delicacies and exquisitenesses which escape our grosser ears; but it is, I suggest, absolutely impossible that the little threads of sound plucked daintily out of the *cithar* or *vina* can betoken any approach to the grasp of mind that weaves, from a thousand filaments of passion, and wonder, and ecstasy and despair, the celestial tissues of the European symphony.

I unfeignedly regret, in conclusion, the controversial and even depreciatory tone of this chapter. Had it been written twenty years ago, its tenor would have been very different. One could then have dwelt with warm appreciation on the numberless beauties of Indian art; one could have noted, without insistence, its obvious defects of exaggeration, excess and monstrosity, and one need not have embarked upon disobliging and quite unnecessary comparisons. The intelligent Indian has undoubtedly a great deal to be proud of in the artistic past of his country. Even its barbarisms are magnificent, while its sane achievements are often of exquisite, sometimes of unique, beauty. Far be it from me to deny that India is, from the artistic point of view, one of the most interesting countries in the world. Her art contributed potently to the spell she cast upon me, but for which this book would never have been written. But when the intelligent Indian is assured that, in almost every branch of artistic activity, his country, by express favour of the gods, stands supreme over all the world, one can only advise him, in his own interest, not to believe it. That way lies—well, not sanity; and sanity is essential to India's salvation.

[255]

IX

NEVER-ENDING are the discussions as to what India ought to learn, and how that knowledge should be imparted to her. But it is much more vital to ascertain what India will consent to unlearn. Upon the answer to that question her future depends.

Someone—is it Sir Alfred Lyall?—tells of an Indian who was thoroughly versed in the mathematics of astronomy, and could calculate eclipses many years ahead, but who confessed that he still believed, and should teach his son, that eclipses were caused by a dog eating the moon. Nothing could be more characteristic.* Indians have an amazing capacity for learning, and for ignoring the consequences of what they learn. They will admit that, for the outer world, two and two make four, but they pin their actual faith to the sages of old whose subtler genius assured them that two and two made five. Not till India has unlearnt this habit of mind will the day of her true greatness dawn.

Many people hold that the worst error of our rule has been the effort to substitute European for Oriental education. This I cannot believe. Our error—our inevitable error, since we knew no better—lay in introducing bad education instead of good. We gave what we had, and it

---

* "A schoolmaster once tried to convince his pupils that the earth goes round the sun. 'Now, do you believe it?' he asked. 'Yes, as long as we are in the class-room.'" James Kennedy, I.C.S., in *Asiatic Quarterly Review*, October, 1910.

was better than nothing; but it was not what the situation really wanted. James Darmesteter put the case accurately, a quarter of a century ago, in his *Lettres sur l'Inde*, when he said that the instruction given by England to India was "superficial and empty, not of set political purpose, but because European instruction in general, and English in particular, was itself superficial and empty."

It is the fashion to denounce Macaulay as the evil genius of Indian education, because he turned the scale in favour of European matter and methods. Let us see what was the actual character of his intervention.

MACAULAY's MINUTE.

A clause in the Charter Act of 1813 empowered the Governor-General in Council to apply one lakh of rupees a year "to the revival and improvement of literature and the encouragement of the learned natives of India, and for the introduction and promotion of a knowledge of the sciences among the inhabitants of the British territories in India." On the face of it, this is a grant for the promotion of Eastern literature and Western science; and at first the money was used in the payment of stipends to students of Oriental subjects. It does not appear that the teaching of science was seriously attempted—perhaps because it pre-supposed on the student's part a knowledge of English, or some other European tongue. But by 1835, when Macaulay was Chairman of the Committee of Public Instruction, it became evident that a great development of education was impending, and a lively controversy arose as to whether it should be predominantly Eastern in its substance and methods, or predominantly Western. The Orientalizers had on their side the plain meaning of the words of the Charter; but Macaulay was not the man to let the literal interpretation of a document stand in the way of what he considered common sense and sound policy. As his famous Minute is not very easily accessible, I may quote some of its most characteristic passages:

I never found one among [the Orientalists] who could deny that a single shelf of a good European library was worth the whole native literature of India and Arabia. . . .

The question now before us is simply whether, when it is in our power to teach [English] we shall teach languages in which, by universal confession, there are no books on any subject which deserve to be compared with our own; whether, when we can teach European science, we shall teach systems which, by universal confession, whenever they differ from those of Europe, differ for the worse; and whether, when we can patronize sound Philosophy and true History, we shall countenance, at the public expense, medical doctrines which would disgrace an English farrier—Astronomy which would move laughter in the girls at an English boarding-school—History abounding with kings thirty feet high and reigns thirty thousand years long—and Geography made up of seas of treacle and seas of butter. . . .

We are forced to pay our Arabic and Sanskrit students, while those who learn English are willing to pay us. . . .

It is confessed that a language is barren of useful knowledge. We are told to teach it because it is fruitful of monstrous superstitions. We are to teach false history, false astronomy, false medicine, because we find them in company with false religion.

There are faults of excess and faults of emphasis in this pronouncement; but it is absurd to talk of the mischief wrought by Macaulay's "blighting rhetoric." Such language can be held only by those who think that England ought to have perpetuated her empire in India by keeping the people entirely ignorant of Western political ideas. Even supposing that this would have been desirable (which

[258]

I do not believe) it would certainly have been impossible. Not in India alone, but all the world over, the day of the ring-fence is for ever past. We might have hindered the percolation of ideas; we could not have prevented it. For the material development of the country, by means of the railroad and the telegraph, a *lingua-franca* was indispensable; and if some other language than English (say Hindustani) had been chosen for the purpose, Western books would have been translated into that language, and discontent would have spread just as surely, though we should probably have known less about it. The people who denounce Macaulay are logically bound to go a step further, and maintain that the railway, the telegraph and the manufactory ought to have been excluded from India, which should have remained a patch of the Middle Ages in the midst of the modern world—a region where time stood still. I am not aware that any of them has explicitly advanced so impossible a theory; but it seems to be implicit in such a passage as the following from Meredith Townsend's *Asia in Europe*. Mr. Townsend tells us that he was one of those who, in the 'fifties, "bestirred themselves to resist Macaulay's ideas."

They maintained that true instruction would never be gained by an Oriental people through a Western language, that education in English would be productive of nothing but a caste, who, like the "scholars" of the Middle Ages, would be content with their own superiority, and would be more separated from the people than if they had been left uneducated: that, in short, English education, however far it might be pushed, would remain sterile. They pressed for the encouragement and development of indigenous culture, and would have had High Schools and Universities, in which men studied, first of all, to perfect the languages and literature and knowledge of their own land. They

[259]

fought hard, but they failed utterly, and we have the Babu, instead of the thoroughly instructed Pundit.*

It is true that we have the Babu, to carry out a thousand duties of civilization for which the Pundit would have been unfit, even if he would have condescended to them. We also have (a more doubtful blessing) the vakil or pleader; and we have the "failed B.A.," and the successful B.A. who feels himself cruelly wronged because Government does not provide for him the comfortable post to which he thinks he is entitled. English education has had many drawbacks, some of them inevitable, some of them arising from defects in our very idea of education. But who can doubt that in the main Macaulay was right? He may even be said to have "builded better than he knew;" for he laid the foundation of a united India, capable—unless it deliberately misuses its opportunities—of taking its place among the great nations of the world. It is never the intelligent Indian who doubts the benefits of English education. He may resent Macau-

* The sort of instruction which would have held the field had these views prevailed may be estimated from Deussen's account of his visit to the Sanskrit College, at Benares, in 1892: "The various sciences, grammar, law, philosophy, even astronomy and medicine, are here taught in accordance with the ancient native handbooks. The absolute dependence upon Indian antiquity, the solution of every dispute by a reference to the ancient authorities, as well as the discussions of their axioms, remind one strongly of medieval teaching in Europe. Equally medieval is the strict adherence to all sorts of superstitions which both limit and dominate the ideas of learned and intellectual men in a most extraordinary manner." *My Indian Reminiscences*, p. 157. At Madhura Deussen met a pundit who "was a medical man, *i.e.*, he had studied the Ayurveda and had an extensive practice in the neighbourhood. 'What is fever?' I asked him. 'Fever,' he replied, 'is a false mixture of three of the juices of the body, wind, mucus, and bile.' 'And how do you cure it?' Here he glibly rattled off a terrific list of drugs, which, after having been pounded and mixed, were to be administered to the patient." "Ayurvedic remedies" are popular and widely advertised in India.

lay's language, but the justice of his conclusion he knows to be beyond dispute. The only rational objector to English education is he who holds (as Lord Ellenborough held a century ago) that it endangers the eternity of English rule. That it certainly does; but if England desired to hold for ever an empire founded on ignorance and mental stagnation, one could only say, "the less England she."

Statistics.

It was not until 1854 that Macaulay's Minute took full effect, and the existing educational machinery was set in motion. After sixty years have passed, we find that (roughly speaking) "rather more than one male in ten and one female in a hundred can read and write; less than one male in a hundred and one female in a thousand can read and write English."

It is estimated that, in all, about one million Indians have some knowledge of our language. Many of them, no doubt, speak and write it very badly; but the amazing thing, as I have already noted, is that thousands of them have mastered it to absolute perfection. Macaulay, indeed, when he wrote his Minute, was probably influenced by his observation of the extraordinary linguistic faculty so common in India. "It is unusual," he writes, "to find, even in the literary circles of the Continent, any foreigner who can express himself in English with so much facility and correctness as many Hindus." I had made the same remark a hundred times before I came across it in the Minute of 1835.

In the decade of 1902-12 the total number of educational institutions in India increased from about 143,500 to about 176,600, and the number of pupils from 4,530,000 to 6,796,000. The total number of boys under instruction

[261]

rose from 4,084,000 to 5,841,000, or by 43 per cent., and the total number of girls from 446,000 to 955,000, or by 114 per cent. These are at first sight large figures; but they mean that, after a decade of steady increase, only 29 per cent. of boys of school-going age, and 5 per cent. of girls, were receiving any sort of instruction. The total expenditure on education had risen during the decade from £2,681,670 to £5,256,223. About half of this expenditure is met by Government, or by municipalities or local boards. About a quarter is covered by fees,* and the remainder by endowments and subscriptions."†

The Next Move: Vernacular Education.

"In one point," said Macaulay in 1835, "I fully agree with the gentlemen to whose general views I am opposed. I feel with them that it is impossible for us, with our limited means, to attempt to educate the body of the people. We must at present do our best to educate a class who may be interpreters between us and the millions whom we govern." In that we have succeeded; and we now cry out, not without reason, that the intermediary class do not interpret us wisely or fairly. Yet we are preparing, with sublime inconsistency, to multiply tenfold the possible readers of the vernacular press; for the day of universal education is rapidly approaching. What was impossible in 1835 will in all probability be an accomplished fact in

* It is stated that the unwillingness of even the well-to-do classes to pay reasonable fees for their children's schooling seriously retards the progress of education.

† The above figures are taken from the *Statement exhibiting the Moral and Material Progress and Condition of India*, 1911-12. In 1915-16 the number of scholars in all institutions was 7,617,496, of whom 5,871,184 males and 1,112,024 females were in public institutions. The total expenditure on education was in that year £7,338,800.

1935. Mr. Gokhale has drafted a bill by which free and compulsory education would, with all reasonable celerity, be established throughout British India; and though the Government, for financial and other reasons, cannot accept that measure, it stands committed to the principle that lies behind it. In a Resolution issued at Delhi on February 21, 1913, we read: "The propositions that illiteracy must be broken down, and that primary education has, in the present circumstances of India, a predominant claim upon the public funds, represent accepted policy no longer open to discussion." And again: "It is the desire and hope of the Government of India to see in the not distant future some 91,000 private schools added to the 100,000 which already exist for boys, and to double the 4½ millions of pupils who now receive instruction in them." And yet again: "The Government of India hope that the time is not far distant when educational buildings will be distinguished as the most modern and commodious buildings in the locality, and scholars in India will have the advantage in this respect of scholars in the West." Critics of the Government, European as well as Indian, hold that this insistence on buildings merely delays progress. "What ought to happen," says Sir F. S. P. Lely,* "is that the department should assign a master and staff to every village where the people undertake to provide a house. . . . The villagers, if left to themselves, could provide a house at a fraction of what the Government department has to pay . . . the Deputy Inspector having no word in the matter, unless only he found the conditions insanitary." It is not necessary for me to take a side in the discussion, though I think there is something to be said for the Government view, that "the influence for good of clean and well-arranged build-

* *Suggestions for the Better Governing of India*, 1906.

ings,* with the concomitant domestic discipline, can scarcely be exaggerated." The essential fact is that a great movement in the direction of vernacular education is formally promised, and that the rooting out of illiteracy is only a matter of time—perhaps of no very long time.

Surely not without reason have I called it a sublime inconsistency, which, in one breath, complains of the results of the education already given, and proposes to extend it to the scores of millions as yet untouched by it. On the theory of never-ending empire—the official theory—it is nothing short of madness. If a little knowledge of English has begotten the agitator and the anarchist, is it not clear that a widespread ability to read the vernacular languages will enormously increase the influence of the makers of political mischief? It may be said, no doubt, that it is in the sheer ignorance of the people that the mischief-makers find their strength. That is true; but ignorance, in this sense, will not be corrected by the mere ability to read and write. If vernacular education means no more than that— if we are not prepared to impart something more than the power of reading seditious newspapers—then vernacular education cannot but enormously increase the difficulty of maintaining our hold upon India. The fact that we blithely proclaim the extinction of illiteracy as a policy "no longer open to discussion" seems to me to prove at once an immensity of honest good-will and an incapacity for clear and consistent thinking. Anything less Machiavellian than our conduct in this whole matter of education it would be

---

* In every Japanese village the school-house is the largest and most prominent structure—a fact which certainly enhances the prestige of education in the eyes of the people. I could not but remember this when, looking into a village school near Poona, during the mid-day interval, I found it an absolutely bare hovel, the earthen floor of which an old woman was busily daubing with cow-dung.

hard to conceive. We do our immediate duty according to our lights, and we let the consequences take care of themselves.

ANGLO-LITERARY TRAINING.

The problem is enormously difficult, for two main reasons: first (as James Darmesteter points out), because we have not ourselves developed a rational system of education; second, because a rational system of education would be resented and resisted by the people whom we propose to teach. How are we to get round this complication of difficulties? Our only chance, it seems to me, is clearly to realize the conditions of the problem, and to call in the best Indian intelligence to help us in solving it. This is as much as to say that we must frankly and sincerely admit our object to be, not to make Indians Englishmen, or even citizens of the British Empire, but to make them competent, clear-sighted citizens of their own country. Hitherto, for the vast majority of Indians, India has not existed in the real world, but in a world of myth, nightmare, and vain imagination. Only by the aid of her own finer spirits can she be brought down from this cloud-cuckooland and anchored on the solid earth. And only by a frank recognition of her right to self-government as soon as she is ready for it can the co-operation of her finer spirits be secured.

It is commonly said that the education we have hitherto given India errs in being too literary. That is true enough; but it would be equally true, and would come nearer the heart of the matter, to say that it is too English. Our aim has been to make of Indians pseudo-Englishmen; and it must be owned that in this endeavour we have attained remarkable success. To their great linguistic gifts Indians add a tenacious verbal memory which enables them to master what may be called the catchwords of culture.

[265]

There are hundreds of Indians who write quite as good English as the average British journalist, and betray their foreignness only in their excessive fondness for quotations and ready-made phrases. "Babu English" is the ridiculous aspect of this characteristic—the English of a man who has stuffed his head with idioms and stereotypes which he pours forth without any sense of fitness, as in the case of the man who announced his mother's death in these terms: "The hand that rocked the cradle has kicked the bucket." But "Babu English" is really a rare phenomenon.* The educated Indian generally uses his quotations and tags with perfect appropriateness, if only he would be a little more sparing of them.

It may have seemed for a brief moment, some thirty or forty years ago, as though this gradual Anglicization of India were destined to solve the problem of her spiritual future. Religious and social reforms appeared to be gradually following in the track of literary education, and such an institution as the Brahmo Samaj, with its eclectic unitarianism, may have seemed full of promise. But it was very soon evident that this apparently marvellous

---

* Perhaps commoner in practice than "Babu English" is the expression of sentiments which seem all the more quaint for being couched in irreproachable language. I have before me a type-written letter from an Indian official to his European superior, complaining that some charitable work he has undertaken has been misinterpreted, and has got him into trouble with his compatriots. "After all," he writes, "I took up the work as it was of public charity, and therefore, His [God's] work, and also the work which interested Government, whose servant I am. It was my ambition to please Him as well as yourself. His verdict we may not know. As for your appreciation, I might as well get it by a small private testimonial." Here is a not very luminous passage from notes on a law-suit under revision. "The issues first and second though they contain automatic points in their latter and former portions respectively, yet the objects which they hide in themselves apply *mutatis mutandis*, differentially to the statements of the parties."

receptivity and adaptability was a surface phenomenon of small significance. The Indians who became effectually Anglicized lost touch with their own countrymen, and carried with them no real following. The genuine outcome of our literary education—our training in Milton and Byron and Shelley, in Burke, Mill, Macaulay and Spencer—was the dissemination of democratic ideals, invectives against tyranny, and violently partisan views of the historical relations between England and India. All this is perfectly natural, and might have been foreseen. You cannot teach the subjects of an alien autocracy to declaim about:

> "Some village Hampden that with dauntless breast
> The little tyrant of his fields withstood,"

and expect them to refrain from making any personal application of the lines. What was less easy to foresee was the recrudescence of aggressive Hinduism, or in other words, of anti-rationalism, which has followed upon the spread of Anglo-literary education. This is, in my view, the really disquieting and baffling feature of the situation. One thing, at all events, that has not resulted from our well-meant educational efforts is any wide dissemination of political or spiritual wisdom. How was it to be expected that India should greatly profit by a course of irrelevant, or, at any rate, premature, politics, unsifted history, and poetry which, to Eastern learners, could at best be little more than half-understood rhetoric?

Let me give one or two instances of what I mean by Anglo-literary education. I once visited a High School for Girls, very well conducted by an English head-mistress. The physical drill and teaching of household occupations seemed to me excellent; it was in the class-room devoted to geography and history that my doubts were aroused by

[267]

two maps displayed on the walls, and pointed out, with
no little pride, as the work of the girls themselves. One
was a map of England, in which the principal products
of the chief towns were shown by means of objects attached
at the appropriate spots. Thus a toy motor-car indicated
Coventry, a ship, Liverpool, a knife, Sheffield, a scrap of
woollen cloth, Bradford, and so forth. In this there was
no harm, if one had felt sure that the local products of
India had been illustrated with similar care; but one or two
maps of India, exhibited at the same time, showed no such
elaboration of detail.*

The second map to which my attention was called belonged to the historical department. The reader would
scarcely guess its subject, if he were to think for a year of
the unlikeliest theme to propose to a class of Indian girls.
It was a plan of the battlefield of Agincourt, showing the
positions of the contending forces! The details of the
battle of Agincourt may be of great interest from a strategic point of view, or from the point of view of a somewhat
narrow British patriotism; but what have Indian girls to
do with either strategy or the quarrels of the Plantagenets?

It was again at a girls' school (this time under Indian
control) that I came across an amusing example of the
value of literary education specifically so called. A show
pupil of fourteen or thereabouts (a married woman, by the
way), was told to recite Thomas Moore's verses, very
popular, I believe, in India, entitled "Those Evening Bells."
In order that I might follow with understanding, the text
had been written out, and was handed to me by the head-

* A schoolboy, it is stated, if asked to enumerate the watering-places
on the south coast of England, will rattle off "Folkestone, Hastings,"
etc., with great volubility, but will be nonplussed if you ask him the
meaning of "watering-place."

mistress. The reciter, however, spoke quite comprehensibly, and I was surprised to hear her say:

> "And so 'twill be when I am gone,
> That tuneful peal will still ring on,
> When other birds shall walk these dells,
> And sing your praise, sweet evening bells."

I turned to the written copy and found that she had followed it exactly. The true text, of course, is:

> "When other bards shall walk these dells;"

but "birds" made quite good enough sense both for the pupil and for the teacher. In India, by the way, the art of recitation is generally understood to mean suiting the action to the word in such detail that every line shall be illustrated by at least one appropriate gesture. If you talk of your heart you must clutch your left breast: if you allude to your eyes, you must point to these organs. I remember hearing a boy recite, "Break, break, break," and accompany it with a whole gymnastic of gesticulation. At the lines:

> "And the stately ship goes past
> To its haven under the hill,"

he shaded his eyes and assumed the attitude of an old coast-guardsman scanning a sail on the horizon. At

> "But, oh, for the touch of a vanished hand,"

he brandished a very visible paw: and at

> "The sound of a voice that is still"

he pointed downwards with a significant flourish, implying, to the European mind, the gloomiest conjecture as to the present location of the owner of the voice. On the other

hand, I have seen Indian schoolboys go through the Trial
Scene in *The Merchant of Venice* with excellent discretion.

THE ARYA SAMAJ.

Whatever the successes or failures of Anglo-literary education, it has at least done one indispensable service in
making the basis of instruction (theoretically, at any rate)
an appeal to reason, in place of the Oriental appeal to sheer
authority, of which something has already been said in
Chapter IV. "The traditional idea of education in India,"
says Mr. S. M. Mitra, "is based on reverence for the teacher
(*guru*) whose word was law, and who was almost worshipped
by his pupils (*chelas*)." Such an ideal was natural enough
so long as all knowledge was held to be stored up in the
past, and thought was conceived as a mere pouring of the
mind into ready-made moulds, or at best as the ability to
perform certain prescribed feats on a mental flying-trapeze.
When European Hinduizers speak with awe of the culture
imparted at the "universities" of ancient India, I cannot
but think of the University of Cairo as it exists to-day,
and of the great mosques in which hundreds of young men
are squatted on the floor, rocking themselves to and fro
hour after hour, day after day, year after year, while, with
closed eyes and muttering lips, they memorize the Koran.
No doubt the Indian *gurus* sometimes inculcated the doctrine of subtler thinkers than Muhammad; but the whole
conception of education as the reverential acceptance of a
set of sacred texts and glosses is fitted only for a static
world which never existed in fact, and has ceased to exist
even in theory. There is too much reliance on authority,
too much mechanical memorizing, in Western systems of
education; but their aim, their ideal, is to make the pupil
think for himself, and accept a formula only when he has
[270]

tested it and found it work. The West has at any rate proceeded some way towards the realization that the true
teacher ought not to strangle, but rather to stimulate, the
critical, the questioning instinct in his pupil. It is clear
that this must also be the ideal of Indian education if India
is to develop her character and make the best of her
intelligence. The relation of *guru* and *chela,* in so far as
it survives, is a thing to be discouraged and finally eradi-
cated. In the modern world, intellectual idolatry is as
much out of place as religious idolatry.

It is for this reason that I look with hesitation upon the
work of the Arya Samaj, a reforming body of great and
growing influence in Northern India. It numbers nearly a
quarter of a million adherents, conducts numerous schools,
and has two great educational centres, the Dayanand Anglo-
Vedic College at Lahore, and the Gurukula near Hardwar,
the sacred spot where the Ganges flows out from the foot-
hills of the Himalayas. The Lahore College takes its
name from the founder of the sect, Swami Dayanand
Saraswati (1824-1883), called by his followers "the Luther
of India." He was a Brahmin from Kathiawar, who broke
away from his caste and preached a doctrine of which the
watchword was "Back to the Vedas." Idol-worship, pilgrimages, child-marriage, enforced widowhood, even caste
itself, Dayanand rejected. He rejected the name "Hindu,"
which he held to be originally a Muslim term of contempt.
"Arya" he declared to be the only name that ought to be
acknowledged by adherents of the Vedic religion. He made
a principle of proselytism, which is to the orthodox Hindu
an impossibility, inasmuch as Hinduism is not a result
of conviction but a privilege of birth. He even "gave practical proof of his moral courage by publicly reclaiming
Hindu converts to Islam."

I have visited both the Lahore and the Hardwar Colleges,

and have been greatly struck by the earnest spirit in which
their work is conducted. Lala Hans Raj, the late Principal
of the Anglo-Vedic College, and Mahatma Munshi Ram,
the present Principal of the Gurukula, will always rank in
my recollection among the most impressive figures I met in
India—which is saying a great deal. Their splendid
physique, and the grave dignity and urbanity of their manners, made them seem, in everything but years—for neither
is more than middle-aged—ideal types of the Eastern sage.
The Gurukula, which represents a different shade of hetero-
doxy from that of the Anglo-Vedic College, is animated by
a spirit of cloistral austerity. It is situated on the eastern
bank of the Ganges, four branches* of which divide it from
the pilgrim-haunted Hardwar. This seclusion is chosen on
purpose that the three hundred pupils may be as remote as
possible from evil influences—"especially those of the home."
Pupils are received at the age of seven and do not pass
out of the college until they are twenty-four. They never
go "home for the holidays," and intercourse with their
parents is severely restricted. They rise at four in the
morning, and bathe either in the Ganges or in the long
bathing-sheds of the College. They do their own menial
work and wait upon each other at meals. Hindi is the
usual medium of instruction, but Western philosophy and
science are taught in English. Sanskrit, of course, bulks
large in the curriculum, and cricket, football, and hockey
are played in that language. Fire—the god Agni of the
Vedas—is prominent in both public and private acts of
worship; but I was assured that it was regarded, not idol-
atrously, but as a symbol of purification. It chanced that
when I arrived at the College, the Principal was kneeling

* I crossed one of these streams on a raft of kerosene-tins, another
by ferry-boat, the third on a bridge of boats, and the fourth on horse-
back.

on the verandah of his bungalow, facing a red sunset over
the green Ganges, and absorbed in prayer, while a tongue
of spirit-flame wavered aloft from a brazen crucible placed
on the ground before him. Assuredly, I never saw a more
impressive act of devotion.

The Arya Samaj is regarded with suspicion by the
authorities, on account of its supposed seditious tendencies.
Several of its adherents, in conversation with me, ener-
getically repudiated this suspicion. "We depend for our
very existence," they said, "on the British Government.
The orthodox Hindus hate us, the Muhammadans hate us,
the Christians hate us. We are encircled by enemies: in
the British Government lies our sole security: why should
we dream of oversetting it?" And again, "One may be
loyal to the King-Emperor and the great officers of the
Government without being loyal to every policeman." And
yet again: "By their fruits ye shall know them. There are
no Aryas in Bengal, and outrages occur in Bengal. There
are no Aryas in Bombay, and outrages occur in Bombay.
In the Punjab the Arya Samaj is powerful, and there are
no outrages in the Punjab."

This reasoning is specious and no doubt sincere. The
wiser spirits of the Arya Samaj realize that British rule
gives India her best chance of moral and intellectual regeneration. It was Mahatma Munshi Ram himself who
wrote (in the *Civil and Military Gazette*):

If any insane persons have for one moment thought that the
Hindus of the present day—the great majority of whom are degraded, hypocritical and base—are fit for governing the country,
and have preached sedition in their madness, surely the teachings
of the great apostle of Vaidic Dharma cannot be held responsible.

A teacher holding these views is not likely to work for
a premature overthrow of the British power. But it must

not be supposed that the missionaries who go forth from the Gurukula—and its pupils are being expressly educated for missionary work—will preach the doctrine of eternal subservience to alien mastery. If it be sedition to work towards the ultimate fitness of India to control her own destinies, then is the Arya Samaj, beyond all doubt, a potent instrument of sedition.

It may appear, then, as if this body were carrying out a scheme of education exactly consonant with the ideas I am trying to set forth. Perhaps it comes, in fact, as near to enlightenment as can reasonably be expected. But its idolatry of the Vedas is a huge set-off to its many merits. How can an education based on so outrageous an excess of authority-worship fit men for rational action in the real world?

Swami Dayanand, it is true, rejected as apocryphal the Brahmanas and Puranas, which orthodox Hinduism accepts, in a general way, as revealed; and in so doing he purified the doctrine of his sect. But at the same time, he, as it were, concentrated and intensified the claim of the Vedas to a superhuman origin. It is impossible to think of God as actually the author of a large mass of heterogeneous literature having its sources in all sorts of historic circumstances. As soon as the heterogeneous nature of the Bible is clearly realized, its claim to divine authorship is fatally weakened. If inspiration is still asserted, it is only in a very attenuated sense. So, too, with the diverse and multifarious "sacred books" of the Hindus: the inspiration claimed for them was not—could not be—very literally understood. But when the heterogeneous mass was thrown overboard, and only the more or less homogeneous Vedas remained—genuinely ancient, and springing from no clearly ascertainable historic soil—it became possible to imagine them as the actual and literal "outbreathings" of the Creator, and to claim for them the full authority attaching to oracles of God. This was the effect of Swami Dayanand's "Back to the Vedas" watchword. On this extreme of bibliolatry the teachings of the Arya Samaj are based.

The Samajists do not fail to make the most of the seeming detachment of the Vedas from history. It is true that the *rishis* who composed the hymns are in many cases named: but this fact is lightly passed over. Here is a specimen of Samajist argument.*

Divine revelation must be meant for all men and consequently given at the beginning of the creation. The Koran, the Bible, and the Puranas are compositions of recent times, and if they are Divine Law revealed to man, we must admit that numberless human beings were left without any guidance. The Vedas are by common consent admitted to be the oldest books in the world's library. Other things being equal, there is a greater probability of their being the Divine revelation. . . .

The Koran, the Bible and the Puranas are full of historical details. It is unintelligible how such books can be called Divine revelations. In historical details, there is no veil that can be drawn only by a supernatural agency. The doings of individuals and tribes can be noticed and recorded by any man; but such records do not deserve to be called a Revelation. The Vedas are free from historical details.†

This is true, in so far that the historical events which manifestly underlie the Vedic literature have remained un-

* From *The Arya Samaj: Its beliefs, aims, and methods of work*, by Diwan Chand, M.A., Professor of Philosophy, D.A.V. College, Lahore.

† The writer proceeds: "The Koran, the Bible and the Puranas are full of contradictions, whereas not one contradiction can be pointed out in the Vedas. As Science advances the teachings of these other books are discovered to be conflicting with the laws of Nature. The advance of Science, on the other hand, furnishes confirmatory evidence in favour of the Vedic teachings." Subtle indeed must be the process of thought by which the manifest contradictions of the Vedas are explained away and the Vedic teachings are brought into harmony with Science.

recorded; but while we cannot bring the Vedas into definite relation with history, it is only too easy to place them in their anthropological context, and to see in them not the oracles of a God, but the artless utterances of primitive men (in some cases highly gifted) personifying and seeking to propitiate the powers of Nature. Anything, on the face of it, less like a divine revelation it would be difficult to conceive. The first condition of a revelation, (as the Samajist pundit justly observes) is that it shall reveal something otherwise unknown; but this condition the Vedas do not fulfil. They "reveal" the hunger of primitive man for all sorts of worldly advantages—for cattle, for rain, for sons, for the destruction of enemies, for long life, etc.—and they show his eagerness, in the pursuit of these blessings, to make friends with every unseen power he can possibly conceive or conjecture. They "reveal" worship and sacrifice as a form of direct bribery, after the fashion of this artless invocation to Indra: "Desirous of milking thee like a milch cow at pasture, Vasishtha has let loose his prayers to thee." They "reveal" the tendency of primitive man to ingratiate himself with one god by outbursts of unmeasured flattery at the expense of all the rest—the tendency which Max Müller has denominated "henotheism." They "reveal" too—but this is infrequent—the perplexities of a reflective mind in view of the mystery of existence. But what is there in all this that needed to be "revealed?" The hymns of the last class* are doubtless the noblest, and are ex-

---

* The 129th Hymn of Book X. of the Rig Veda is, as rendered by Max Müller, a remarkable utterance of a sort of agnosticism. It ends thus:

> Who knows the secret? Who proclaimed it here,
> Whence, whence, this manifold creation sprang?
> He from whom all this great creation came,
> Whether his will created or was mute,
> The most high seer that is in highest heaven,
> He knows it, or, perchance, e'en he knows not.

tremely interesting; but it is surely the business of "revelation" not to utter perplexities, but to solve them.

No doubt the Samajists explain away the manifestly human and non-divine contents of the Vedas, by processes not unknown to other theologians. For one thing, they profess to extract monotheistic teaching from documents which breathe polytheism in every line. But though I believe the Vedas to be, of all the "sacred" books of the world, perhaps the most unpromising materials for deification, it is not on their individual demerits that I wish to dwell. What I cannot but deplore is the fact that the Arya Samaj, so enlightened in many of its tenets, should give its soul into bondage to any "holy texts" whatsoever, and should simply substitute an intellectual idolatry for the worship of stocks and stones. The childish incompetence of thought revealed in the expository tracts of the Samaj is only accentuated by a parade of modern scientific method. We are offered, for example, "internal" and "external" evidences that "the Vedas are the Word Divine." The internal evidences are simply assertions contained in the Vedas themselves: for example:

He from whom the Rig Veda sprang, He from whom the Yajur Veda sprang, like unto whose hairs are the Samas, and like unto whose mouth is the Atharva-Angiras—what is that Being like? Him do thou declare, O Sage.

Answer: Know, O mortals, that this Being is Skambha (Pillar of the universe or Fulcrum of all existence).—*Atharva* X., 7-20.

The external evidences are similar assertions occurring in other writings; such as this from Manu:

To the wise elders, to the sages and saints and mankind in general, the scripture is an eye giving constant light; nor could the Veda-Shastra have been made by human faculties, nor can it be measured by human reason (unassisted by revealed glosses and comments): this is a sure proposition.

It would seem that the followers of Dayanand, if not he himself, admit "revelation" in glosses and comments subsequent to the Vedas; but it would be mere waste of time to examine the evidential value of such statements, whether "internal" or "external." Argument in a circle is everywhere a pleasant intellectual exercise, but nowhere is it more popular than in India. You prove an author inspired by showing that he was inspired to assert his own inspiration, and that other (uninspired) authors have repeated his assertion.

Dayanand, indeed, must not be held responsible for the logic of his followers. Here, however, are a couple of extracts from the writings of the Maharishi himself, which sufficiently disclose the intellectual level upon which he moved.*

"The Rig Veda, the Sama Veda, the Yajur Veda, and the Atharva Veda are the outbreathings of that great being."—*Shathapatha*, Kan. I., Chapter 5.

To make this clearer:

"Maitriya (says Yajnavalka) by Him who encompasses even Space, the Rig Veda as well as the other Vedas—all four of them—are breathed forth without effort." This is a fact. And as the vital air issuing from the body is breathed in again, even so are the Vedas breathed forth and finally breathed in again by God. This is certain.

On this subject many people say: "How could the Veda which is in *word form* have proceeded from God who is incorporeal and without parts?" To this we reply: "Such an objection cannot hold good when urged against an *almighty* God. Why? Because

* From *An Introduction to a Commentary on the Vedas.* Young-men's Arya Samaj Tract Society, Lahore.

even in the absence of mouth, the *pranas* (breathing power) and other appliances in the Supreme, the power to do His work, is ever present (or manifest) in Him. And even as in the mind of man, when absorbed in silent thought, words in question-and-answer form are being constantly pronounced, even such (we must believe) in the case with the Supreme also. He whose omnipotence is undoubted, taketh not the help of anyone in doing His work. Mortals cannot do their work without the help of others, but such is not the case with God. When He, though incorporeal and without parts, made the entire universe, then how can the fact of His having made (revealed) the Vedas be doubted?"

Just as a father ever does kind offices unto his children, even so does God, in His infinite Mercy, preach His knowledge unto all men. If He did not do this, then, as the result of ignorance and barbarism transmitted from age to age, men would find it impossible to realise *Dharma* (duty), *Artha* (wealth), *Kama* (felicity), and *Moksha* (salvation), and hence would be shut out from the enjoyment of supreme bliss. When the merciful God has created roots, fruits, and so forth for the enjoyment and happiness of His creatures, how could He then have left out vouchsafing to them the Vedas, the source of all bliss, the record of all Law and Knowledge? The happiness which accrues to man from the possession of the most enjoyable things in the universe, does not come up even to a thousandth part of that which the possession of knowledge gives. It follows from all this that God is the author of the Vedas, and even this must be believed.

And Swami Dayanand is one of the great thinkers of modern India! That India which we are asked to regard as possessing a unique spiritual genius! That India which proposes to send forth its Swamis to spiritualize the Western world, the world of Berkeley and Kant, of Bergson and William James.*

* "Once more," said Swami Vivekananda, "the world must be conquered by India. This is the dream of my life. . . . We must conquer the world through our spirituality and philosophy, we must do it, or die.

[279]

"But is not this Veda-worship better, after all, than the worship of Siva and Kali, of Ganesh and Hanuman? Since the Arya Samaj renounces caste,* child-marriage, enforced widowhood, *sraddha* (ancestor-worship), pilgrimages and other abuses of Hinduism, and since it is admitted on all hands that, in India, at any rate, education must proceed upon some religious basis, may not 'Back to the Vedas' be the very idea predestined to solve the great and pressing problem of discovering a principle of instruction at once fairly enlightened and fairly acceptable to the Indian people? Ought not the Government, perhaps, in its promised campaign against illiteracy, to take a leaf out of the book of the Arya Samaj? Might it not even entrust to the Samaj, at all events in Northern India, the working-out of its proposals?" Such thoughts as these have again and again beset me, in reflecting upon the difficulties of the situation. "Assuming," I have said to myself, "that some compromise with unreason is inevitable, might not this compromise prove the least injurious?"

To these questions there are many answers; but the most conclusive is that the compromise would not be even "fairly acceptable to the Indian people." The Arya Samaj is, after all, only a heretic sect, and the Government is forbidden, by its essential principle of religious impartiality, to endow any sect whatever. It might almost as well

The only condition of Indian national life . . . is the conquest of the world by Indian thought." An "eminent Hindu teacher" entitling himself "His Holiness Swami Sri Shankeranand Sannyasi" has recently been evangelising in South Africa. His doctrine is that "When man through the help of a real spiritual teacher has realised that he is only a stranger here, and that his original and proper residence is the eternal happiness, he cannot be entrapped into the net of illusion, and thus he reaches the supreme stage of the Highest—the Ultimatum."

* It is reproached with many backslidings in the matter of caste (see p. 91). There is no doubt, however, that the Samaj does excellent work among outcasts and untouchables.

A GHAT, BENARES

endow Christianity while it was about it, and try to force Christian education upon the masses. The attempt would be scarcely more shocking to the general sentiment.

THE CHANCES OF CHRISTIANITY.

Here a word may be said in passing as to the prospect of a solution of India's problems through the spread of Christianity. It is a vision that has haunted many fine spirits, from Herbert Edwardes in the past to the Rev. C. F. Andrews in the present. *The Renaissance in India: Its Missionary Aspect,* by the last-mentioned writer, is certainly one of the most helpful books of recent years. Its ardent humanity, its faultless sweet-reasonableness, almost persuade one to share the writer's hopes that in Christ lies "the key to India's future." But what are the chances? After many centuries of occasional missionary effort, and a century of constant labour by many European and American organizations, the tale of Indian Christians does not amount to quite four millions! In other words there are three hundred and eleven millions still awaiting conversion. It is true that the influence of Christianity is not to be measured by the number of actual converts. It is traceable in all the intellectual movements of modern India —in every reform, indeed, which does not proceed directly from the Government, and in many which do. But this merely means that Western enlightenment has come to the East in such close association with Christianity that it is impossible to distinguish between the one influence and the other. Christian missions—and not least among them the Salvation Army—have assuredly done splendid work. I brought with me (I confess) a vague prejudice against the missionary and his calling, but it did not take me long to throw it off. After a few weeks in India, one fully enters into the spirit of Sir Alfred Lyall's *Theology in Extremis,* and feels that here one would die for a religion which elsewhere one would disown. Certainly it would be to the immeasurable advantage of India if the great landslide in the direction of Christianity, which Mr. C. F. Andrews seems to anticipate, were one day to occur. So strongly do I feel this that I should be sorry to say a word that might have a featherweight of influence in impeding such a movement. Christianity would be for India a halfway house to civilization—of that there is no doubt. But if you ask for the evidence portending a mass-movement towards the halfway-house, I confess that I cannot find it either by observation or in the writings of the missionaries. Some people hold that the current is rather setting towards Islam, and that view seems to be quite as plausible.

The coming education for the masses, at all events, cannot be Christian. So far as it is directed by Government —and no other agency is adequate to the gigantic task— it must be wholly dissociated from sect or creed. But a host of authorities rise up to assure us, theoretically, that "education without a religious basis is like building a house without foundations," and practically, that under the system of secular education hitherto pursued by the Government "no appreciable rise in morality can be observed." It would seem, then, that we are in a cleft stick: that we cannot give religious education, and that non-religious education is powerless for good.

A little examination, however, may perhaps lead us to a more cheerful view of the case. To take the question of experience first, the weight of evidence is against the assertion that secular education is powerless for good. Grave as have been the defects of the methods hitherto adopted, the saner view seems to be that they have done much to raise the average character of those who have come under

[282]

their influence. It would take pages to marshal the evidence on both sides. Here it need only be said that, from the nature of the case, the failures are more apt to be noted and remembered than the successes, and that large allowance must be made for the point of view. The British official may sometimes record as moral delinquency what is, in fact, the awakening of a (perhaps misguided) sense of moral responsibility.

Passing now to the theoretical question, is it, in fact, impossible to devise a form of education which, without affirming or denying anything as to powers unseen or other lives than this, may have a definite and potent effect in the upbuilding of character? It does not seem to me impossible at all, if India will faithfully apply her best intelligence to the task, and if the British Government, on its part, will place no hindrance in the way of a scheme of instruction which shall answer to the legitimate aspirations of intelligent India.

It is true, no doubt, that little is to be expected from the administration of the three R's with a "cauld clash o' morality." * The mistake lies in imagining that it is

---

* Something, however, can be done on these lines. The Government Resolution of February, 1913, lays it down that "Excellent materials for ethical teaching are available in the Mahabharata, the Ramayana, portions of Hafiz, Sadi, Maulana Rumi, and other classics of Sanskrit, Arabic, Persian, and Pali." I imagine that this remark was partly, at any rate, inspired by the success which is said to have attended the introduction into some schools of *Youth's Noble Path*, by Mr. F. J. Gould —a book of moral lessons extracted from the classics aforesaid. Mr. Gould himself visited India at the invitation of the Bombay Government, and gave some lessons, with encouraging results. It is reported that in the schools of the State of Mysore "direct moral teaching is given by capable men who make their discourses interesting and instructive by illustrating moral precepts with examples taken from the Ramayana and the Mahabharata, history, fables, folk-lore, etc." If material for the up-building of character can be extracted from the Epics, so much the better; but certainly the process must be one of drastic expurgation.

supernatural religion alone that can "touch morality with emotion." If a fervent sense of supernatural religion were necessary to the formation of character, then England herself would be in a parlous case; for who can allege that any deep personal religion is generally characteristic of the British schoolboy of any class? In nine cases out of ten, it is not devotion but loyalty that keeps a young man straight—loyalty to his family or school traditions; loyalty to his class, or (if you will) to his caste; loyalty to his country, or to some larger, yet still mundane, ideal—to science, to art, or to social service. It may be religious fervour, in the narrower sense, that makes the saint, though even that is not always true; but if it needed religious fervour, or even conviction, to make an upright man and a good citizen, then, I repeat, England's case would be desperate indeed. The crying fault of English education, to my thinking, is that we do not make strong enough and definite enough appeal to the largest loyalty of all—the loyalty to that great host of Humankind, which has won such splendid victories (though here and there chequered with defeats) on its march out of the dim and tragic past, and is clearly destined to far greater triumphs in the immeasurable future, if only each man does faithfully the duty that falls to his lot. This is not an appeal to any Religion of Humanity in a technical, Comtean sense, but simply to the plain facts of anthropology and history, which, rightly presented, are just as capable as any creed of touching morality with emotion, and have the great advantage of being unassailable by criticism. Not until we place our moral teaching on a historic basis, and admit that its sanctions are antecedent to, and independent of, theology, will the problem of English education be ultimately solved.

This, however, is a digression, intended merely to illustrate the fact that it is not through religion alone that morality can be raised to the temperature at which it passes into our blood and nerve—into the very fibre of our being. All that is needed is to kindle a sentiment, or (one might almost say) to awaken an instinct, of loyalty to something higher than our own personal or family interests—"something, not ourselves, that makes for," or rather demands, "righteousness."

PATRIOTISM AS AN INSPIRING PRINCIPLE.

Where are we to find in India this "something not ourselves?" To appeal to the Indian masses on the ground of world-citizenship—of their participation in the onward march of humanity—would be so premature that the suggestion sounds ironic. But may not the necessary stimulus be found in that very idea of India, of the Motherland, which a timorous or merely selfish policy would have us proscribe as seditious? Just as the loyalty of an English, French, or German schoolboy ought to be extended so as to embrace, not only his country, but the world, so the loyalty of the Indian schoolboy of the near future should be encouraged to attach itself, not merely to his caste or sect, but to his country. Whether we like it or not, this is what will happen—nay, is happening in certain parts of India. It seems to me that the only true wisdom for the Government is to recognize that the inevitable is also the desirable, and to seek in patriotism that reinforcement of character which is falsely declared to be the peculiar property of religion. "Bande Mataram" should no longer be the watchword of sedition, but should be accepted as the inspiring principle of a great effort of national regeneration. It should be the motto, not only of the schoolroom, but of the secretariat.

[285]

"Is national patriotism," some people may ask, "the only, or the best, inspiring principle? What about imperialism? Why should not the loyalty in which you would have us seek the starch of character be loyalty to the British Empire?" I do not discuss the question, because to anyone who has a living vision of India it is merely absurd. What can the British Empire mean to the Indian schoolboy? What has it meant to the Indians who have actually put the idea to the test in South Africa and Canada? The question of the ultimate relation of India to the British Empire will be solved, when the time comes, by considerations of statesmanship which we cannot yet foresee, in a world very different from that of to-day. In the meantime, of course, loyalty to India need not exclude loyalty to the King-Emperor, the head of the actual Government. The best way to endanger the latter loyalty is to declare it inconsistent with the former.

Let it not be thought, however, that I consider the problem solved by the mere mention of the word "patriotism" as the inspiring principle of the new education. The real difficulty lies in disengaging patriotism from the ignorant or misinformed vanity to which India is already far too prone. The battle will lie, not between patriotism and no patriotism, but between enlightened and misguided patriotism; and if, by a narrow and jealous policy, we strengthen the worser cause, nothing but disaster can follow. By misguided patriotism I mean that which declares India to be a land specially favoured by heaven; the home of the loftiest religions, the profoundest philosophies, the noblest civilizations, the world has ever seen; a land whose divine genius has passed under the eclipse of brutal foreign domination, which it has but to cast off in order to shine forth in redoubled radiance, the wonder and envy of mankind. Of this vision of India, what can one say but that "history

[286]

laughs and weeps it down?" It should be the task of the
true scholar-patriot to teach his country that no region
of earth is specially favoured by heaven; that to India's
lot has fallen many glories, but also many calamities; that
if we regard the past alone, we are bound to admit that the
balance deflects on the wrong side; but that it lies with
this and the coming generations to redress the balance, and
make the real India of the future far greater and more
splendid than any of the fabled Indias of the past.
Especially should the teacher show that, whatever may be
the truth about these vanished glories, it will be time to
boast of them when they are restored, and not till then.

It may be thought that the whole tenor of this book
is to depreciate and belittle the past of India; but I attack
only the legendary and fictitious past which threatens to
enslave and blight the future. No one feels more keenly
than I do that a reasonable and well-founded patriotic pride
is possible to every Indian. His country is one of the most
beautiful and wonderful in the world. The very legends
that have gathered round it, the very superstitions that
have weighed it down, are among the most fascinating
phenomena in the history of the human spirit. In philosophy, in art, it has been, though not supreme, as its
idolaters would have us think, yet nobly distinguished. It
has set the world's standard of spectacular magnificence.
If it has been the prey of many conquerors, that is only
because it has been the dream of all. Had India never
existed, history would have lacked many of its most marvellous pages, and the imagination of the world would have
been immeasurably the poorer. The children of the Motherland have ample grounds for legitimate, though chastened,
pride; and unchastened pride is, in any people, only another
name for ignorant vanity. If India can but find the wise
teachers she needs, she may one day exchange that chastened

sentiment for the exultant pride which says: "These and these evils were, and are no more."

What is wanted, then, is a sound course of Indian elementary education, and especially a series of text-books written by Indians for Indians, which shall place India before the youthful mind as a real country in a real world. There is no lack of men qualified to produce such books—men familiar with the results of modern scholarship and science, and capable of expressing them clearly and acceptably. European help should doubtless be called in—the help, I mean, not only of books, but of men—but information must be conveyed through Indian channels and under Indian sanction. The theological difficulty is surely no greater in India than in England. Hinduism, though it has talked much of "righteousness," has never claimed moral teaching as one of its functions, so cannot hold its privileges invaded. Moreover with all its *sruti* and *smriti*, it has no definite canon of sacred books—none, at any rate, that is accessible to the masses—so that the inconsistency between the theological and the scientific conceptions of the world need not become so definite and clear-cut as it is with us. Even the Koran stands in no more flagrant conflict with astronomy, geology and anthropology than does the Bible. Moreover, the accommodating nature of the Indian intellect in regard to the acceptance of contradictions ought to smooth away certain initial difficulties. No desperate conflict between science and theology need arise in minds which are capable of believing, at one and the same time, that the world is round, and that the world is flat. This capability must, in time, be eliminated; but in the first stages of mental awakening it may prove convenient. Not, indeed, that India is the only country where enlightenment and superstition can co-exist comfortably in the same mind. They do so in every clime—one might almost say in every brain, excepting those in which superstition reigns supreme. It is all a question of proportion, of degree; and the growth of world-realization must of course be gradual in India, as it has been everywhere else.

The true difficulty, I conceive, will not be theological, but social. What attitude is the new education to adopt towards those social institutions, with caste in their fore-front, which have no inherent and necessary connection with religion, but are inseparably bound up with it in the popular mind? This is a problem which the intelligence of India must solve for itself; and it is just here that the patriotic ideal, judiciously brought into play, ought to be the determining factor. It may be said that the patriotic ideal can never take hold upon the popular mind until caste, its negation, is vanquished. But this is to assume that India is exempt from the providential muddle-headed-ness with which, as we have just noted, she is, in fact, rather superabundantly endowed. The idea of caste and the idea of a great united India, though essentially incompatible, may quite well be housed in the same head; but under the right system of education, the larger, saner, wholesomer idea ought gradually to eliminate its rival. So too, with immature marriage and enforced widowhood: it is one thing to cling to them in opposition to European prejudice and Christian disapproval, quite another to close the ears to the remonstrances of Indians who have obviously nothing but the welfare and greatness of India at heart. While social reform means, or appears to mean, the victory of Europe over the national ideal, it is natural enough that many otherwise enlightened Indians should view it with coldness, and even hostility; but if once it is seen and admitted to be an indispensable preliminary, not to the defeat, but to the triumph of the national ideal, patriotism cannot but rally to its support.

Even now, it seems to me, enlightened "Servants of India"—to use the title of Mr. Gokhale's nobly-inspired confraternity—might set about the composition and compilation of vernacular text-books, and thus show the Government the way it ought to go. What books already exist I do not know; but they can scarcely be informed by the ideal here propounded. Perhaps a Central Committee might be formed which should distribute the different tasks among men of known competence. It would, I assume, matter little in what language the books were originally written, since they could be translated into all the others. But each division of the country should have its special historical-geographical handbook in its own idiom.

And here we come upon a point to which I cannot find that sufficient attention has been given. "It is an amazing fact," writes the Rev. J. Knowles,* "that the Indian Empire has a greater number of alphabets than there are for all the other languages in the world." This statement may, perhaps, be open to criticism; but the fact that it can be made without patent absurdity is sufficiently significant. Mr. Knowles continues:

"There are about 50 recognised indigenous alphabets, and there are probably twice as many varieties of scripts used in writing them. Most of the sounds are common to all languages . . . but it is remarkable that hardly any of the letters for the same sound have the same form in any two different vernaculars. No less than 10,000 symbols are in use to represent the 64 sounds which are all the vernaculars contain.

To print the most ordinary book in the Devanagari character, a fount of some eight hundred types is required;

* *Our Duty to India and Indian Illiterates;* London, Christian Literature Society, 1910. See also the same writer's: *Common Alphabet for Indian Languages,* Eastbourne, W. H. Christian, 1913.

[290]

Malayalam and Sinhalese require over seven hundred each.*
The great number of syllabic characters renders it very
difficult to learn to read and write in these languages;
and even if the number of types required were smaller, the
necessity for employing so many different founts must
enormously enhance the cost of providing books for a
general scheme of vernacular education. A quarter of a
century ago, Sir M. Monier-Williams wrote: "Britain is
bound to give her unlettered millions of subjects the option
of acquiring a simple alphabet, which would, if adopted,
reduce the labour of education, now much increased by the
complexity of indigenous graphic systems." I cannot
learn that any definite steps in this direction have yet been
taken; but surely an All-Indian Alphabet is the most indispensable of pre-requisites for a campaign against
illiteracy. Mr. Knowles, the unwearied champion of this
idea, reckons that fifty-three alphabetic characters would
be sufficient to represent all the sounds in the Indian vernaculars, and has actually designed such an alphabet, based
on our ordinary Roman types. I am told that his phonetic
analysis is defective, and that his scheme would require
serious modification. On this point I can have no opinion;
but, whatever the merits or defects of his system, the principle remains unaffected. If it be true (and there is no
reason to doubt it) that all, or even the chief, vernacular
languages of India could be printed and written by means
of a single alphabet of from fifty to sixty letters, it would
seem to be the plainest duty of the Government to appoint
a commission of experts to devise such an alphabet.†

* There are great discrepancies in the numbers stated by different
writers, and even by the same writer at different times. It is sufficient
for the argument that the number of types required by any syllabic
system of notation is necessarily very large.

† There would be some opposition to the introduction of a reinforced

Though there should certainly be no unnecessary delay in setting about the great effort of enlightenment now formally promised, I would suggest to the Indians who are impatient for sweeping measures that a well-considered and thoroughly-prepared movement is better than a hasty rush at so difficult a problem. For one thing, the training of teachers is an indispensable preliminary, and for this the best European aid should be called in. For another thing, it is of vast importance that female education should not be left to lag hopelessly behind, but that measures should be taken to bring it more or less into line. Better, for a beginning, comparatively few schools taught by competent and tolerably-paid masters,* than a great number taught by starved incompetents. Better schools attended by a thousand boys and five hundred girls than schools attended by two thousand boys and no girls, or only a handful. Into questions of ways and means, I have no space to enter, even if I had the knowledge. Let me only say that in such a country as India, there must always be differences of opinion as to the relative importance of the various purposes to which public funds are applied, and that, for some time to come, the Government will scarcely escape the charge of lavishing money on other objects which its critics consider less essential, and treating education with parsimony. But if the Government gives proof of the sincerity of its intentions, it seems to me that fair-minded critics should not complain too bitterly if the rate of progress does not quite answer to their wishes.

Roman alphabet on the score of its being un-Indian. But this opposition could surely be overcome; unless, indeed, one of the indigenous syllabaries could be so adapted as to give it the advantages of an alphabet.

* How low is the standard of remuneration may be gathered from the fact that the Resolution of February, 1913, lays it down that "trained teachers should receive not less than Rs. 12 per month,"—that is, sixteen shillings.

[292]

India has been content with illiteracy for thousands of years; it does not so very greatly matter whether it takes twenty, or forty, or even sixty years, to root it out.

A Literate India.

But when once illiteracy becomes the exception instead of the rule, how marvellous will be the change! On the material side, the whole working of the machinery of civilization will be greatly facilitated. The peasant will be much better able to hold his own against the village accountant, the landlord and the money-lender. He will be able to make free use of agricultural banks, and perhaps he will put his savings into the savings-bank instead of hanging them on his wife's nose, wrists and ankles. On the intellectual side he will gradually pass into a world of new interest—a world bearing some resemblance, at any rate, to the globe on which he is actually placed. The ferment in his mind will doubtless take strange and possibly dangerous forms. He will exchange apathy for mobility, excitability, and will be very accessible to suggestion, good or bad. The vernacular press will then have ten times its present power; the rhetorician and the sophist will be loud in the land. If the Government be determined to remain obstinately hostile to national aspirations, it is, as I have already said, pursuing the maddest of policies in educating the masses. Even if it adopted (as it will surely be driven to adopt) the view that its great function is precisely to train India for *Swaraj*, it may have to face a difficult period of turbulent impatience, to which, in the interest of the country itself, it must not yield. I cannot but think that one way to avoid or minimize this danger would be for the Government to become itself a purveyor of vernacular literature, both in the shape of books and periodicals. If you create a reading public, it is but reason to provide it with something good to read. Well-edited, interesting, well-illustrated papers, to circulate through each of the great regions of the country, would be only a logical corollary to the whole theory of popular education. There is no harm in a subsidized press, so long as its position is frankly avowed. A secret bribe paid to a paper which professes independence is a totally different matter.*

In this chapter, even more than in its predecessors, I am only too well aware that I must have been guilty of many superficialities, and doubtless of not a few errors. The one theory which I advance with perfect confidence, is that the educational problem falls into line with all the rest, inasmuch as the key to it lies in the recognition that our rule in India is a means, not an end, and that the end is none other than the addition of a great self-sufficing, self-respecting civilized community to the free and equal nations of the earth.

* Scarcely had I written these lines when I came across a letter from Sir Henry Lawrence to Lord Canning, written shortly before the Mutiny, in which he speaks of incendiary newspapers. "I would not trouble any of them," he says, "but, with your Lordship's permission, I think we might squash half the number by helping one or two of the cleverest with information, and even with editorials and illustrations. . . . An illustrated vernacular, cleverly edited, would tell well, and do good both politically and morally."

EPILOGUE

In attempting to think out a problem like that of the future of India, one must inevitably take as a starting-point some more or less definite expectation, or, at any rate, desire, regarding the future of the world at large. The fundamental assumption on which my argument proceeds is that some rational and stable world-order is ultimately attainable. If that be denied—if it be asserted, for instance, that the more prolific nations and races will always tend to encroach upon the territory of the less prolific, and that the struggle for existence, in the shape of wars for territorial expansion, must go on to the end of time—then the attempt to apply reason to international problems becomes, if not absolutely futile, at any rate, comparatively uninteresting. Blind instinct being, by hypothesis, the determining force in human affairs, and periods of civilization and rational progress being simply lucid intervals between recurrent crises of barbarism, why should we toil and struggle towards a foredoomed and self-defeating ideal? And why, in particular, should we trouble our heads as to the future of India? Let British rule maintain itself as long as it can, and then pass away in the welter of the next world-convulsion. Progress being illusory, or at best evanescent, why force it upon a country which, in its inmost heart, resents and despises it?

This argument, pushed to its limits, would imply that constructive thought, in the political sphere, is an absurdity, since there is nothing ultimately good or ultimately bad in an incurably chaotic world. The wise man will confine his care to matters of immediate expediency, knowing that every seeming triumph of reason and order will, in the long run, have to be paid for—perhaps with usury.

But if, on the other hand, a rational world-order be not, in the nature of things, impossible, the future of India becomes a matter of absorbing interest, because it offers, so to speak, a test case. One of the great obstacles to a stable equilibrium among the peoples of the earth lies in the immense differences in the development of the different races. If, in a case so conspicuous as that of India, the obstacle can be overcome, and one-fifth of the human race can, in the course of a couple of centuries (say from A.D. 1800 to A.D. 2000) be emancipated from medievalism, and fitted to take an equal place among the peoples who are shaping the future, then the solution of the whole problem will at last be definitely in sight.

As to the general justification of our rule in India, up to the present point, we need have, I think, no qualms. It is rather surprising to find a philosophic historian like Lord Bryce—and, after him, Lord Morley—raising the question whether "the immediate result" of the influence of Europe upon Asia will be "to increase the sum of human happiness." * One is inclined to answer as Robert Bruce, in John Davidson's play, answers the question whether it might not have been better for Scotland if Rome had conquered her:

> A subtle question, soldier,
> But profitless, requiring fate unwound.

The influence of Europe upon Asia is no mere accident which we can, as it were, think away, in order to speculate upon the course things would have taken if it had not

* Lord Bryce in *The Roman and the British Empire*, p. 73. Lord Morley in a speech at Manchester, June, 1912.

happened. There is a sense in which (for instance) the result of the battle of Waterloo was an accident. A very slight difference in the balance of motives governing the conduct of Grouchy would have led him to "march to the cannons," and would in all probability have turned the fortunes of the day. We can then, rationally (if not very profitably), conjecture what would have happened if Napoleon had won the battle—as Mr. G. M. Trevelyan has, in fact, done, with much ingenuity. But in order to imagine events so shaping themselves that Asia should not, in the nineteenth century, have undergone the influence of Europe, we have either to unmake and remake human nature, or else to go back into the prehistoric past, and, standing beside the conjectured cradle of mankind, speculate on what would have happened if the children had climbed out of the cradle on different sides, or in a different order. In other words, the relations between West and East proceed from causes so infinitely remote as to baffle analysis and present themselves to our imagination in the guise of fatality.

They were determined from the moment when the East adopted the static ideal of civilization, which happens to be in the long run false and impossible, and left the West to discover the dynamic ideal, which happens to be alone consonant with the inmost nature of things. From that moment it was inevitable that in the fullness of time—which practically means when the ocean had been transformed from a barrier into a highway—the East should be awakened, and to some extent dominated, by the West. Movement must always have the advantage over immobility, momentum over inertia. The ring-fence ideal broke down, not so much by reason of violence from without, as of disaffection from within. However intense may be the innate and cultivated conservatism of a people, it cannot resist the infiltration of knowledge; and when it becomes known that other peoples exercise certain marvellous powers of locomotion, communication and production of commodities, whereby they attain great riches and power, the desire to share in these benefits becomes irresistible. In vain do the sages proclaim that they are not benefits at all, and strive to stop the breaches in the ring-fence. Human nature is too strong for them. When desirable things can be done and procured rapidly and economically, no section of mankind can, in the long run, be persuaded that it is better to go without them, or to do and procure them slowly and with infinite labour. Surely the one unmistakable lesson of the history of the past hundred years is that great disparities of material civilization cannot for ever co-exist on this tiny globe of ours. The railway, the telegraph and the automobile are penetrating, and are bound to penetrate, everywhere. Should they be superseded by still more efficient and economical devices, all the more rapidly will the whole world be permeated by the filaments of one great nervous system. The East was fated to fall under the influence of the West, because the East denied, while the West affirmed, the potency of Time as a factor in human affairs.

Therefore I am unmoved by the sarcasm of that able Japanese writer, Okakura Kakuzo, when he exclaims: "You talk of the Yellow Peril—but what about the White Disaster?" It was because Asia misread the essential nature of things that she was fated to undergo the influence of Europe. To ask whether that influence makes for happiness seems to me not unlike inquiring whether a child would not be happier if it could remain a child for ever.

It is true that the ring-fence theory was never formally adopted in India, as it was in China and Japan. How could it be, in the most invaded country in the world, with the possible exception of Italy? There were too many practicable gaps in the physical ring-fence. But India fell a victim, no less than her neighbours, to the spiritual disease, endemic in Asia, of which the ring-fence theory is the most familiar symptom. Even to-day, do we not find pundits solemnly discussing whether it is lawful for a Hindu to cross the *kala pani*, and deciding in the negative by a majority of forty-five to one? A century ago, the prohibition was absolute and unquestioned—and what clearer evidence could one require of unfitness to take part in the inevitable development of the real world? A race which thus walled itself in behind Himalayas of arrogant ignorance, and then split itself up into a thousand segments of no less arrogant mutual exclusiveness, was manifestly predestined to a period of tutelage and probation ere it could fall into step with the advancing host of civilization. Ignorance and arrogance are poor defences against the resistless trend of human affairs, nor can any race, by taking council with its gods and its *rishis*, elect to stand still in a moving world.

The task of opening passes through the mountains of ignorance fell to England, and not to France or another, because England, at the critical period, happened to command the sea. The bait which lured her on was commercial advantage, and for some time, before she realized her true mission, she pursued that advantage unscrupulously and even ruthlessly. But it was not long before her better instincts awoke, and she saw herself, not in the light of an irresponsible trafficker, but of a guardian and trustee. It is upon her more and more perfect realization of the duties involved in this relationship that the success of her great undertaking, in my judgment, depends.

In any picture that we can form of a stable world-order, can we possibly imagine three hundred million people abjuring for ever the exercise of their will on political matters of any importance, and resting content to leave their national fortunes and their individual welfare in the un-

[299]

restricted charge, primarily, of a body of alien administrators, and ultimately of the elective assembly of an alien nation, nearly half the world away? If these three hundred million people belonged to an essentially low and unimprovable stock, such a solution of their destiny might be thinkable, though scarcely desirable. But, as we have seen, this is by no means the case. They are a blending of various races, almost all of relatively high potentialities. There is, indeed, a large infusion of a breed neither higher nor lower than our own, since it is ultimately the same. Nor is this composite race, when once awakened from the sheer apathy of a meagre life on the soil, by any means inclined to humility and subservience. It is much more apt to overvalue than to underrate its grounds for racial and historical self-complacency. Who can possibly believe that such a people will passively submit to perpetual tutelage? Or that any other people, which has its own work to do and its own troubles to face in the world, can permanently afford to hold them in subjection by what service-club declaimers call "the sword"?

No doubt one may be deceived in anticipating that the coming world-order will be in the main democratic. The apparent drift towards democracy may be a false start, and order may be ultimately imposed by a confederation, or a conspiracy, of military autocracies. But that would mean a rearrangement of world-forces in which, most assuredly, the British rule in India could not subsist in anything like its present form. If, on the other hand, democratic institutions survive and develop, it is wholly inconceivable that an educated and civilized India should never aspire to take its fate into its own hands, or, so aspiring, should be forcibly balked of its will by a far smaller nation at the other side of the planet. This autocracy of a democracy is a paradox and a marvel which may, if we are wise, work out

[330]

beneficently for the one party and gloriously for the other. But work out it must, for good or for ill—it cannot endure for ever.

Meredith Townsend, a man of long (unofficial) Indian experience, and author of a clear-sighted though rather too pessimistic book, *Asia and Europe*, goes to the root of the matter when he writes:

> The Indian Empire is a miracle, not in the rhetorician's sense, but in the theologian's sense. . . . It is a miracle, as a floating island of granite would be a miracle, or a bird of brass which flew and sang and lived on in mid-air.

That is the fundamental fact which was more and more impressed on me every day I spent in India—a fact which people who have not been there do not realize, and which those who pass their lives there, forget. Lord Bryce, a very observant traveller, realized it to the full; but, rather oddly, he writes as though the very wonder of the miracle were a source of strength to us. "The English," he says,

> have impressed the imagination of the people by their resistless energy and their almost uniform success. . . . That over three hundred millions of men should be ruled by a few pale-faced strangers from beyond the great sea . . . this seems too wonderful to be anything but the doing of some unseen and irresistible divinity. I heard at Lahore an anecdote which, slight as it is, illustrates the way in which the native thinks of these things. A tiger had escaped from the Zoological Gardens, and its keeper, hoping to lure it back, followed it. When all other inducements had failed, he lifted up his voice and solemnly adjured it in the name of the British Government, to which it belonged, to come back to its cage. The tiger obeyed.

Perhaps; but how long will the tiger obey? I do not doubt that Lord Bryce has rightly discerned one element in the complex feeling with which British rule is regarded by the mass of the people; but it is necessarily a diminishing element. Familiarity, if it does not breed contempt, at any rate takes the edge off wonder. Our military successes are a mere legend to this generation; our administrative successes are contested by Indian opinion, and are not, at best, of an awe-inspiring nature. It is hard to believe, in short, that our position can be permanently strengthened by its very marvellousness. Sir Alfred Lyall wrote in the eighties: "One thing is sure: the natives all discuss our rule still as a transitory state of existence, a huge structure that may vanish any day inexplicably as it appeared."

In the following passage, however, Lord Bryce puts his finger on one of the cardinal facts of the situation. "In the higher grades of the civil administration," he says, "there are only about twelve hundred persons; and these twelve hundred control three hundred and fifteen millions, doing it with so little friction that they have ceased to be surprised at this extraordinary fact." That is exactly true. The British official goes to India young, before he has begun to think very seriously about things; and by the time his mind has matured, he has become so habituated to the smooth working of the administrative machine that he regards it as a matter of course, and quite in the natural order of things. He is acutely conscious of imperfections in the mechanism, both from his own point of view and from that of the people entrusted to his charge; but in the very existence of such a mechanism he sees nothing surprising. I do not say that this frame of mind is universal. On the contrary, one finds cases of a just appreciation of the marvel, and cases, too, of an exaggerated fear of it. But on the whole one may say that the typical Anglo-Indian (and still more, the typical memsahib) is serenely unconscious of the utter astoundingness of his and her position.

[302]

On the other hand, when we turn to the great men who built up the Indian Empire, we find that many of them fully realized that they were not laying bases for eternity. They saw, indeed, that the very success of their work must make the position of a foreign ruling caste ultimately untenable. Here is the passage—much better known, unfortunately, in India than England—in which Macaulay forecasts what seemed to him the most desirable development of the relation between the two countries:

> The destinies of our Indian Empire are covered with thick darkness. . . . It may be that the public mind of India may expand under our system till it has outgrown that system; that by good government we may educate our subjects into a capacity for better government; that having become instructed in European knowledge, they may in some future age demand European institutions. Whether such a day will ever come I know not. But never will I attempt to avert or retard it. Whenever it comes, it will be the proudest day in English history. To have found a great people sunk in the lowest depths of slavery and superstition, to have so ruled them as to have made them desirous and capable of all the privileges of citizens, would indeed be a title to glory all our own.

These words were spoken in 1833, before Macaulay went to India; but there is not the slightest reason to suppose that experience led to any change in his views. A somewhat older contemporary of his, and an empire-builder in the sanest sense of the word, was Mountstuart Elphinstone, administrator of the Maharashtra and Governor of Bombay, where his ardour in the cause of education is commemorated in the Elphinstone College. No abler man has England sent to India; and he spoke in the same sense as Macaulay, without Macaulay's note of hesitation. We find him writing to Mackintosh in 1819:

I am afraid the belief that our Indian Empire will not be long-lived is reason and not prejudice. It is difficult to guess the death it may die. . . . The most desirable death for us to die of should be the improvement of the natives reaching such a pitch as would render it impossible for a foreign nation to retain the government; but this seems at an immeasurable distance. . . . A time of separation must come; and it is for our interest to have an early separation from a civilized people rather than a violent rupture with a barbarous nation.

This was not the utterance of a mood, but of a settled conviction; for thirty-five years later we find him writing to his biographer, Sir T. E. Colebrooke:

The moral is that we must not dream of perpetual possession, but must apply ourselves to bring the natives into a state that will admit of their governing themselves in a manner that may be beneficial to our interest as well as their own and that of the rest of the world; and to take the glory of the achievement, and the sense of having done our duty, for the chief reward of our exertions.

Very similar was the view of Sir Charles Metcalfe, who, in defending his policy of granting liberty to the press, wrote: "If my opponents' argument be that the spread of knowledge may eventually be fatal to our rule in India, I close with them on that point, and maintain that, whatever may be the consequences, it is our duty to communicate the benefits of knowledge. If India could be preserved as a part of the British Empire only by keeping its inhabitants in a state of ignorance, our domination would be a curse to the country, and ought to cease." He went on, indeed, to argue that our rule was endangered by ignorance rather than by knowledge; but he had at best no great confidence in the security of our position. "Our hold," he wrote in

[304]

another place, "is so precarious that a very little mismanagement might accomplish our expulsion; and the course of events may be of itself sufficient, without any mismanagement. . . . All our native establishments, military and civil, are the followers of fortune; they serve us for their livelihood, and generally serve us well. From a sense of what is due to the hand that feeds them—which is one of the virtues that they most extol—they may often display fidelity under trying circumstances; but in their inward feelings they partake more or less of the universal disaffection which prevails against us, not from bad government, but from natural and irresistible antipathy." This, to be sure, was written before the Mutiny, at a time when our military position was much weaker than it is now; but it certainly cannot be said that we are more generally beloved than we were in Metcalfe's day.

Of Sir Henry Lawrence, "one who had known him well" wrote, "With all his love for the people and their interests, he felt that the rule of strangers was only tolerated because they could not help themselves." Lawrence himself is reported to have said: "We measure too much by English rules, and expect, contrary to all experience, that the energetic and aspiring among immense military masses should like our . . . arrogation to ourselves, even when we are notorious imbeciles, of all authority and all emolument." Though we have somewhat relaxed our exclusive grasp upon authority and emolument since Lawrence's day, on the other hand, the class of persons who have, at any rate, a plausible claim to share in these advantages has increased out of all proportion, and the resentment of exclusion has grown far more acute.

A year or two after the death of Henry Lawrence, we find a much younger man, Alfred Lyall, expressing the same disquietudes. Writing to his family at Harbledown, he says:

I always find myself diverging into Indian politics, for I am interested heart and soul in the affairs of the country, and am always thinking of the probable fortunes of our Empire, and trying to conceive it possible to civilise and convert an enormous nation by the mechanical processes of the present times, by establishing schools and missionary societies. Also, having civilised them, and taught them the advantage of liberty and the use of European sciences, how are we to keep them under us, and to persuade them that it is for their good that we hold all the high offices of Government? Well, it does not matter much to Harbledown.

Pity that it does not matter more to Harbledown—to the homes of England. It must matter much to them all some day whether England understands India or not.

Returning to the subject a little later, he writes:

The wildest as well as the shallowest notion of all seems to me that universally prevalent belief that education, civilisation, and increased material prosperity will reconcile the people of India eventually to our rule. De Tocqueville's study of the *Ancien Régime*, and the causes of the Revolution . . . appears to me to demonstrate most logically that it was the increased prosperity and enlightenment of the French people which produced the grand crash.*

Must we not hold it significant that men like Elphinstone, Lawrence and Lyall—men distinguished no less for their character and intelligence than for their sympathetic understanding of the Indian people—express freely their sense of the unnaturalness and probable impermanence of our power, while those who loudly postulate in the Englishman an indefeasible right to rule, and in the Indian an innate craving to be ruled, are apt to be men whose intelligence

* Sir Mortimer Durand's *Life of Sir Alfred Comyn Lyall*, pp. 89 and 95.

we must take on trust, since they have given no other conspicuous proof of it?

In point of character, Sir Herbert Edwardes ranks very
high among the heroes of British India. He was one of the
strongest men of a masterful generation; and he was the
bosom friend and confidant of John Nicholson, a man not
to be suspected of taking or tolerating sentimental or pusillanimous views of any situation whatever. Hear, then, what
Herbert Edwardes has to say:

If we would but think of it a bit, is not our Indian Empire just
the most abnormal and unnatural thing in all this topsy-turvy
fallen world of ours? And is it not, then, the most unreasonable
thing to take it so easy as we do, and assume that it will go on
for ever? Surely it would be no great wonder if India, now so
topsy-turvy, were to go turvy-topsy some fine day, and right
itself, as it were, in the creation. . . .

God would never have put upon two hundred millions of men
the heavy trial of being subject to thirty millions of foreigners,
merely to have their roads improved, their canals constructed
upon more scientific principles, their letters carried by a penny
post, their messages flashed by lightning, their erroneous notions
of geography corrected; nor even to have their internal quarrels
stopped and peace restored, and life in many ways ameliorated.
. . . This free and sympathising country, which has now a heart
for Italy, and shouts across these narrower seas "Italy for the
Italians!" should * lift that voice still higher and shout across the
world "India for the Indians!" In short, England, taught by
both past and present, should set before her the noble policy of
first fitting India for freedom and then setting her free.

It may take years, it may take a century, to fit India for self-
government, but it is a thing worth doing and a thing that may
be done. It is a distinct and intelligible policy for England to

---

* The omission, for brevity's sake, of a portion of this paragraph,
has forced me here and in the following sentence, to substitute "should"
for "would." The sense is unaffected.

pursue—a way for both countries out of the embarrassments of their twisted destinies.*

It is only fair to add that Edwardes believed in the conversion of India to Christianity. "Until she is leavened with Christianity," he wrote, "she will be unfit for freedom." And again: "If we pursue the *ignis fatuus* of secular education in a pagan land, destitute of other light, then we English will lose India without those Indians gaining any future."

The half-century which has elapsed since these words were written does not seem to me (though it does seem to others) to lend encouragement to the idea of a formal Christianization of India. But if we give a liberal interpretation to the phrase "leavened with Christianity," we may perhaps admit that even here Edwardes was not so far wrong. And, this question of method apart, do not sound sense and right feeling breathe from every syllable of the passage I have quoted?

In calling the course he advocated "a distinct and intelligible policy," Edwardes went to the heart of the matter. He might justly have called it "the only intelligible policy;" for the alternative policy of staking our all on the permanence of the *raj* postulates a rigidity of conditions unknown in human affairs. Everyone admits that India is changing rapidly before our eyes, and that measures to which the Government is committed must accelerate the process. Is the dogma that, change how it may, it can never so change as to be capable of managing its own affairs, a reasonable, an intelligible doctrine?

There is, indeed, one intelligible argument in favour of the assumption of permanence, though, for obvious reasons,

* *Our Indian Empire: Its Beginning and End*, by Major-General Sir H. B. Edwardes, K.C.B. (1861).

[308]

it is not often openly stated. "Of course," it may be said, "we do not deny the ultimate mutability of human affairs, or doubt that our Indian Empire is subject to the law of change. But it is for the good of India that we should hold on as long as possible; and to that end we must loudly assert that we are here for ever and a day, since any admission to the contrary would fatally diminish our prestige." I do not say that this argument is quite without weight, or that inconveniences would not result from any sudden and sensational proclamation of the temporary nature of our rule. But, closely examined, the argument will be found to move in a circle. For the prestige which would be impaired is needed to support a permanent, autocratic rule, imposed without regard to the will or feelings of the people. If the nature of our rule can be gradually altered—or rather, not its nature, but its theory—so that it shall be recognized as a collaboration with all that is best in the Indian character towards the great end of creating a united, self-respecting India, then the prestige of the heaven-sent autocrat, the infallible, inevitable, immovable sahib, will no longer be essential to the efficiency of government. In other words, by insisting on the perpetuity of the *raj*, we create the conditions which compel us to rely upon prestige, which means, after all, a certain measure of illusion. I am a great believer—as it would seem Herbert Edwardes was too—in the ultimate wisdom of looking facts in the face. If both England and India can be induced to do so, the romance of their association may resolve itself into beneficent reality for themselves and for the world.

But it is necessary that both parties should adopt this salutary principle, and that India should realize how much she has to learn and to unlearn before she can reasonably claim an equal place among the civilized nations of the world. Rapid as her progress has been in some respects, the essential fact is that the great mass of her people are at this moment given over to beliefs, prejudices and habits a thousand years behind those of races who live efficiently in the real world. A country which has lain for twenty or thirty centuries under the maleficent spell of caste, fetishism, cow-and-Brahmin worship, and almost equally enervating metaphysics, cannot all of a sudden wake up, rub his eyes, and claim to be a civilized nation. There is now, as we have seen, every likelihood of a great and fairly rapid change in the mental condition of the masses; and until that change has had time to make itself felt, it would be madness for India to attempt to stand alone.

Another fact which must be looked in the face, is that the unification of India is not an accomplished reality, but a far-off ideal. British rule has done much to promote it, but it is still a vision of the educated few rather than an efficient factor in the general consciousness. * Mr. Edwyn Bevan, in his thoughtful book on *Indian Nationalism*, uses a telling and very just image, when he speaks of India as a patient who has suffered many fractures, and British rule as the plaster-of-Paris packing round the broken limbs. The premature removal of the casing would undo all the surgeon's work, and leave the patient a hopeless cripple.

A third fact is that, even if India threw off British rule,

---

* Sir Madhava Rao, formerly Minister of the Baroda state, said to Lord Roberts: "We have heard the cry of 'India for the Indians' which some of your philanthropists have raised in England; but you have only to go to the Zoological Gardens and open the doors of the cages, and you would very soon see what would be the result of putting that theory into practice. There would be a terrific fight among the animals, which would end in the tiger walking proudly over the dead bodies of the rest." "Whom do you consider to be the tiger?" Lord Roberts inquired. "The Muhammadan from the North," was the reply. *Forty-one Years in India*, Vol. II., p. 388. This conversation dates from more than a quarter of a century ago; but the condition to which it points is not one to be quickly remedied.

and deliberately made up her mind to relapse into eighteenth-century anarchy, she would certainly not be permitted to do so. The world would not stand by and see the chaos of Mexico repeated on a vaster scale. There is more than one Power that would ask for nothing better than a pretext for stepping into England's shoes, and forcing peace and order upon India by methods probably far more drastic than those of the British Administration. When Rajah Dinkur Rao, the Gwalior Prime Minister, assured Sir Alfred Lyall that "the natives prefer a bad government to our best patent institutions," Sir Alfred's comment was: "I know he is right;" and we hear the same story on every hand. But the alternative of reverting to the sort of bad government they are said to like, is not, in fact, open to the Indian people. They may easily fall under a worse government than ours, but it will have none of the imagined charms of the good old days of Maratha and Pindari, *begar* and *chauth.* * For a brief interval, no doubt, chaos may be revived; but assuredly it will not be suffered to endure. India has once for all been drawn into the stream of the world-movement, and her ancient backwater is for ever closed to her.

Impatient spirits are fond of urging that political freedom should precede social reform: and I certainly would not maintain that the one should be entirely postponed to the other. If a nation had to be thoroughly civilized before it was fit for self-government, the world would indeed be in a parlous state. What people can boast itself fully emancipated from degrading superstitions, and evil traditions, and survivals of ancient blindness and folly? If India's feet .were once firmly set upon the upward path, we might reasonably fall to discussing the point at which she might be left to her own devices without danger of relapse. But the truth is that the upward movement has barely begun, and only in

* Forced labour and blackmail.

certain limited classes. The great mass of the people are practically untouched by the spirit of progress; they do not want it; they resent it; and so long as that frame of mind subsists, some outward stimulus is necessary to prevent a general slip-back. The actual resentment of the rudiments of civilization is, I believe, dying away, at all events in certain districts. It is quite conceivable that, when once the decisive impulse is given, things may move with gathering momentum, and that fifty or sixty years may see a surprising change. But, in the meantime, to start India off on an independent career would be like sending a great liner to sea with wrangling landsmen for officers and a crew of children.

There exists as yet (so far as I have been able to discover) no plausible scheme for national organization apart from British rule. The Gaekwar of Baroda, speaking to Mr. Price Collier, "hinted at a federation of states under a central government;" and this, no doubt, is the idea which naturally suggests itself. But no one has applied any constructive imagination to the task of drawing up detailed proposals for serious discussion. When I have asked why this obvious preliminary to self-government was neglected, the answer has been that anyone who dared to put forward such proposals would be prosecuted, and perhaps deported. If this be so—if a calm and unprovocative survey of possibilities in the matter of national organization would be treated by the Government as seditious—there could not be a better example of the purblind policy against which my whole argument is directed. Government ought to place no obstacle in the way of any feeling-forward of the Indian mind towards a stable and ordered method of self-regulation. If the ideal to be aimed at were, in a general way, clear and accepted, the course of intellectual and social training necessary for its realization would be immensely facili-

[312]

tated. It is because no ideal is proposed—no goal, however distant, offered to hope and endeavour—that national sentiment is so apt to wander off into visions of catastrophic revolution, without plan, without forecast, without any reasonable or probable expectation of the achievement of lasting good. Mr. E. B. Havell enlarges on the splendid results attained by Indian master-builders (as distinct from architects) who go to work, it would seem, without any definite plan. That may be possible in building palaces, but not in building states. * It would be madness for India to throw off her present organization without any clear conception of that which was to take its place. Her architect-statesmen ought to devote earnest thought and care to designing her ultimate polity, and the Government ought to encourage them to do so. If she has no architect-statesmen capable of working out the problem, and producing a scheme or schemes which shall offer reasonable chances of success, the inference is that she is still more unripe for self-government than I, for my part, imagine her to be.†

It may be asked who is to be the judge as to when India is ripe for *swaraj*, and whether there is any likelihood that India and England will ever come to a peaceful agreement on that point. I reply that we need not cross this bridge before we come to it. Let me add that I do not think the difficulty at all a serious one. If India earnestly applies herself to the task of qualifying for recognition as a self-

* It may be said that the British constitution was not designed, but grew. Yes: but a modern state, which aspires to peaceful development, cannot wait for its constitution to grow. It must start with some definite scheme of national life, which does not exclude, of course, the probability of subsequent growth.

† So, too, it were greatly to be desired that at least one or two Indian politicians should show a statesman-like realisation of the larger issues of the emigration question discussed in Chapter VII. I have not come across any very penetrating forecast of the economic future of India, though in such a work there could be no question of "sedition."

respecting, self-directing member of the Grand Committee
of civilized nations, she will one day make foreign tutelage
such a manifest superfluity that it will cease and determine
almost by process of nature. One imagines that the ultimate discussion may be rather between the forward and the
backward party in India itself, than between India as a
whole and England. It is almost inconceivable, at any
rate, that England should attempt to maintain by force of
arms her autocracy over a country unanimously demanding
independence, and giving evidence, by that very unanimity,
of a highly-developed national self-consciousness. As soon
as the Indian people are capable of forming a sane political
judgment, that judgment will command respect. So long,
on the contrary, as the withdrawal of outside control would
hand over the patient, inarticulate masses to mere anarchy
and class-exploitation, we cannot honourably renounce the
responsibility which, wisely or unwisely, we have once for
all assumed.

Indian patriotism should take particular note of the
history of the Mutiny, and realize the causes of its failure.
They fall, as I understand the matter, under three heads.
In the first place, there was no national idea for the people
to rally to; and this, it may be said with some truth, is
now changed; a similar movement to-day would probably
call forth a wider popular response. In the second place,
there was no statesmanship or generalship behind the revolt;
and who can say that, now or in the near future, a similar
movement would bring to light a more adequate provision
of these qualities? "You give us no opportunity to develop
them!" it may be said; but, in the case of statesmanship, this
is not true. Many able politicians have, in fact, been developed; but is there any one of such conspicuous genius that
he could reasonably hope to command universal respect,
and grapple successfully with the giant problems, first of the

[314]

war itself, and secondly of the reconstruction that would
have to be faced after the overthrow of the British
power? I have a sincere admiration for some of the leaders
of the National movement, but, frankly, I do not see a
Cromwell on the horizon; and no lesser man could, under
present circumstances, give to insurrection the slightest
chance of a prosperous issue. The third reason for the
failure of the Mutiny is intimately connected with the
second, and may almost be said to be included in it. If there
had been any brain, any insight or foresight, behind the
movement, it would not have taken the form of a headlong
relapse into barbarism. In Deussen's very instructive book,
which I have already quoted more than once, there occurs
the following curious passage:

The chief sights of Cawnpore consist of a Memorial Church,
a disused well, surmounted by a beautiful statue of an Angel, and
other monuments, all referring to the Mutiny, as the English term
the rebellion of 1857. Had the rebels attained their end . . .
they would have been held in honour by their nation, as we honor
Schill, Scharnhorst, Blücher, and the other heroes of the Wars of
Independence. As they were overthrown, they are now termed
mutineers and their memory decried.

Dr. Deussen omits to mention the reason why the well is
"disused"—namely, that it contains the bodies of some
six-score butchered women and children. And the infamies
of Cawnpore were only the culmination of a campaign of
massacre, which, in its very nature, was foredoomed to
failure. Had the British been encountered by civilized,
enlightened, organized patriotism, which offered them, if
beaten in fair fight, an honourable retreat from the country,
with their women and children unharmed, it is not at all improbable that they might have weakened in the unequal
struggle. Faced with the alternative of victory or massacre,

they set their teeth and chose victory. That is why to-day, over the battered ruins of the Residency at Lucknow, "the banner of England blows." And that is why no fair-minded Indian ought to blame us if we take all reasonable precautions against the recurrence of a frenzy which was, and would be again, far more calamitous to his country than to ours.

The moral of these reflections is that Indian self-government is bound to come, almost automatically, as soon as the country is intellectually, morally and socially prepared for it; whereas any attempt to upset the existing order, while the nation is imperfectly welded together and but slowly emerging from barbarism, would, even if it nominally succeeded, mean a reversion to anarchy which the world could not and would not permit. Should England get into serious trouble elsewhere, India might doubtless achieve the expulsion of her depleted garrison and her "sun-dried bureaucrats" with their mountainous "files." But they would in all probability only make room for a more domineering garrison, and another breed of bureaucrats, perhaps congenitally yellow of hue.

I suggest, then, that patience and unwearied effort in the cause of enlightenment ought to be the watchword of sane Indian patriotism. It should in especial devote itself, not merely to the ventilation of grievances, but to constructive thinking-forward. Nothing could more effectually reinforce the demand for ultimate self-government than some unmistakable proofs of the power of reasoned political forecast, as distinct from the power to carry on a mere campaign of criticism and opposition, however able. But if we ask for patience, sanity and constructive thought on the part of our Indian friends, we must meet them with similar qualities on our own side. We must not take our stand on a dogma of perpetuity which is as unpractical as it is unphilosophical. We must recognize—I repeat the phrase for the twentieth time, for it puts the matter in a nutshell—that our rule is a means, not an end. It is not a good in itself, but an alternative to greater evils. Only on condition that it is recognized as such can it ever be tolerable to enlightened and self-respecting Indians—the class which we have ourselves done so much to enlarge, and which must inevitably go on growing. We can reasonably ask these Indians to co-operate with us in the enfranchisement of their countrymen —enfranchisement, in the first instance, from age-old spiritual and social bonds—but we cannot expect them to co-operate loyally in measures confessedly directed to perpetual enthralment.

I am no belittler of our work in India. In my heart I am perhaps irrationally proud of it. We have lavishly spent on India the best we had to spend in talent and in character. It has been a very real sacrifice, not only national but individual. For, though the Indian services may offer "the lordliest life on earth," it is also one of the most laborious and most thankless. Anglo-Indian biography is, in the main, very tragic reading. In saying so I do not think merely of the thousands who have laid down their lives in and for India, but also of the two or three-score men, from Viceroys downwards, who might be called conspicuous successes. Many of them have sacrificed their health, almost all their peace of mind, to their splendid but almost superhuman responsibilities. The "land of regrets" is also, and above all, the land of disappointments, and of the patient endurance of misunderstanding, misrepresentation, and, not infrequently, bitter and undeserved humiliation.

> "If tears be the price of empery,
> Lord God! we ha' paid in full—"

[817]

and most of all in those unshed tears that, dropping inwardly, sear the greatest souls.

Without skulking behind a "perhaps" or an "almost," I make bold to call our rule in India the most heroic adventure in history. But every adventure must have an end; and if this one could, by miracle, be eternalized, that would only mean that it had missed the highest success. An end must come; and this book is inspired, however inadequately, by the desire and hope that it may be a glorious one. Or at least, if fate has otherwise decreed, and a tragic doom impends, let us endeavour that history may not have to find the *tragische Schuld* in our own unintelligence.

INDEX

INDEX

Abdul Qadir, Shaikh, 123.
Abu, Mount, 210, 241.
Aga Khan, H.H. the, 119.
Agra, 1, 105, 153, 242.
Ahmedabad, 148.
Ajanta frescoes, 245.
Akbar, 152, 253.
Alexander the Great, 1, 16.
Allahabad, 12, 153.
Amaravati stupa, 198.
Amritsar, 1, 13.
Andrews, Rev. C. F., 105, 281.
"Anglo-Indian," 7, 123.
Animals, Cruelty to, 87.
Animism, 68.
Antiochos, 16.
Aranyakas, 59.
Architecture:
  Hindu, 239.
  Muhammadan, 241, 249.
Arjuna, 50, 74, 78, 218, 227, 232, 250, 252.
Art:
  Hindu, 186-211.
  Muhammadan, 237-244.
Aryans, 25, 56, 66, 68, 118, 190.
Arya Samaj, 62, 97, 270-281.
Aryavarta, 23, 73, 206.
Asceticism, 79-82, 206, 218.
Asoka, 28, 252, 253.
Aurungzeb, 51, 152, 239, 248, 253.
Ayodhya, 221, 236.

Babar, 1.
Babu, The, 122, 260.
Babu, English, 266.

Badami, 201.
Baden-Powell, B. H., 164.
Baluchistan, 139.
Bana, 230.
"Bande Mataram," 122, 285.
Bangalore, 9.
Baroda, Gaekwar of, 312.
Benares, 1, 12, 260.
Bengal, Partition of, 46.
Bernier, 153, 155.
Besant, Mrs., 22, 56, 81, 116.
Bevan, Edwyn, 310.
Bhagavad Gita, 74, 252.
Bhagiratha, 225.
Bharata, 217.
Bhavabhuti, 232.
Bhima, 218.
Bijapur, 1.
Bikanir, Maharaja of, 122.
Birdwood, Sir George, 189.
Bombay, 11, 98, 110, 114, 117, 148.
Bodhisattvas, 202.
Boro Budur, Reliefs at, 200.
Brahma, 65, 69, 75, 217.
Brahmanas, 59, 65, 274.
Brahminism, 68, 84, 85, 102.
Brahmins, 38, 50, 65, 76.
Brahmo Samaj, 97, 266.
Bramachari Bawa, 57.
British Empire, 21, 166, 185, 286.
  India its strategic frontier, 140.
British rule:
  A means, not an end, 17, 90, 186, 317.
  "A miracle," 301.
  Indictment by Mr. Gokhale, 130.

British rule:
  Is India overcharged for, 128–138.
  "Most abnormal and unnatural thing," 307.
Bryce, Lord, 296, 302.
Buddha, Gautama, 65, 66, 74, 86, 195, 253.
  Images of, 201.
Buddhism, 70, 74, 97, 245.
Buland Darwaza, 243.
Burdwan, Maharajadhiraja Bahadur of, 105.
Burke, Edmund, 117.
Burn, Mr., 72.

CALCUTTA, 11, 31, 86, 114, 146.
Caird, Sir James, 165.
Caste, 27, 47, 85, 89–109.
  Brahmins, 27, 38, 50, 65, 76, 92, 93, 94, 117, 215.
  Classification, 94.
  Dhoomnas, 96.
  Kshattryas, 92, 94, 105, 216, 219.
  Pariahs, 27, 93, 94, 95.
  Pleas in defence of, 89, 107.
  Rejected by Arya Samaj, 280.
  Sudras, 92, 95, 218.
  Vaisyas, 92, 94.
Caste-marks, 32.
Cawnpore, 95, 315.
Central Hindu College, 94.
Chandavarkar, Sir Narayan, 16, 98.
Chandragupta, 234, 252.
Charlton, Hon. Mrs., 87.
Chirol, Sir Valentine, 168.
Chitor (Towers of Victory), 241.
Christ, 72, 87, 281.
Christianity, 91, 263, 281, 288, 308.
Civil and Military Gazette, Letters to, 191.
Civil employment, Exclusion from, 172.
Clubs, 13, 110.
[322]

Collier, Price, 41, 53, 110, 119, 312.
Colombo, 29.
Commercial subjection of India, 145–151.
Conjeevaram, 108.
Coomaraswamy, Dr. A. K., 194.
Cousin, Victor, 64.
Crewe, Marquis of, disavows Lord Hardinge's despatch, 4.
Curzon, Lord, 20, 46, 158, 182.

DADA HARRI's well, 244.
Darmesteter, James, 257.
Dasaratha, King, 217, 221.
Dayanand Anglo-Vedic College, 271.
Dayanand Saraswati, Swami, 271, 274.
Delhi, 1, 153, 228, 242.
"Demartialisation," 176, 178.
Deussen, Paul, 59, 63, 66, 106, 244, 260, 313.
Dilwarra Temples, 241.
Diwan Chand, 275.
"Drain, The" (financial), 82, 140, 154, 163.
  Theory examined, 131–138.
Draupadi, 250.
Dravidians, 25, 118, 206.
Dritarashtra, 218.
Drona, 218, 219, 222, 250.
Dubois, Abbé, 43, 55, 94, 127.
Durga, 39, 209, 211.
Duryodhana, 218.
Dushyanta, 235.
Dutt, Romesh Chunder, 65, 93, 99, 223.
Dutt, Pundit Rambhaj, 96.

EAR-RINGS, 33, 150.
East India Company, 151.
Education, 256–294.
Education:
  Anglo-Literary, 265.
  Female, 267.

Education:
  Government resolution on, 263,
    283.
  Macaulay's Minute on, 257.
  Need of standard alphabet, 290.
  Neglect of, 170, 171.
  Patriotism as inspiring princi-
    ple, 285.
  Schoolhouses, Importance of,
    263.
  Statistics, 261.
  Vernacular, 102, 172, 262.
Edwardes, Sir Herbert, 281, 307.
Ekalavya, 218.
Elephanta, 200.
Ellenborough, Lord, 261.
Ellora, 200.
Elphinstone, Mountstuart, 151, 154,
  170, 203.
Emigration, 108, 156-159, 166-170.
Examinations, Simultaneous, 173.

Famine relief, 147, 164.
Fatehpur-Sikri, 1, 154, 229, 243.
Fergusson, James, 198.
Fuller, Sir Bampfylde, 3, 87, 89,
  104.

Gait, Sir E. A., 100, 101, 161.
Gambling, 109, 222.
Ganesh, 37, 86, 196, 206, 262, 280.
Gangetic Valley, 65.
Ghosh, Sarath Kumar, 104.
Gilgit Protectorate, 139.
Gokhale, Mr. G. K., 129, 139, 140,
  141, 145, 146, 165.
Gould, F. J., 283.
Griffith, R. T. H., 224.
Growse, F. S., 225.
Gujrat, Battle of, 1.
Gunga (The Ganges), 224.
Guru and Chela, 63, 187, 270.
Gurukula, The, 271.

Halebid, 210.
Hans Raj, Lala, 272.

Hanuman, 86, 228, 280.
Hardinge, Lord, his despatch of
  1911, 4.
  Attempted assassination of, 5.
Hardwar, 271.
Harsa Carita, 230.
Hastings, Warren, 117.
Havell, E. B., 190-201, 225, 238,
  241, 247, 313.
Hawkins, William, 155.
Hearn, Lafcadio, 70.
"Hewers of wood and drawers of
  water," 146, 148.
Hindu drama, 239.
  Epics, 211.
  Sculpture, 197-211.
Hinduism, 24, 36, 41, 47, 49, 56,
  74, 84, 89.
  Higher and lower, 67-88.
Hinduizing movement, 102.
Hindus versus Muhammadans, 48,
  49, 112.
Hoernle, Dr., 97.
Holderness, Sir Thomas, 46.
Horrwitz, Ernst P., 209.
Hoysalesvara Temple, 210.
Humayun's Tomb, Delhi, 154, 243.
Hunter, Sir William, 152.
Hyderabad (Deccan), 10, 153.
Hyder Ali, 253.
Hyslop, Professor, 72.

India:
  Barbarous or civilised, 6, 28, 33,
    34, 40.
  Area, 10.
  Population, 10.
  Population problem, 157, 165
  British territory, 10.
  Native states, 10, 135.
  "Golden Age," 23, 28, 57, 66.
  Racial diversities, 43.
  Compared with Italy, 2, 43, 249.
  Compared with Greece, 249.
  Geographical unity, 44.

India:
  Multiplicity of languages, 46.
  The "Motherland," 49, 168.
  "Idealism," 59, 109.
  Philosophy, 61-65, 196.
  Poverty, 127, 150.
  Causes of poverty, 151, 165.
  Lack of capital, 133, 148-150.
  Taxation, Incidence per head,
    135.
  Defence, Cost of, 136.
  Her value to Britain, 143.
  Trade with Britain, 144.
  Commercial subjection, 145, 150.
  Land revenue, 159.
  Agriculture, 164, 165.
  Death-rate rising, 165.
  Sanitation, 166.
  Her "greatest asset," 168.
  Magna Charta of, 172.
  Contrasted with Japan, 177.
India Office, Cost of, 144.
Indian Mutiny, 10, 51, 180, 315.
  Music, 254.
Indians:
  In Government service, 14.
  Physical types, 26, 29, 30.
  Had no word for patriotism, 47.
  Hindus *versus* Muhammadans,
    49, 50, 112.
  "Vain and self-sufficient people,"
    55.
  Character and religion, 83.
  Emancipated, 114, 125.
  Assimilative talent, 125.
  "Chosen People," 185.
  Psychology, 252.
Indra, 62.
Infanticide, 100.
Irrigation, 169.

Jagannath car, 37, 38.
Jahangir, 155.
Jainism, 38, 85, 97, 202.
Japan contrasted with India, 177.

Jewellery, 33, 150.
Jumma Musjid, 154, 243.

Kaikeyi, Queen, 226.
Kala pani, Prohibition of crossing,
  108, 299.
Kali, 39, 49, 209, 280.
Kalidasa, 81, 232.
Kalighat, The, 86.
Kanishka, 252.
Kapila, 225.
Karma, 69-73.
Karna, 227, 250.
Kashmir, 1.
Kennedy, James, 256.
Khyber Pass, 1.
King-Emperor's visit to India, 4.
Kipling, Rudyard, 22.
Knowles, Rev. R. J., 290.
Kohat, 95.
Koran, The, 270, 288.
Krishna, 50, 75, 78, 209, 246, 252.
Kunti, 250.
Kurukshetra, Battle of, 1, 58, 75,
  222, 229.

Lahore, 1, 12, 95, 141, 153, 242,
  271, 301.
Lakshman, 217, 232, 250.
Lanka (Ceylon), 228.
Lawrence, Sir Henry, 294, 305.
Lely, Sir F. S. P., 263.
Leopardi, 73.
Loti, Pierre, 36, 38.
Low, Sydney, 2.
Lucknow, 12, 316.
Lyall, Sir Alfred, 36, 44, 84, 116,
  170, 173, 256, 282, 302, 305,
  306.

Macaulay, Lord, 160, 303.
  His Minute on education, 257.
Macdonald, Rev. K. S., 61.
Madhura, 260.
Madras, 11, 110, 117.

Madura, 31, 49, 197, 241.
The great temple, 35.
Magic, 207, 68, 79, 219.
Mahabharata, The, 50, 80, 217, 229, 283.
Malati and Madhava, 233.
Malavikagnimitra, 238.
Mamallapuram, 201.
Manners and customs:
Of British, 14, 110-126.
Of Indians, 117, 120.
Manu, Laws of, 100.
Marriage, Infant, 96, 99, 102, 106, 280.
Marriage of widows forbidden, 99, 280.
Megasthenes, 28.
Memsahib, The, 13, 112, 115.
Menander, 16.
Mendicants, 81.
Metaphysics, Indian, 196.
Metcalfe, Sir Charles, 170, 304.
Metempsychosis, 69-73, 85.
Military expenditure, 131-136, 138-145.
Military training, Denial of, 176-181.
Mitra, Mr. S. M., 270.
Mogul Empire, 151-158, 178, 243.
Monier-Williams, Sir M., 214, 215, 290.
Morison, Sir Theodore, 59, 132, 151, 156, 163.
Morley, Lord, 296.
Mudra Rakshasa, 234.
Muhammad, 87.
Muhammadanism, 47, 48, 83, 91, 114, 238.
Muhammadans, 47, 51, 150, 168.
Muhammadans *versus* Hindus, 48, 51, 112.
Müller, Max, 60, 92, 276.
Munro, Sir Thomas, 151.
Munshi Ram, Mahatma, 272, 273.
Mysore, 10.

Nadir Shah, 1.
Naidu, Sarojini, 23.
Nakula, 218.
Nana Sahib, 95.
Naoroji, Mr. Dadabhai, 22, 133, 140, 160.
Nevinson, H. W., 2.
Nicholson, John, 115, 307.
Nirvana, 74.
Nose-rings, 33, 150.

Okakura, Kakuzo, 298.
Olcott, Colonel H. S., 56.
OM (mystic syllable), 64.
Oman, Professor, 57.

Painting, 245-248.
Panchagavya, 86, 98.
Pandu, 218.
Panipat, Battles of, 1.
Pariahs, 27, 93, 94, 95.
Parsis, 22, 110, 148.
Parvati, 113.
Paul, Saint, 87.
Peacock throne, 154.
Pessimism, 73-79.
Pindaris (marauders), 104.
Pinjrapole hospitals, 86.
Plassey, Battle of, 1, 29.
Poona, 12.
Ptolemy, 16.
Punjab, 65.
Puranas, 64, 274.
Purdah women, 47, 111.

Rajputs, 1, 100, 110.
Railways, 53, 98, 102, 146.
Rama, 113, 218, 221, 225, 226, 227, 232, 236, 250.
Ramanujachariar, Mr. N., 108.
Ramayana, The, 50, 212, 214, 217, 223, 232, 239, 283.
Ranade, Mr. Justice, 184.
Rao, Rajah Dinkur, 311.
Rao, Sir Madhava, 310.

Ravan, 214, 217, 226.
Rebellion, Possibility of, 18.
Retnaeali, 224, 233, 238.
Rishis, 1, 57, 61, 79, 109, 235.
Risley, Sir Herbert, 94, 96, 109, 118.
Roberts, Lord, 141, 143, 310.
Roe, Sir Thomas, 153, 156.

Sadhus, 82.
Sahadeva, 218.
Saint Nihal Singh, 47, 92.
Sakuntala, 76, 219, 221, 81, 232, 235.
Salisbury, Lord, 22.
Samudragupta, 26.
Sannyasis, 82.
Satrugna, 217.
Savings Bank statistics, 150.
Schopenhauer, Arthur, 64.
Sculpture, Hindu and Buddhist, 189.
  Gandharan, 202, 205.
Sect-marks, 32.
Secunderabad, 10.
"Servants of India," 129, 290.
Shah Alam, Tomb of, 241.
Shah Jahan, 152, 239, 253.
Sidi Sayyid, Mosque of, 241.
Sikhs, 1, 85, 97.
"Sister Nivedita," 113, 116, 217.
Sita, 113, 222, 232, 236, 250.
Siva, 32, 113, 207, 209, 210, 235, 280.
Sivaji, 253.
Smith, Vincent A., 16, 44, 196, 201, 231.
Sobraon, Battle of, 1.
"Spirituality," Hindu, 55-66.
Sri Shankaranand Sannyasi, 262.
Steevens, G. W., 2.
Sujampur, 97.
Surpanakha, 222.

Suttee, 99, 101, 104, 229.
Swadeshism, 122.
Swaraj, 293, 313.

Tagore, Abanindro Nath, 251.
Tagore, Sir Rabindra Nath, 205.
Taj Mahal, The, 154, 243.
Tanjore, 37, 197.
Theosophy, 69, 184, 190, 193.
Thugs, 104.
Tirthankaras, 202.
Timur, 1.
Townsend, Meredith, 259, 301.
Toy-Cart, The, 233.
Transmigration, 69-73.
Trichinopoly, 37, 197.
Tulsi Das, 215, 235.
Tuticorin, 31.

"Untouchables," 27, 92.
Upanishads, 59, 63, 66.
Uttara Rama Cheritra, 236.

Vasishtha, 216, 223, 276.
Vedanta, 59, 68.
Vedas, 59, 60, 65, 69, 84, 92, 109, 188, 271.
  "Back to the Vedas," 264-280.
Viddha Salabhankija, 238.
Vidura, 218.
Vijayanagar, 200.
Vikrama and Urvasi, 236.
Vikramaditya, 252.
Vishnu, 32, 74, 217, 236.
Visvamitra, 216, 223.
Vivekananda, Swami, 279.
Vyasa, 218.

Wells, H. G., 57.
Wilson, H. H., 236.

Yoga, 75, 79, 193, 196.
Yudishthira, 218, 222, 250.

RETURN TO: **CIRCULATION DEPARTMENT**
198 Main Stacks

LOAN PERIOD | 1 | 2 | | 3
Home Use | | | |
| 4 | 5 | | 6

ALL BOOKS MAY BE RECALLED AFTER 7 DAYS.
Renewals and Recharges may be made 4 days prior to the due
date Books may be renewed by calling 642-3405

DUE AS STAMPED BELOW.

FORM NO DD6
50 M 1-06

UNIVERSITY OF CALIFORNIA, BERKELEY
Berkeley, California 94720-6000

CPSIA information can be obtained
at www.ICGtesting.com
Printed in the USA
LVHW060610220321
681992LV00064B/35